PARANOID PARENTING

WHY IGNORING THE EXPERTS MAY BE BEST FOR YOUR CHILD

FRANK FUREDI

Library of Congress Cataloging-in-Publication Data

Furedi, Frank, 1947–
Paranoid parenting : why ignoring the experts may be best for your
child / Frank Furedi.
        p.   cm.
     "... was previously published in a substantially different form
in the U.K. in 2001."
     Includes bibliographical references and index.
     ISBN 1-55652-464-1
     1. Parenting.   2. Parents—Psychology.   3. Child rearing.
4. Parent and child.   I. Title.

HQ755.8 .F87   2002
649'.1—dc21   2002004121

Cover design: Rachel McClain
Interior design: Pamela Juárez

Paranoid Parenting was previously published in a substantially different
form in the United Kingdom in 2001.

Published by Chicago Review Press, Incorporated
814 North Franklin Street
Chicago, Illinois 60610
ISBN 1-55652-464-1
Printed in the United States of America
5 4 3 2 1

 # Contents

Preface and Acknowledgments

During my travels around the world, I have become convinced that children do not have to be regarded as always at risk. In many parts of the world, parents do not continually worry about the safety of their children. The idea that responsible parenting means the continual supervision of children is a peculiarly Anglo-American one. Consequently, in many societies children enjoy a far greater freedom to explore the outside world than their counterparts in the United States.

I am always envious when I travel to Spain or France and see that children as young as six or seven are able to walk to school on their own. Last summer, when I visited northern Italy, I encountered busy playgrounds where adults were conspicuous by their absence. In Norway, they are actually building playgrounds that are designed to inspire children to take risks. In Karmoy, on the west coast of Norway, Asbjorn Flemmen has constructed an outdoor play area where children have an opportunity to climb and jump in an environment that many American adults would consider dangerous. Yet the children thrive because they have an opportunity to explore the unknown.

In the United States, anxiety regarding children's safety is at an unprecedented level. Accidents, which were hitherto regarded as an integral part of children's lives, are increasingly represented as a danger that we must avoid at all cost. Professionals no longer use the word *accident*. They prefer to describe a child's bruised knee as *unintentional injury* and insist that such an event can and must be avoided. Such paranoid attitudes toward childhood safety impose a heavy burden on our youngsters. They force parents into a life of permanent alertness. This book aims to explain why parents have allowed themselves to accept the ethos of paranoid child rearing. It provides plenty of arguments for parents who want to question this ethos and assert control over their lives.

After a radio debate on parental anxieties in London, England, a listener e-mailed me, stating, "You've got to write a book on this subject." It was my partner, Ann, who convinced me that I ought to put my academic training toward something as practical and worthwhile as a book on paranoid parenting. I received great encouragement from mothers and fathers to whom I talked. The unwavering support of my agent, Maggie Pearlstine, somehow made this project more real. Helen Searls in Washington, D.C., and Bruno Waterfield in London assisted with the research and managed to discover more material than I needed. Finally, my six-year-old son, Jacob, has convinced me that childhood does not need to be colonized by adults. This one is for him.

Introduction

I am not sure if this book is written by a sociologist who happens to be a father of a six-year-old or a father who possesses an intense sociological curiosity about the relationship between generations. My academic training did not prepare me for the strange world of parental anxiety that seems to afflict so many fathers and mothers. Since my son, Jacob, was born, I have been reminded time and again that life is perilous and the peril starts at birth.

The alarm began almost at once. At the hospital, nurses carefully explained the in-house measures in place to thwart baby snatchers. Concerned friends made sure that we were fully aware of the latest crib death advice. Relatives weighed the risks of different child-care arrangements, debating the dangers of a nanny (potential baby abuser) versus the dangers of a child-care center (potential neglect). But it was when my mother announced that she could no longer bring herself to watch any television programs about babies because they made her nervous about Jacob that the intensity of parental paranoia was fully brought home. It was as if my child's survival was constantly under threat.

It does not take long for parents to realize that everyone today holds strong opinions about the problems of raising a child. While the politicians regularly hold forth what they believe makes a good or responsible parent, an industry of experts bombards parents with helpful insights drawn from the science of child rearing. This science produces an endless stream of manuals, pamphlets, and leaflets that claim to provide crucial knowledge for the now terrified mother and father.

Paradoxically, it seems as if the only people who lack confidence in their opinions about what is good for children are parents themselves. Experts have assigned them the role of bumbling amateurs. Consequently, a lack of self-belief tinged with an intense level of anxiety informs the parenting style of our times. Most parents I know are not just *worried* about how they are performing as fathers and mothers, they are *paranoid* about it. Having a child appears to change people's worldview. Once a man becomes a father and a woman becomes a mother, other adults are suddenly transformed into potentially threatening strangers. As one mother explains: "I took James to the grocery store this morning, and a man about fifty years old was talking to him. The first thought that came into my head was *get away from my child*, and of course he was probably only being nice. I hate it, but I can't let anyone touch him or talk to him without getting suspicious." Parents not only seek to protect their children from strangers—they distrust even those they charge with the care of their offspring. Neighbors, nannies, day-care workers, and other children—no one is above suspicion.

Although children are rarely mistreated by their caretakers, and certainly no more frequently today than in past decades, it only takes one high-profile case of nanny abuse to unleash a wave of parental anxiety. In recent years, security has become one of the primary concerns of parents choosing preschool care for their children. A survey carried out by the advocacy group Public Agenda in 2001 indicates that 63 percent of parents say they worry about neglect or abuse at day-care centers. The survey also found that 57 percent claim that trust, not cost or convenience, was the hardest part of finding good day care. Not surprisingly, many day-care centers now vie with minimum-security prisons in their security arrangements. Concern with children's safety has spawned an industry. Companies such as Toddlerwatch.com, Inc.; ParentWatch, Inc.; and Kinderview, Inc. provide services that let parents watch their children live on their own computer screens. "You can watch your child at any time of the day on any computer," boasts Ucando Preschool, a company marketing a secure day-care environment. Digital Monitoring and Recording Systems offers "the ultimate in child monitoring and security." "Monitor your child from your office or even from another continent," it exhorts anxious parents. Some day-care centers possess the latest security technology, including a palm recognition system. Adults who wish to enter the nursery must type in their personalized four-digit PIN number and place their hand on a scanner that will either let them enter or keep them out, depending on whether it recognizes the palm print.

Spying on nannies, day-care workers, and children has become associated with good parenting. It shows you care. Throughout the nation, moms and dads are bugging their children's telephones, installing secret cameras in their bedrooms, and sending strands of hair retrieved from pillows for analysis at drug laboratories. Parental paranoia leads to mistrust and renewed demands for even more drastic security measures. Predictably, the commercial sector is more than happy to feed parents' appetite for greater security.

Companies promoting safety gadgets both foster and prey on parents' anxieties. Safety Shield offers a child-protection package that "can be instrumental in preventing your child from being kidnapped." Its promotional material is designed to put the fear of God into every adult reader. "Did you know that more than one million American children are kidnapped, lost, missing, or run away every year?" it asks, before warning, "Don't delay one minute, the quicker you order the quicker your child can be protected." One company peddling its Child Abduction Alarm tells potential customers:

Criminally insane child killers can strike anywhere at any time. Churches, shopping malls, playgrounds are all targets for these deranged dregs of subhumanity. Unfortunately these individuals are protected by unjust and dangerous liberal laws allowing them to be released back on the streets to kill again. Now through the marvels of space aged electronics you can be alerted the moment your child wanders out of a selected safety range.

Such alarmist warnings are echoed throughout the land. Their aim is to create a market of terrified parents. Safe Kids International, Inc., sells child-security emergency cards. Its promotional material cites a father who writes, "I don't think I could live with myself if anything ever happened and I had not taken every precaution possible." The message is crystal clear—unless you purchase the latest child-security system, you are an irresponsible parent.

It is not just aggressive child-security companies who use parental anxieties as a marketing tool. Businesses in a wide variety of fields know that they can improve their profile through adopting child-security measures. Code Adam, one of the country's largest child-safety programs (created by Wal-Mart), is a textbook example of how this issue can help a company gain goodwill and increase its market share. Even small family businesses have jumped on the child-security bandwagon. The other day I received a flyer in the mail. On one side of this flyer, a Washington-based glass installing company offered to replace a broken windshield for ninety-nine dollars, and on the other side were pictures of two beautiful missing children. Missing children are now an advertising gimmick. The relentless bombarding of parents with such images inevitably takes its toll.

The surveillance technology that is designed for the paranoid parent market can have the effect of distracting mothers and fathers from their real lives. All this new technology is wonderful, and no doubt many working moms and dads would enjoy sneaking off for a few minutes to watch their children play in their day-care center or preschool. But do parents really *need* to know just exactly what their children are up to? Do they *need* to constantly monitor their activities? Is there not something a little sordid in parents spying on their children and their caretakers? There was a time when mothers and fathers assumed that child-care centers were safe places where caring teachers looked after their toddlers. Thankfully, most still trust their children's sitters and teachers. But the fact that many of them are inclined to rely on a camera rather than a teacher's word does not bode well for the future.

Unfortunately, there are no technological solutions to parental anxieties. Even if it were desirable, it is humanly impossible for parents to monitor the lives of their children twenty-four hours a day. Surveillance is far more likely to intensify rather than allay parental fears. A parent who has no means to check on a caretaker has to trust or suspend suspicion. Someone who cannot do that is likely to grow increasingly neurotic. A mother with access to a Webcam is likely to feel guilty when she does not check it. The very fact that it has been installed suggests to her that there is a need for it.

This obsessive fear about the safety of children has led to a fundamental redefinition of parenting. Traditionally, good parenting has been associated with nurturing, stimulating, and socializing children. Today, it is associated with monitoring their activities. An inflated sense of risk prevails, demanding that children should never be left on their own and that preferably they should be within sight of one of their parents at all times. An army of professionals advises that children are never safe. Today, allowing a child to play outside on his own is seen as an act of neglect. Permitting youngsters to be home on their own after school is presented as an act of parental irresponsibility.

The media play a significant role in provoking these irrational attitudes. There is no such thing as good news when it comes to children. In January 2000, a report by the National Center for Missing and Exploited Children indicated that no babies were abducted from U.S. hospitals in 1999. This story could have been used to reassure expecting mothers but was swiftly buried. On the other hand, every negative incident involving a child serves as a pretext for demanding greater vigilance and new forms of supervision. In February 2001, a five-year-old boy died when a table fell on him at a northeast Philadelphia elementary school. Such tragic accidents are fortunately very rare, but child-safety advocates and newspapers responded by demanding a stricter regime of regulation. Their message was that everyday objects can kill. Yes, they can. But do we need to turn every extraordinary tragedy into an alarmist spectacle? Too often, the media cannot resist the temptation of transmitting a scare story involving children, even if it is unsubstantiated. Recently the *Today* show news anchor Ann Curry introduced a report that claimed that children were at risk of radiation-induced cancer from computed tomography (CT) scans. In her introduction, Curry emphasized that this study provided "very important information" that was "very scary for parents." It was, and numerous physicians reported that they were overwhelmed with questions from anxious parents. Scary stories about children have a predictable outcome—even if they are just stories. Fortunately, CT scans are very safe; since their introduction, the death rate from childhood cancer has been cut in half.

Every aspect of a child's experience can be transformed into a scare story. These days a responsible parent is not simply expected to buy toys—she is instructed to engage in a protracted process of risk assessment to ensure that the doll she bought for her seven-year-old daughter is safe. Many toys "from scooters to tiny toy animals can be hazardous to children," warns an earnest *Los Angeles Times* staff writer in his lecture to parents searching for Christmas gifts.[1] Safety experts have turned summertime into a horror story. The advocacy group Safe Kids frightens parents about every aspect of children's summer experiences. Parents are warned about the peril of summer heat and told to keep their eyes firmly fixed on their children to prevent them from drowning or crashing their bikes or scooters. The magazine *Family Life* gravely informs its readers to take their "cue from emergency-room doctors" who call summer the "trauma season." *Family Life*'s idea of a safe summer includes forcing your child to wear a pair of slip-on shoes in the shower and changing room, and waterproof footwear for in-pool play. Why? To prevent uncomfortable fungal infection![2]

Scare stories always conclude with the demand for greater vigilance, creating an impossible strain on fathers and mothers while helping to reinforce their already intense sense of insecurity. Since supervision can never be constant, the pressure to monitor every aspect of a child's life reinforces paranoia. Mothers and fathers have responded to this pressure by fundamentally altering their relationship to their children.

In order to monitor children's activities, parents have reorganized children's time. A growing number refuse to allow their children to play outdoors on their own. Activities that were normal even in the seventies—children walking down the street on their own or playing outdoors with friends—have become increasingly rare. Instead, parents drive their kids to school, drive them to after-school care, or take them to other types of organized activities supervised by adults.

The irony is that many of those concerned with the institution of the family complain that parents do not spend enough time with their children. It is widely believed that a new generation of selfish career-oriented adults are refusing to take responsibility for bringing up their children. But such complaints fail to mesh with reality. One of the big myths of our times is that mothers and fathers spend less time with their children than previously. The new cultural norms that demand the constant supervision of children in fact represent a major new claim on parents' time. According to a recent Cornell University study, *Child Rearing Time by Parents*, parents with two children put in seven and a half hours a day raising their children. Another study, published by the University of Michigan in the summer of 2001, reports that children between the ages of three and twelve in two-parent families spent about thirty-one hours per week with their mothers in 1997 compared with about twenty-five hours in 1981. Time spent with fathers increased from nineteen to twenty-three hours.[3]

One consequence of parents spending more time with their children is that children spend less time playing together or alone without the company of adults. Allowing children to play unsupervised or leaving them at home on their own is increasingly interpreted as a symptom of irresponsible parenting. No doubt, some parents are neglectful and make decisions that put their children at risk. However, chaining children to their parents will benefit no one. Allowing children to play on their own is essential for their personal development. Children thrive when they have the freedom to explore the world with their friends. For their part, parents also need their own space.

Those who question the merits of the constant supervision of children are sometimes accused of reckless parenting. Parents who allow their children to walk to school unsupervised may find themselves the subjects of local gossip. Mothers and fathers who allow their children to stay at home on their own after school are regularly admonished for courting danger.

Family Life advises the anxious parent to find out what the local law says about when you can leave your child alone at home and warns that "you still won't know how the police might interpret the law if your child gets hurt when she is alone."[4] "Good parenting" now seems to mean protecting children from the experience of life—supervising them and chaperoning them to keep them safe.

This book explores the phenomenon of paranoid parenting. It makes no apology for failing to provide answers to the many questions that people ask in the course of raising their children. Instead, it tries to explain why parenting has become such a troublesome enterprise and encourages parents to believe in their innate capacity to act as capable fathers and mothers. There is little basis to the fears that fuel parental paranoia. Children are far healthier and safer now than at any other time in history, and if we can resist subjecting them to our anxieties, they are likely to thrive and develop into well-balanced adults.

Anxious Parents, Battered Children

Every message directed at parents comes with a health warning. "It's 4 P.M. Do You Know Where Your Children Are?" asks a headline in *Newsweek*, before informing parents that the most dangerous time of day for kids is between 2 P.M. and 8 P.M.[5] Experts use the word *alarming* to describe every conceivable child-related setting. "While the actual numbers of students injured in and around schools in the United States is not known, the estimates are alarming," warns a report on the subject.[6] It appears that lack of reliable facts is not a barrier to transmitting "alarming estimates" to parents. The objective of these warnings is to put pressure on moms and dads to alter their approach to child rearing. So the Safe Kids Campaign's survey of sports injuries to children directly targets parent behavior. According to the campaign chairman, C. Everett Koop, the attitude of parents needs to change, since many of them accept "that getting hurt is part of playing the game."[7] Safe Kids is uncomfortable with the fact that many parents do not turn their children's routine sports injury into a drama and demands—you guessed it—yet more adult supervision. The cumulative impact of these scare tactics is to transform normal parental anxiety into paranoia. If so much of a child's life needs to be regulated, then the only responsible solution is to never let children out of your sight and never allow them an independent existence.

Some observers may finally be recognizing the damaging consequences of paranoid parenting. "Is the war on risk scaring our kids to death?" asks Robert Wright in an essay critical of America's obsession with child safety.[8] Dave Shiflett has challenged the way in which child-safety advocates have constructed a world that takes on "the appearance of a big death trap."[9] Some experts are concerned about the way that safety-conscious recreation fails to engage the creative side of children. Roger Hart, the codirector of the Children's Environments Group at the Graduate Center of the City University of New York, believes that childproofing the world has led to the decline of rough-and-tumble play. "We don't understand that play is important enough to allow children to get dirty," argues Hart.[10]

For some time now, educators and psychologists have been concerned that young children are turning into couch potatoes as timid parents stifle their sense of adventure. Numerous studies document how children's independent activity has contracted. Since the 1970s, a growing part of children's lives is devoted to adult-supervised structured activities. According to a study carried out by the University of Michigan's Institute for Social Research, the time children spend in school is on average up by more than ninety minutes a week since 1981. This is happening because more children spend more time in preschool and before-and after-school child-care programs.[11] In 1981, the average American school child had 40 percent of the day for free time—meaning hours left over after sleeping, eating, studying, and engaging in organized activities. By 1997, the figure was down to 25 percent.

Unfortunately, this small band critical of paranoid parenting is overwhelmed by the majority of professionals, who are committed to putting more structure into children's lives. They have invented the term "self-care" to describe what children do on their own at home. Typically, parenting experts claim that self-care limits a child's horizons, "while good child care will offer stimulating, enriching situations and help develop social skills and confidence."[12] Of course good child care can provide a stimulating environment for youngsters, but what children learn about their environment through self-care is no less important. Professionals may distrust independent activities and prefer structured ones because only the latter justify their existence.

Unsupervised children's activity—it used to be called *play*—is now defined by child professionals as a risk. Some professionals regard play as an inferior form of activity that children can well do without. "Unlike the rather serendipitous learning that can occur through play, project-based activities can provide more intentional and planned learning experiences, while still offering many of the attractive qualities of play," argues the National Institute on Out-of-School Time.[13] One of the most destructive consequences of this denigration of free play is the decline of children's independent activity. Supervised play is virtual play. Unsupervised activity—where children can test their limits independent of an adult framework—is crucial for their development. They should be allowed to make mistakes, and to learn from them. Children must learn to make decisions for themselves, something they can never do under a parent's watchful eye. They need street smarts. Supervising children, cocooning them, can seriously damage their health. Why? Because when children are with adults, they tend to remain childish at precisely the time when they need to learn to grow up. Playing, imagining, and even getting into trouble has contributed to the sense of adventure that has helped society forge ahead. A community that loses its sense of adventure and ambition does so at its peril, and yet that is precisely what may happen when socializing children consists, above all, of inculcating fears into them.

Children now spend so much time cooped up at home that the safety of their indoor environment has come under intense scrutiny. Parents are continually warned about the dangers that toys represent to their children's well-being. The U.S. Consumer Product Safety Commission exhorts parents to monitor children playing with their toys. "Play is safer when adults are involved than when toys are given to children and parents supervise from a distance," it observes.[14] Since they see child's play as life threatening, safety experts cannot resist the temptation of portraying popular toys as potential death traps. Recently, children's scooters have provided a focus for their obsession. Typically, their propaganda inflates the risk of scootering in order to force parents onto the defensive. Talking up this "alarming trend," Heather Paul, executive director of the Safe Kids Campaign, reprimands moms and dads with a lecture. "Parents and care givers must do better," she observes.[15]

Health warnings do not attach themselves only to new toys—but also to products that have been trusted by generations of parents. "I consider myself a cautious parent, but I was recently surprised to learn that bagels, balloons, and hot bulbs can all be hazardous to my kid's health," writes a contributor to a parenting magazine.[16] The article explains how bagel-cutting invites injury to an uncoordinated child and how an eight-year-old who bites an inflated balloon could die from choking on it. The message of the article is that since nothing is safe, you would do well to be paranoid. Safety professionals and parenting experts are continually looking for risks that no mother or father has ever thought about. The periodical *Parents* publishes a regular feature titled "It Happened to Us." Every issue contains a story about an unusual accident that happened to a family—the moral of the story is that it can happen to you, too. "Our Child Got Burned by a Cellar Door," "My Baby Fell Down the Basement Stairs," "My Baby Was Nearly Strangled by My Hair," or "A Bouncy Seat Hurt My Baby" are some of the stories recounted. While it is not evident what these articles aim to accomplish, their only possible effect is to scare parents about one more trivial aspect of their children's lives. Scare stories about cellar doors, basement stairs, bouncy seats, and the length of a mother's hair are not important in and of themselves. But they feed into and reinforce a climate that continually forces parents onto the defensive.

Relentless Advice

Well-intentioned advice has become the bane of parents' lives. As I am writing, the radio has just announced a new study revealing that since children absorb up to 50 percent more radiation from mobile phones than adults do, these gadgets represent a serious risk to their health. Dr. Gerald Hyland, a physicist at Warwick University, England, warns that parents who dish out phones as presents to their children are making a dangerous mistake. "It's totally irresponsible for parents to allow their children to have these," argues Hyland. Ironically, many parents issue phones as a safety measure in case a child is stranded and needs a lift home.

Health scares affecting children are a particularly invidious source of anxiety to parents. It only takes one speculative study on a potential new risk to set off another parental panic. According to a recent survey of 1,600 parents of young children in the journal *Pediatrics*, 25 percent worried that routine vaccinations could weaken their infants' immune systems.[17] Such fears, completely unsupported by scientific evidence, are the product of ill-informed gossip transmitted through the media.

Every parent is plagued by the media-fueled fear that crib death, or sudden infant death syndrome (SIDS), might suddenly snatch their child away in the night. These apprehensions are regularly reinforced by new studies that claim to have discovered yet another cause of crib death. Small, obscure studies contradicting previous findings are reported as serious news. In 1998, there was widespread public discussion around a study claiming that crib death was caused by pollution from traffic and industry. This report was followed by another that insisted that quilts put babies at risk of crib death. And this was succeeded by a study of thirty-four infants suggesting indirectly that babies flying on airplanes faced a significant risk of crib death. A few weeks later, parents were reassured that flying does not kill their babies.

The relentless publicity that surrounds crib death produces anxieties that are completely disproportionate to the scale of the problem. Sudden infant death syndrome is very rare and declining steadily. The number of such deaths in the 1990s fell from 5,000 to less than 3,000 yearly. Yet campaigns around this issue continue to generate a sense of insecurity among parents, who fear a tragedy that is extremely unlikely to happen. This can only undermine their enjoyment of their baby's early life and encourages them to be overattentive and overprotective. It almost seems that campaigns around SIDS seek to guilt-trip parents. In February 2001, the American Academy of Pediatrics recommended that child-abuse specialists should investigate all SIDS cases. The implication is that parents of a child who died of SIDS are guilty until proven innocent. Through promoting the presumption that fathers and mothers are likely to be responsible for SIDS, the Academy sends out the message that parents cannot be trusted to look after their babies.

It is a sign of the pervasiveness of parental fear that many scare stories about children's health touch upon practices that were in the past advocated as beneficial. Parental advice is not rocket science. Reports on children's safety often contradict one another, and experts seem unable to agree which end of the baby is up. In recent years, many professionals have advocated the practice of co-sleeping on the grounds that it promotes breast-feeding and strengthens bonds between parents and child. The practice has gained popularity with young couples who, absent during the day, are reluctant to be separated from their children at night. However, in September 1999, the U.S. Federal Consumer Product Safety Commission issued an alarmist statement warning parents not to sleep in the same bed with infants under the age of two. It claimed that sleeping together poses a significant risk of accidental smothering or strangling. "Don't sleep with your baby or put the baby down to sleep in an adult bed," counseled Ann Brown, the commission's chairwoman. One would think that a pronouncement like this one, which directly affects the daily practice of millions of parents, was based on research conclusively showing that babies died specifically because they were sleeping in their parents' bed. But the study did nothing of the sort. The authors acknowledged that they did not take account of any other risk factors. They merely noted that 557 children under the age of two died while sleeping with their parents in their beds. Although the report could not substantiate a direct causal relationship between co-sleeping and infant death, it could clearly offer one more problem for parents to worry about.

Yet according to some experts, sleeping with your baby is of tremendous benefit to the child's development. William and Martha Sears, in their *The Baby Book: Everything You Need to Know About Your Baby—from Birth to Age 2*, insist that sleeping with your baby is a natural way to bond. There can be no doubt about this advice. The Searses ask rhetorically, "which do you think your baby prefers: to drift off to sleep peacefully at his mother's breast or to soothe himself to sleep with a tasteless, emotionless rubber pacifier?" But hold on! A very different message is conveyed in *What to Expect the First Year*. This successful manual, written by three American mothers backed by an army of doctors and caring professionals, says that "those who opt for the family bed" need to be made "aware of the possible risks" of letting their child sleep with them. Such as? Sleep problems, developmental problems, peer problems, marital problems, safety problems, "drawing the line" problems—even dental problems.

On the other side of the argument, Sheila Kitzinger, author of *The New Pregnancy and Childbirth* and other parenting texts, assures readers that leaving a child to sleep alone in his crib "may not be the safest arrangement . . . there is some evidence that a mother's movements during sleep, and the noises that she makes, stimulate a baby's breathing." But just as mother rushes to bring baby into her bed, pediatrician Bradley Thatch of Washington University School of Medicine in St. Louis tells us that an adult bed can be a potentially dangerous place for a tiny infant because it has other bodies, blankets, pillows, and crevices in which he could get lost. So we are damned if we do and damned if we don't. The people who definitely will not get any sleep after reading all this are petrified parents.

Of course, getting babies to sleep has always been a fundamental problem. In his classic child-care manual *Baby and Child Care*, the late Dr. Spock says that if you are having trouble getting your baby to sleep, the cure is simple: "Put the baby to bed at a reasonable hour, say goodnight affectionately but firmly, walk out of the room, and don't go back." What could be clearer than that?

Unfortunately, in the book *Your Baby and Child*, Penelope Leach is equally clear that "tearing yourself away, leaving him to howl, cannot be the right answer." If "your baby cries when you leave, go back," she counsels. But as you quietly make your way back to the baby's bedroom, Spock's warning rings in your ears: "It's important not to tiptoe in to be sure the baby is safe or to reassure her that you are nearby. This only enrages her and keeps her crying much longer." So you turn away again, only to be confronted by a recently published study claiming that leaving your baby to cry will not only spoil her night's sleep but could ruin her entire life.

The sleeping debate rages on. Parenting guru Richard Ferber champions the strategy of letting your baby cry for a while before you comfort her. His rival, Dr. William Sears, adopts the no-wait approach and lectures parents to be at the beck and call of their crying baby.

Toilet training has also become a battlefield for rival child experts. John Rosemond, a bestselling author of parenting books, has published articles in more than one hundred newspapers attacking wishy-washy parenting. Rosemond demands a return to traditional child-rearing practices and advocates that children should be toilet trained by the age of two. The process, he says, should be as simple and straightforward as housebreaking a four-month-old puppy. Dr. T. Berry Brazelton, a well-known pediatrician, is horrified by Rosemond's approach. He argues that parents who force toilet training can cause long-term problems for their children. In the meantime, parents are left wondering as to whether they should let their children decide when they are ready to use the toilet or take matters into their own hands and train their offspring into the mysteries of this science. And whatever they decide, they will get a slap on the wrist from some expert for doing things wrong.

This slap may be a metaphorical one, but when it comes to the highly charged issue of parents spanking their children, the debate is venomous. Many child-protection experts believe that spanking children constitutes a form of abuse. Their sentiment was upheld in 1997 by the European Court of Human Rights in Strasbourg when it awarded ten thousand pounds in damages to a British boy who sued his stepfather for a beating he received. For its part, the British government indicated that while it would make sure that children were protected from severe beatings, it would defend the right of parents to spank their children. Most parents continue to believe that it is acceptable for them to spank a naughty child. The American Academy of Pediatrics (AAP) took a firm stand against spanking in April 1998. However, a survey of its own members indicated that four out of ten participating pediatricians recommended spanking as a form of discipline "under limited circumstances and with specific conditions and rules." The AAP's survey showed that 90 percent of American families use spanking as a means of discipline. Parental insecurities about this subject have been exploited by a New Zealand Company called Safe Smack Limited. In October 1997, it marketed a Safe Smack Parenting Program, which included a patented leather strap known as the "Uncle Sam

Smacker." The company claimed that this strap was "the only safe way to smack children" and assured potential customers that its product was good for children. Predictably, child-protection advocacy groups denounced the Uncle Sam Smacker as dangerous.

Controversy surrounds not only spanking but the exercise of parental discipline itself. Some experts criticize even the concept of "time-out." Dr. Otto J. Arnoscht believes that time-out is an effective teaching tool that demonstrates acceptable behavior to a child. In contrast, Dr. Peter Haiman contends that instead of correcting bad behavior, time-out may actually aggravate it.

The controversy that surrounds the question of how adults should discipline their children exposes the highly politicized character of parenting. Advice on spanking has little to do with the specific needs of an individual child. Instead it is driven by competing ideologies about what constitutes an appropriate form of family life. Many opponents of spanking are suspicious of parents' motives toward the disciplining of their children. Those who support the right of parents to spank their children are often motivated by the objective of restoring traditional family values. Highly polarized advice about spanking undermines the ability of mothers and fathers to negotiate the difficult choices they have to make when forced to discipline their children. There will always be some expert who will criticize parents for being too robust or too soft in their approach to child rearing.

The discussion on spanking is part and parcel of the current tendency to question every aspect of parental behavior. Parents who place pressure on their children to perform well in sports or in school are sometimes denounced as emotional abusers. In contrast, parents who leave their children's education to their teachers are stigmatized for neglect. Either way, it is always assumed that parents who ignore one side or the other are highly irresponsible individuals. Thus it is that the advice givers—sometimes inadvertently—transform routine aspects of parenting into major scientific or ideological issues. Probably the main consequence of their advice is to intensify parental paranoia.

The Assumption of Parental Incompetence

Parents are not just continually bombarded with advice, they are also labeled incompetent. A study of 1,025 parenting articles and advice columns in the United States, carried out by Mary McCaslin and Helen Infanti, indicated that parents were presented as the problem in 97 percent of the entries. At the same time, although parents were deemed to be responsible for causing problems, they were not perceived to have the competence to deal with them. Sixty-eight percent of the entries advised parents to follow the advice of an expert, while parents were counseled to act on their own judgment in just 29 percent of the entries. Most research carried out on parenting has as its premise the view that parents have less expertise on the subject than the professional mounting the research. Surveys of professional attitudes toward parents suggest they hold them in low regard and mistrust parent competence and commitment to the education and upbringing of their children.

Parenting experts often complain, only partly in jest, that child rearing is the only profession that does not require rigorous training or qualification. Some experts take the view that parents are not only incompetent but also too stupid to learn the necessary skills. Consequently, the efficacy of parenting classes has come under scrutiny. Experts claim that parenting classes get in between them and the child. Matthew Melmed, executive director of the Washington-based advocacy group Zero to Three, says that "for programs to be effective, what seems to matter is the child's direct involvement in the services." Cutting parents out is the secret aspiration of some child experts.

The impulse to transform parenting into a hugely complicated skill that requires special training can take highly intrusive and totalitarian forms. In the United States, some experts have proposed that parents be required to obtain a license from the government to raise their children. Jack C. Westman's book *Licensing Parents: Can We Prevent Child Abuse and Neglect?* offers an extreme variant of the conviction that many mothers and fathers are not fit to parent children. Such authoritarian experts seldom say what they would do with women who became pregnant without a license. Most experts are far more restrained in their advocacy of parenting education and stop well short of demanding parental licensing. They tend to confine themselves to simply drawing attention to parental shortcomings. For example, Professor John Gottman, author of *The Heart of Parenting*, pontificates: "There is a big difference between wanting to do right by your children and actually having the wherewithal to carry it off." Gottman's message is clear: "Read my book or you will fail as a parent."

Some parenting guides and magazines seem to assume that their readers are pathologically stupid. Scolding parents for their incompetence usually serves as a prelude to scaring them with the terrible consequences that their failure represents to their children's futures. Such advice undermines parental confidence while inflating the responsibility of mothers and fathers for every aspect of their children's lives. The paradox that drives parents paranoia is being told that although they are hopelessly incompetent, they also bear greater responsibility for the well-being of their children than did parents of previous generations. To parent acceptably, mothers and fathers should be permanent supervisors, be experts in literacy skills, and possess a university degree in counseling. Only professionals can cope with the basics of bringing up children. Parents in turn end up treating their offspring as an endangered species. Every aspect of conceiving, bearing, and raising children is subject to professional advice, since, the experts agree, child rearing is too important a task to leave to parents.

Since parenting has been transformed from an intimate relationship that depends on emotion and warmth into a skill involving technical expertise, the role of the expert assumes a special significance. Let's take parenting out of the family so that enlightened professionals can put things right. Those who advocate parental training justify their proposal on the grounds that it helps to empower confused adults. In fact, despite the claims of empowerment, this approach can only have the effect of further undermining parents' confidence in their abilities. No doubt it has been assumed that all this professional advice and intervention leads to a more confident and informed generation of proud new parents. Instead, it seems that today's parents are less secure and less confident than their own parents ever were.

The truth, of course, is that the relationship between parent and child is a qualitative one that cannot be improved by the application of a technical formula. Such intervention can, however, undermine the integrity of the parent-child relationship. When professionals encroach on this relationship, it necessarily weakens the authority of parents. And parents with weak authority are unlikely to become confident at handling their children.

Professional intervention rests on the bureaucratic conviction that because parenting has got to be learned, it must also be taught. This misguided approach fails to grasp the elementary relationship between human experience and learning. We learn many things in life in our own way, through experience. Such lessons cannot be taught through a course drawn up by experts. These courses encourage the parents to develop a relation of dependence on the professional.

To make matters worse, child professionals do not merely give advice, they intrude into parents' lives. Recently, when my wife took Jacob into his preschool and explained that he had bruised himself falling over, one of the staff joked that social services would have to be informed. Everybody laughed—if a bit too nervously. Afterward, one of the mothers whispered to my wife, "Amy had two bruises last week. You have no idea how nervous I was in case people jumped to the wrong conclusion." This exchange of confidences is symptomatic of the temper of our times. Something has clearly gone wrong when parents live in fear that the most innocent incident can be interpreted as malign and lead to intrusive inquiries. In such circumstances, parents are quite entitled to feel paranoid.

During the course of researching this subject, I learned a lot from the parents that I interviewed. Probably the main insight that I gained is that, although not all of us are paranoid parents, none of us is immune from the climate of insecurity that afflicts child rearing today. But if we can understand why we behave the way we do, I hope we can do something about its dreadful effects on our youngsters.

Making Sense of Parental Paranoia

Tony is giving up teaching. Although he would not use the words, it was parental paranoia that drove him out of the elementary school where he had taught for three years. During his teacher training, Tony had anticipated that he might be stretched by the challenge of dealing with rowdy children. But he was not prepared for the task of coping with difficult, anxious parents. The most taxing moments of his working life were to be spent dealing with worried moms. He sighs as he tells of the mother who insisted on driving behind her son's school bus to ensure that he arrived safely. He wearily recalls how a school trip to the seaside, planned for a class of five-year-olds, was cancelled because two parents were concerned that the trip would involve their children in a forty-five-minute journey in a private car. Would the cars be roadworthy? Who would accompany a child to the lavatory? Who would ensure correctly fitting seat belts? Were these normally nonsmoking cars, or would the children be made victims of passive smoking? The planned pirate's day on the beach ended up being confined to the school field—sea, sand, and adventure confined to the imagination, and many of the trip's educational aims undermined. Exasperated by "problems—all in the minds of parents," Tony sought, and found, a career outside teaching.

Of course, it is normal for parents to be concerned about the well-being of their children. A brief inspection of the pages of *Parents* magazine from the 1920s and 1930s shows that our grandparents were haunted by many of the doubts, worries, and preoccupations that torment fathers and mothers today. A frequently revisited topic was: Is my child's development normal? Child tantrums, shyness, aggression, jealousy, thumb sucking, nail biting, and refusing to sleep were regularly raised in letters from concerned parents. Many begged an answer to the age-old problem of how to get children to obey their parents.

It might seem that not much has changed. But the superficial similarities betray some big differences. In the past, parental anxiety focused on problems within the family. Infant health—physical, psychological, and moral—was an important preoccupation, as was preparing children for the outside world—school, career, marriage. And of course, the older generation was often anxious about their children falling in with bad company and generally getting up to no good.

Reading parental worries published in the 1920s, the overall impression is something like this: family life is fine, but there is just this *one* little thing that we need to sort out. Today the discussions in parenting magazines suggest that family life is far from fine, that most parents feel out of control, and that everything is up for question. Instead of being troubled by a specific concern, parents seem to be suffering a general loss of confidence.

The parents who write to magazines today seem overwhelmed by the sheer scale of troublesome issues confronting them. Every little issue— how to toilet train a child, when you can leave a child home alone, whether to force children to eat their greens—is made into a bigger problem by an overall crisis of parental nerve. This suggests that there must have been some major changes in the way that adults negotiate the task of looking after kids. The clearest symptom of this trend is the public panic about child safety.

I am looking at an ad inside a 1950 copy of *Life* magazine with Myra, a mother of a three-year-old, from Boston. The picture shows a multitude of babies sitting in their buggies outside a large A&P supermarket. Their mothers are inside the store doing their shopping. The byline to the ad states, "It's a pretty good sign, when you see a pram parade lined up outside a store, that mothers are inside doing a smart bit of shopping." There is a look of incredulity on Myra's face. We both know that today, these mothers doing a "smart bit of shopping" would be reported to the police.

In recent years, no issue has come under closer scrutiny than the question of children's safety. It has become so highly charged that a single incident can spark a major public debate and demands for new regulations. The tragic school shootings at Columbine have turned youth violence into an immediate problem facing all parents. The frightening images associated with school homicide have led to a flurry of legislative activity. New zero-tolerance policies in schools have helped create the impression that American schools are a uniquely dangerous territory for children. Millions of parents have concluded that no child is safe anymore. Eighty-one percent of parents surveyed in a *Newsweek* poll took the view that there has been an increase in gun-related incidents at schools. Yet in fact, violence in the classroom has declined dramatically during the past decade. The chances of being murdered at school are less than those of being struck by lightning.[1] However, it only takes one terrible tragedy to incite parents to become apprehensive about yet another danger facing their youngsters.

One reason why the issue of school violence has had such an impact on mothers and fathers is that parents are often blamed for every tragedy involving children. In the aftermath of the Columbine shootings, the question "Where were the parents?" was repeated time and again. Many observers assume that parents are morally culpable for every misfortune involving children, and thus parents feel under considerable pressure to demonstrate that they are fanatically committed to policing their children.

Public concern with safety has reached obsessive proportions. The remote possibility that children might choke on small toys in packets of cereals, chocolates, and potato chips has provoked demands to ban them. Baby walkers, which have been used for years to allow infants to whiz about before they can walk alone, have been condemned because of the possibility that children may topple over or fall down the stairs. Admittedly, this danger is more real than that of death by Pokemon card ingestion, but it is still triggered by the idea that something might happen and not by specific evidence that anything has happened.

Once in place, parental paranoia easily attaches itself to any new experience. Take in-vitro fertilization (IVF). Rather than celebrating the potential of IVF to create wanted children, researchers have recently warned about hypothetical dangers to the children being brought to life. There have been warnings that IVF could induce changes in children's genetic makeup and impair their mental development, and speculation about whether sperm that have to be assisted to fertilize an egg will produce babies as healthy as sperm that can swim on their own. Psychologists muse about whether people who become parents by artificial means after years of infertility will be able to relate, in an emotionally stable manner, to their much-wanted children. It has even been suggested that IVF children will be loved too much and may not be able to live up to their parents' hopes for them. It is only a matter of time before the fertile imagination succeeds in turning IVF into a child-safety issue.[2]

The Internet has a remarkable potential to enhance young people's lives by providing educational opportunities. Yet it is widely seen as another new technology that poses *dangers* to children. Much of the discussion about the World Wide Web has focused on how to protect young people from its perils, to prevent innocents from stumbling across adult sites or into the clutches of pedophiles. "The Internet can be a big and dangerous place for your children, but for the price of a local phone call, it needn't be," promises a newspaper advertisement for an Internet provider specializing in protecting children in cyberspace. Such manipulative marketing schemes are confident that they can convert parental paranoia into hard cash.

Virtual reality provides infinite space for the exercise of the anxious imagination, an unknown world where our fear of invisible strangers can run riot. Since children are often more adept at negotiating the Net, parental control is forced to confront uncomfortable new challenges. "You don't know what's out there," a group of fathers confided in me. One raised the specter of pedophile rings lurking in the shadows online, ready to pounce on his unsuspecting teenagers by e-mail. Nobody I talked to had actually heard of any child being damaged, but nevertheless they regarded the Internet as a really big problem. As one parents' guide to the Internet warns: "You might think you have taken adequate steps to protect your child, but please beware that a determined child might nonetheless be able to circumvent any protective software or security measure."[3] And apparently, there are other risks to worry about. A London conference on parenting in April 2000 was informed by Dr. Jane Healy, an American educational psychologist, that computers can also damage children's brain development.[4]

Old-fashioned television is often indicted for its negative impact on children. Parents complain that television is teaching their children to be violent shopaholics. They protest that video games distract children from reading or riding bikes. Even parents who rely on the VCR to keep their children busy feel guilty about their pragmatic embrace of this electronic babysitter. The experts encourage these concerns. One American study warns that the impact of the media on children "should be eliciting serious concern, not just from parents and educators but from physicians, public health advocates, and politicians as well."[5] In a world where they already feel powerless, parents experience television as yet another threat to their authority.

Parents mistrust the Internet and television because of a more general unease about having to cope with external influences upon their children. Many of these influences—television advertising, consumerism, the Internet—are portrayed as part of a complex new world that is causing parental insecurity. But adult overreaction to new technology is a symptom and not the cause of the problem. Many parents now feel so insecure and fearful of what they do not understand that virtually anything can be turned into a potential child-care crisis.

Most parents I interviewed appear to regard child rearing as something akin to preparing for war. They regard the world out there as hostile territory, inhabited by dangerous strangers devoted to the objective of hurting children. The gap between adult perceptions and the reality of the risks faced by children is confirmed by other studies in the Anglo-American world. A survey of U.S. pediatricians carried out in 1995 claimed that parental anxieties were on the rise among the parents of their patients— and that these anxieties tended to be significantly out of proportion to any real risks. The discrepancy between actual and imagined risks was particularly striking in relation to the dramatic issues of child welfare, such as abduction, environmental poisons, and cancer.[6]

Parents are particularly apprehensive about the threat of abduction of their children, creating a climate hospitable to rumors that can generate an atmosphere of panic. Take the following e-mail circulated to mothers of toddlers in a playgroup in Washington, D.C.:

CHILD ALERT!!!!!
Even if you do not have little kids, pass this one on to everyone you can think of. You never know who you might save by sending this e-mail! Please take the time and forward this to any friend who has children, baby-sits or has grandchildren! Thanks! I wanted to share something that happened today while shopping at Sam's Club. A mother was leaning over looking for meat and turned around to find her four-year-old daughter was missing. I was standing there right beside her, and she was calling her daughter with no luck. I asked a man who worked at Sam's to announce it over the loud speaker for Katie. He did and let me say he immediately walked right past me when I asked and went to a pole where there was a phone. He made an announcement for all the doors and gates to be locked, a code something. So they locked all the doors at once. This took all of three minutes after I asked the guy to do this.

They found the little girl five minutes later in a bathroom stall. Her head was half shaved, and she was dressed in her underwear with a bag of clothes, a razor, and wig sitting on the floor beside her to make her look different. Whoever this person was, took the little girl, brought her into the bathroom, shaved half her head, and undressed her in a matter of less than ten minutes. This makes me shake to no end. Please keep a close eye on your kids when in big places where it's easy for you to get separated. It only took a few minutes to do all of this—another five minutes and she would have been out the door.

I am still in shock that some sick person could do this, let alone in a matter of minutes. The days are over when our little ones could run rampant all over the place and nothing worse would happen than them annoying people. The little girl is fine. Thank God for fast workers who didn't take any chances.

BE SURE TO FORWARD THIS TO EVERYONE, SO THEY KNOW JUST HOW SICK PEOPLE ARE OUT THERE!!! (This happened at the Sam's Wholesale Club in Omaha, Nebraska.)

Yet another reminder of the sick people out there is of course the last thing that anxious parents need. Such reminders are continually transmitted through the media and by child-protection advocacy groups, politicians, and members of the public. A culture of fear has been constructed around the issue of stranger danger. Most recent national surveys indicate that as many as three out of four parents fear that a stranger will kidnap their child. This reaction is not surprising, since it is common to read alarmist claims that suggest that more than one million American children are kidnapped, lost, or missing or run away each year.[7] In reality, two to three hundred children are abducted yearly by nonfamily members and kept for a significant time or murdered. Such horrible tragedies do take place—but very rarely, and not more often than in the past. The risk of being kidnapped facing America's 64 million children remains very, very, very remote.

Fear of adult strangers has led parents on both sides of the Atlantic to restrict their children's independent outdoor activities. In 1971, in Britain, eight out of ten eight-year-olds were allowed to walk to school alone. Now it is less than one in ten. At age eleven, almost every child used to walk; now it is down to 55 percent and falling. A report published by the Children's Play Council in 1997 argued that children had become virtual prisoners in their own homes. American play activists contend that society is "robbing children of physical activity."[8]

Research has linked the decline in British children's fitness to the decrease in the amount of time they spend walking and cycling. The First National Travel Survey reported a fall of about 20 percent in the annual distance walked and 27 percent in the distance cycled by children between 1985 and 1993. An average British schoolgirl now walks for less than seven minutes a day. Deprived of the opportunity to burn calories by racing around outside, children grow fat.

A study published in the *British Medical Journal* in September 1999 found an alarming proportion of preschool children to be overweight and even obese. Among those aged two, 15.8 percent were considered overweight and 6 percent obese. By the time they reached age five, 18.7 percent were deemed overweight and 7.2 percent obese. In the United States, the problem of child obesity is even more extensive. According to the American Academy of Child and Adolescent Psychiatry, between 16 and 33 percent of children and adolescents are obese. A government report states that the percentage of children who are overweight has doubled since 1980.[9] Poor diet contributes to child obesity—but so does lack of physical exercise.

The Precautionary Approach to Parenting

Parental paranoia today is more than simply a worse version of past anxieties. For instance, a common target of child-rearing manuals before World War II was the overprotective parent; parents worried that they might be smothering their children. But how many times do we hear parents criticized for being overprotective today? Many of the traits associated with the classic overprotective father or mother are likely to be praised by today's child experts as responsible parenting.

Researchers advise parents to supervise children, not only outdoors, but even when they watch television. The term *coviewing* has been coined to describe the practice of hands-on parents playing the role of a "media value filter and a media educator." Other researchers claim that parental supervision inoculates children from many of the dangers they face. They contend that "parental monitoring has been inversely associated with antisocial behavior, drug use, tobacco use, and early sexual activity."[10] There is obviously some truth in this. The more time a child spends in the company of his or her parents, the less time is available for smoking, drinking, and sex. But to equate the amount of parental supervision directly with behavioral outcomes tells parents that the more time they manage to spend with their children, the better off their offspring will be. This raises the question of where to draw the line. How do parents decide how much monitoring is reasonably required, as opposed to optimally possible?

Unfortunately today, parental supervision is always interpreted as a positive virtue—so parents can never spend too much time supervising their youngsters. Child-rearing experts occasionally concede that it is simply impossible to keep children and young teenagers under constant adult supervision. But even then they insist that alternative, indirect forms of child surveillance be employed. One American expert argues that if a child has to be left under self-care, then parents must do whatever they can to supervise in absentia, by liasing with a trusted adult who knows what the youngster is up to. The message is clear: if you are going to shirk your responsibility toward your child even for a few hours, you must at least make sure that somebody else is doing your job for you.[11]

Parents are not just *advised* to supervise their children. This advice contains the implicit threat of legal sanction. Although in most states there is no statutory age at which it is illegal to leave children unattended, many counties and municipalities have issued guidelines. For example, the Department of Family Services in Fairfax County, Virginia, suggests that eleven- to twelve-year-olds should not be left alone for more than three hours. Some child professionals go so far as to claim that it is wrong to allow even a thirteen-year-old to be left alone.[12] What a shock this would have been to the parents of latchkey kids in the 1970s! In those days, many thirteen-year-olds were charged with the responsibility of looking after their younger siblings. Then, debate about the children of working mothers returning from school to empty homes focused on whether it was right for women to have jobs, which deprived their children of a welcoming smile and the smell of home baking. The issue was not seen as one of child safety and certainly not of abandonment. Yet today, the very act of allowing children to play at home on their own after school is perceived as court-ing danger. Many child professionals consider leaving a child on his own an act of neglect. Even though few parents are prosecuted in these cir-cumstances, the strict guidelines convey a clear message about what soci-ety expects of parents. And that expectation is founded on the premise that parents can never do too much to protect their children.

And it gets worse. It appears that even older teenagers require constant adult supervision. A report released by the YMCA in March 2001 claimed that unsupervised teens are four times more likely to be D students than teens supervised every day. The report targets fourteen- to seventeen-year-olds as potential recruits for organized-supervised activities.[13] How long before college students are transformed into vulnerable children in need of constant parental monitoring?

Twenty or thirty years ago, authors of child-rearing manuals had their own way of making parents feel guilty. But they would have reacted with disbelief to the proposition that it was wrong to leave children under age thirteen alone in their home. Fortunately, there are still some societies where the overprotective parent is not promoted as a role model. Children in Norway and Finland "enjoy being at home without their parents from about seven onward," records Priscilla Alderson, a Reader in Childhood Studies at the Institute of Education in London. According to Alderson, Finnish children start school at seven years and sometimes go home at 11 A.M., where they play with friends until their parents arrive home in the late afternoon.[14] In Anglo-American societies, such practices would be condemned as child abuse.

The view that children cannot survive without the constant presence of a responsible adult is continually reinforced. Parents are often warned to use only babysitters who are over age sixteen. Even the time-honored practice of hiring fourteen- or fifteen-year-olds eager to earn some pocket money by helping moms and dads look after their children is now dis-missed as an act of gross irresponsibility.

Today's parenting style sees safety and caution as intrinsic virtues. Paranoid parenting involves more than exaggerating the dangers facing children. It is driven by the constant expectation that something really bad is likely to happen to your youngsters.

A morbid expectation that something terrible can happen any moment means that parents avoid many risks that are well worth taking because of their stimulating effect on a child's development. Child rearing today is not so much about *managing* the risks of everyday life but *avoiding* them altogether. As child psychologist Jennie Linden argues, the adult "preoccupation with risk can create too much emphasis on removing every conceivable source of even minor risk." The characteristic feature of such an obsession is, according to Linden, "to speculate excessively on what can go wrong rather than on what children may learn."[15] It is this precautionary approach that defines the parenting culture of contemporary society.

Parents have always been concerned about protecting their children from harm. Asking what can go wrong is a sensible way of dealing with the many new experiences children encounter. To weigh up probabilities before doing something is an informed way of managing risk. But asking what can go wrong is very different from acting on the assumption that things will go wrong. Such a fatalistic outlook reduces the power of parents to make informed, intelligent judgments. A more appropriate approach might be to follow an assessment of what can go wrong with two other questions—does it matter, and what might the child learn from the experience? The precautionary approach continually encourages adults to adopt the same one-dimensional response: beware!

It is tempting to interpret the precautionary approach to child rearing as the irrational reaction of individual mothers and fathers. Child professionals sometimes point the finger at overanxious parents and advise them to be more sensible about managing the risks their children face. Some old-fashioned observers blame a generation of timid parents for stifling the sense of adventure in American children. However, it is a mistake to reduce the problem to the personalities of some parents. How individual adults relate to their offspring at any time is inseparable from the parenting style encouraged by our culture and society.

The Erosion of Adult Solidarity

Christina Hardyment, in her excellent study of baby-care advice past and present, is struck by the intensity of parental paranoia today. She senses a climate of permanent panic that invites a guilt-ridden style of parenting. The loss of small children's freedom is one consequence.[16] In the past, not even the archetypal overanxious parent would have taken the precautionary approach that is now seen as the norm. Even though children have never been safer or healthier, at no time has so much concern and energy been devoted to protecting youngsters from harm.

Although surveys confirm that paranoid parenting is widespread, there has been little attempt to understand its causes. The most common explanation is that it is all the fault of the sensationalist media. Panics about children's safety are interpreted as "media led," and television is accused of making parents unnecessarily apprehensive. "Increasingly, we are bombarded by the news media with spectacular accounts of violence, illness and health concerns, as well as varied opinions about appropriate diets and child rearing practices," concluded the authors of one study of parental worries in the United States. They certainly have a point. Media focus on the tragic abduction of a child has a profound impact on the imagination of a parent. Through the media, an individual tragedy, such as the kidnapping at knifepoint of Polly Hannah Klaas, becomes the personal property of every parent. Not surprisingly, the images of a child victim stay fresh in their minds.

So yes, the media helps shape adults' perception of the risks faced by children. But it is far too simple to blame the media for the problems of parenting. Moms and dads do not need high-profile media horror stories to provoke their insecurities. Parents worry about all manner of everyday things, all the time. They can be anxious about Mary's weight on Monday, Tim's refusal to eat vegetables on Tuesday, the poor state of Mary and Tim's education on Wednesday, and so on. A heightened sense of insecurity can attach itself to relatively mundane experiences such as whether a child is too fat or too thin. The media do not cause paranoid parenting. Their main role is to amplify society's concerns, to give shape to our fears. Confusing the messenger with the bad news is an understandable reaction, but not one that will help illuminate the issues at stake.

So what is the bad news? In the chapters that follow, it should become clear that a variety of influences helps to shape contemporary anxieties about parenting. But if one thing above all others has created the conditions for today's parenting crisis, it is *the breakdown of adult solidarity*.

Adult solidarity is one of those unspoken facts of life that people used to take for granted. Most of the time in most places, people practice adult solidarity, even though they have never heard the term. In most communities throughout the world, adults assume a modicum of public responsibility for the welfare of children even if they have no ties to them. When the local newsagent or postman scolds a child for dropping a chewing gum wrapper on the road, he or she is actively assisting that boy's parents in the process of socialization. When a retired woman reprimands a young girl for crossing the road when the light is red, she is backing up her parents' attempts to teach her the ways of the world. These displays of public responsibility teach children that certain behavior is expected by the entire community, not just their mom and dad.

It has long been recognized that the socialization of children relies on a wide network of responsible adults. Parents cannot be expected to act as twenty-four-hour-a-day chaperones. Across cultures and throughout history, mothers and fathers have acted on the assumption that if their children got into trouble, other adults—often strangers—would help out. In many societies, adults feel duty-bound to reprimand other people's children who misbehave in public.

As every parent knows, in America today, fathers and mothers cannot rely on other adults to take responsibility for looking after their children. American adults are hesitant to engage with other people's kids. This reluctance to assume responsibility for the welfare of the young is not simply a matter of selfishness or indifference. Many adults fear that their action would be misunderstood and resented, perhaps even misinterpreted as abuse. Adults feel uncomfortable in the presence of children. They don't want to get involved and, even when confronted by a child in distress, are uncertain about how to behave.

Take the following scene in an elementary school in Bristol, England, during the spring of 2000. The teachers have organized a group of seven-year-olds to go outside the schoolyard to count the cars that pass by. Little Henry is bored and proceeds to poke his head through the railings that separate the schoolyard from the street. He gets his head stuck. The teachers are at a loss to know what to do. A crowd gathers around the trapped child. One teacher finds a jar of hand cream and applies some of it to the railing to help Henry wriggle out. It doesn't work. Parents begin to arrive to pick up the children. The teachers are standing around. Not one of them has attempted to pull Henry out. Not one of them has put an arm around the distressed boy in an act of reassurance. They are afraid of touching the child. Finally, Henry's mom arrives. She takes one look at her son, grabs hold of him, gives him a yank, and he is out. Henry's one-hour-and-twenty-minute ordeal is over.

The story was recounted to me in horror by a young teacher, as a statement about the world we live in. When I asked why she didn't do something to help little Henry, she said that she had already been reprimanded a year earlier for being "too physical" with one of her pupils.

Tragically, the same story is repeated time and again throughout the United States. An obsessive preoccupation about good touch and bad touch has made many teachers—even preschool teachers—wary about holding and comforting small children. "We advise our members not to touch children, especially as the children grow older," states a spokeswoman for a New Jersey teacher's union.[17] A climate of suspicion has led many day-care centers to prohibit workers from changing a baby's diaper without an another adult present. Gone are the days when day-care workers can feel relaxed about holding toddlers on their laps.

When we live in a society that warns off teachers, traditionally seen as in loco parentis, it is hardly surprising that strangers hesitate before becoming involved with other people's children. If a teacher is not allowed to cuddle a crying child for fear of the action being misinterpreted, no wonder that a passerby will turn her back on a weeping infant.

Awkward adults uncomfortable in the company of children represent a serious problem for parents. Mothers and fathers feel that they are on their own. Worse, many parents are convinced that it is best if other adults don't interfere in their children's affairs. Parents regard other people not as allies but as potential predators of their young ones. Clumsy adults inept at relating to kids and anxious parents concerned about stranger danger are two sides of the same coin.

This breakdown in adult solidarity breeds parental paranoia. The fear of the other person is the most tangible expression of parental insecurity. A 1998 survey carried out by the British advocacy group Families for Freedom noted that 89.5 percent of the respondents had a general sense of foreboding about the safety of their children. This general sense of alarm became more focused when other adults were brought into the equation. Seventy-six percent said that they were "very worried" about their children's safety in relation to "other people." The other person is the stranger. Research carried out by Mary Joshi and Morag Maclean in 1995 found that more parents gave "stranger danger" as a reason for using cars for school journeys than any other reason.[18]

Perhaps that is why parents in Britain are more likely to drive their children to school than in Germany, Scandinavia, and other parts of Europe, where the distance between home and school may be far greater. In societies where neighbors and other adults assume a degree of responsibility for keeping an eye on children, attitudes toward their safety are far less obsessive. A comparative study of children's independent mobility concluded that there is far less parental supervision in Germany than the United Kingdom. According to the authors, one reason why German parents are more likely to allow children out on their own is because they expect other adults to keep an eye on them; in turn, German children reported feeling that they are watched over by the adult world. This culture of collaboration creates a sense of security for German parents. The expectation that other adults will do the right thing helps them to take a more relaxed attitude toward letting their children out of the door than might be the case in America or Britain.[19]

A Poisonous Atmosphere for Parenting

The finger does not only point at other adults; American and British parents themselves have come under suspicion. The public is frequently warned that children are at risk from their own parents. Parents who find it difficult to deal with the pressures of everyday life have been portrayed as potential abusers. In May 2000, the UK National Society for the Prevention of Cruelty to Children (NSPCC) launched its Full Stop campaign.

Shocking pictures on billboards show a loving mother playing with her baby. The caption reads, "Later, she wanted to hold a pillow over his face." Another picture highlights a loving father cuddling his baby. The words *That night he felt like slamming her against the bed* serves as a chilling reminder not to be deceived by appearances. The NSPCC justified its scare-mongering tactics on the grounds that it was telling parents that it is normal to snap under pressure and that they need to learn to handle the strain. But this alleged link between parental incompetence and abusive behavior has disturbing implications for every father and mother. If anyone can snap and smash the head of his baby against the wall, whom can you trust?

It is easy for a mother or a father to lose control and lash out at a youngster. Regrettably, most of us have done it on more than one occasion. Snapping under pressure is a normal if unfortunate fact of life. But when we snap, we don't go on to smash our baby's head against the wall. The implication that parenting under pressure is an invitation to abuse is an insult to the integrity of millions of hardworking mothers and fathers. It also helps to create a poisonous atmosphere of suspicion and mistrust.

A booklet called *Protecting Our Children: A Guide for Parents*, sponsored by British Labor member of Parliament (MP) Dan Norris and with a foreword by Prime Minister Tony Blair, asserts that anybody can be a pedophile. "They live in our communities, in our families, and may even be someone we know and love," the booklet informs the reader. "How can seemingly kind and even respectable people abuse children?," it asks.[20] Anyone reading this book is invited to look at people "we know and love" with a newly suspicious eye. If it is indeed the case that anyone and everyone in our communities and our families should be treated with caution, then trust and collaboration between adults become impossible. The same message is echoed in the United States. Time and again the public is reminded that it is not just strangers but also family members who pose a danger to children. David Finkelhor, director of Crimes Against Children research center at the University of New Hampshire, claims that the "biggest perils are close at hand." "Between 50 to 100 kids are killed a year by strangers," said Finklehor, "whereas there are 1,000 killed by parents."[21] The message is clear—a far more formidable threat than stranger danger is parent danger.

Family life, once idealized as a haven from a heartless world, is now widely depicted as a site of domestic violence and abuse. If victimization within the family is pandemic, then clearly we are obliged to mistrust even those closest to us. The focus of anxiety can no longer be the alien stranger or criminal, but our closest family relations, neighbors, friends, lovers, and colleagues. Such a suspicious attitude toward everyday life redefines how people are expected to relate to those closest to them. Every year in Britain, some 120,000 parents experience the nightmare of being wrongly accused of child abuse.[22] Since normal parents are now portrayed as potential abusers, it is not surprising that so many face investigation on the basis of hearsay and rumor.

Scare campaigns that target parents represent a blow to the authority of every mother and father. Here and there, public figures still pay lip service to the great job performed by parents. But the ceaseless reminders of parental failure take their toll. Everyone now feels entitled to speculate about what Mary's dad is up to. Under this pressure, parents will openly criticize other parents—sometimes in front of the children. A society that expects parents to teach children to avoid strangers and to regard them with dread is storing up big problems for the future. When parents instruct children about stranger danger these days, they are also communicating a negative statement about the adult world—and, by implication, about themselves.

The Code of Mistrust

If family life is seen as suspect, if parents, brothers, and sisters cannot be entirely trusted, how can we have faith in the integrity of more distant acquaintances? This is the message conveyed on a daily basis through television and popular culture. Not a day goes by without another sordid tale of some professional abusing the trust that has been placed in him. The suspicion of abuse that hangs over the family has spread like a disease to infect other institutions from schools to Scout and Guide groups.

An editorial in the *British Journal of Sports Medicine* claims that sport is "the last refuge of child abuse." "I know it is going on from hundreds of interviews with athletes but it is difficult to get any statistical evidence," writes Celia Brackenridge.[23] Many sports organizations have issued guidelines about how to spot potential abusers working in their midst. In December 1998 the Amateur Swimming Association, in conjunction with the NSPCC, set up a help line for children on the grounds that their sport might be targeted by pedophiles like the Olympic swimming coach jailed for child sex abuse. In 1999, the England and Wales Cricket Board issued child-protection guidelines. At least one commentator blamed the collapse of English cricket on pedophiles, who made parents reluctant to allow unsupervised children to play the game.[24]

Predatory pedophiles have also become an issue with the St. John ambulance service, after three of its officers were jailed for the long-term abuse of cadets in 1998. The British Scout Association has been implicated in sex scandals. After a Coventry Scout master was jailed for indecency offences against two boys and a Hampshire Scout master was sentenced to six years for sexually abusing eight boys, the association adopted a policy to "safeguard the welfare of all members by protecting them from physical, sexual and emotional harm."

Even religious organizations have been implicated in this climate of fear. Almost every day we hear of a new scandal implicating pedophile Catholic priests.[25] In Australia, Roman Catholic bishops have sought to ban their priests from having any private contact with children. Guidelines drawn up with the approval of the Vatican mean that confessionals have to be fitted with glass viewing panels. Priests are also banned from seeing any child alone with the door closed.[26] Closed doors and private interaction are no longer acceptable to a society fed a constant diet of mistrust. It is as if by definition the closed door is an invitation to abuse.

Any one-to-one contact between adults and children has in effect been stigmatized. A guideline published by the Salvation Army advises its members to ensure that "an adult is not left alone with a child or a young person where there is little or no opportunity for the activity to be observed by others." It adds that this "may mean groups working within the same large room or working in an adjoining room with the door left open."[27] Salvation Army members were far from happy with this rule, since many of their activities involve musical practice. Since band members play different instruments at various levels of proficiency, a lot of the training took place one-on-one in separate rooms.[28] Nevertheless, the new order dictates that doors should be left open—and, presumably, ears closed.

A guideline issued by the British Home Office to voluntary organizations recommends that activities "which involve a single child working with an adult" should "take place in a room which can be observed easily by others in nearby areas, even if this is achieved simply by leaving doors open."[29] Scout Association guidelines warn scout leaders to avoid one-on-one situations and contact sports. Guidelines issued by the England and Wales Cricket Board tell coaches not to work with a child "completely unobserved" and suggest that "parents should take on the responsibility for their children in the changing room."[30]

The return of the medieval chaperone in Britain provides eloquent testimony to the regulation of adult contact with children. In one case, a rector at a village church was forced to disband a choir because of new guidelines on child protection. Up to twenty child choristers met weekly for rehearsals and sang every Sunday at St. Michael's Church in Northchapel, West Sussex. Rev. Gerald Kirkham had to stop recruiting because, under the new code, at least two adult chaperones were needed at choir practice.[31]

Mistrust of adults, especially of men, has had a destructive impact on working relations between adults and children. The British Scout Association faces a shortage of volunteer leaders. "If a man says he wants to work with young boys, people jump to one conclusion," reported Jo Tupper, a spokeswoman for the Scouts.[32] A similar pattern is evident in primary school education. Research carried out by Mary Thornton of Hertfordshire University suggests that men are turning away from primary school teaching because of fears that that they will be labeled perverts. Thornton claimed that men in teacher training programs "felt they had no idea how to deal with physical contact." Some of the trainees asked questions like "Should they cuddle a distressed child"?[33] When physical contact with children comes with a health warning, teachers face a continuous dilemma over how to handle routine issues in the classrooms. In August 1998, the Local Government Association even went so far as to advise teachers not to put sunscreen on pupils because it could lead to accusations of child abuse. Lord Puttnam, the inaugural chairman of the General Teaching

Council, has warned that when teachers are regarded as potential rapists and pedophiles, their authority is very seriously undermined.[34]

In November 1999, it was reported that "teachers, fearful of accusations of any kind of inappropriate touching, are increasingly wary of direct contact with the children in their charge, even if tears are involved." One school in Glasgow has responded to this "affection-phobic culture" by introducing special massage classes for children. The idea is that pupils will stay fully clothed and standing upright while they take turns massaging each other's heads, backs, and shoulders. While the teacher reads a story, they will also take turns massaging each other's forearms with plain, unscented oil.[35] A new ritual for an age that dreads physical contact between adult and child.

Fear of adults victimizing children is fueled by a child-protection industry obsessed with the issue of abuse. The NSPCC's *Safe Open Spaces for Children*, launched in August 1999, advises parents never to make their children "kiss or hug an adult if they don't want to." The justification for this proposal was that it would make children confident about refusing the advances of a stranger.[36] From time immemorial, parents have pleaded with their children to kiss or hug grandmothers and aunts. The call to ban this innocent practice is symptomatic of the intense professional mistrust of adult behavior toward children.

All this hysteria about physical contact actually does little to protect children. By casting the net so wide and expecting child abuse to be a normal occurrence, we run a danger of trivializing it. A climate of suspicion will not deter the child abuser, but it will undermine the confidence of all parents. And at the end of the day, confident parents are best placed to educate their children to deal with risks and danger.

The Flight from Children

From voluntary organizations to primary education, well-meaning adults are being put off from playing a valuable role in instructing and inspiring young children. At a conference organized by Playlink and Portsmouth City Council in November 1999, the delegates were enthusiastic professionals committed to improving children's lives through outdoor play. But several of the play workers felt that their role was diminished by bureaucratic rules designed to regulate their contact with children. One play worker complained that she often could not do "what's right" by the children, because not following the rules would threaten her career prospects.

Those who work with children are undermined by new conventions that control their behavior. If it is assumed that professional caretakers need to be told how to relate to the children in their charge, why should parents—or children—trust them? But it is not only professional caretakers or volunteers who are affected by this climate of paranoia. Suspicion toward them reflects and reinforces a more general distrust of adults. It is assumed that none of us can be expected to respect the line between childhood and adulthood, that we need to be told what almost all of us know by instinct—children are vulnerable creatures who need protection. This means comforting a distraught child with a cuddle just as much as it means not abusing those young people who have put their trust in you.

The negative image of adulthood enshrined in the new conventions has far-reaching implications. The healthy development of any community depends on the quality of the bond that links different generations. When those bonds are subjected to such intense suspicion, the ensuing confusion can threaten the very future of a community. After all, warmth and affection are inherent in family relationships, and in relations between children and other caretakers. If an adult touching a child comes to be regarded with anxiety, how can these relations be sustained?

It should really come as no surprise that some children have begun to play off this general distrust of adults to make life difficult for those they don't like. Most children are enterprising creatures, for whom adult insecurities provide an opportunity to exercise their power. Every year hundreds of teachers face false allegations of abuse. A teacher wept openly at the April 2000 conference of the Association of Teachers and Lecturers as he recounted his three months of agony after being falsely accused of punching a twelve-year-old pupil. Other teachers recounted cases of false accusation and demanded that school staff should not be treated as guilty until proven innocent.[37] It is tempting to blame malicious children for making life hell for some of their teachers. But it is not really their fault. They are merely manipulating a dirty-minded world created by obsessive adults.

The distrust of adult motives has encouraged a flight from children, a distancing between the generations. In some cases it has led to an avoidance of physical contact, in others the reluctance to take responsibility. Elderly people in particular are often unclear about what is expected of them in dealing with children. An eighty-two-year-old man with numerous grandchildren and great-grandchildren provides a classic illustration of this dilemma:

> I was in a shop and this woman came in who the wife knew, with her little granddaughter. I was eating a candy, and this little girl looked up at me, so I said, "Would you like a candy?" She got all scared and jumped back. And I said, "Well, that's the best thing you want to do. Never take a candy from anybody." She did right, but it made me feel cheap. It made me feel awful really, to think I was offering a little girl a sweet. And I love kiddies. In the paper you hear there are horrible people and it's awful, but it made me feel cheap.[38]

This octogenarian has internalized the new mood of suspicion toward adult motives. His mental retreat from following his well-meaning instincts toward the young girl is part of a general pattern. Sadly, this flight from children means that adult collaboration in raising the young rests on a fragile foundation. Parents of course cannot flee from their children. They are left to deal with the damage caused by the erosion of adult solidarity. They are truly on their own. The decline of adult solidarity means that parents must pay the cost of society's estrangement from its children.

Parents on Their Own

More than ever, parents are on their own. According to Professor John Adams of University College, London, we live in an age of hypermobility, where the car has facilitated a new level of social dispersal. Adams believes that hypermobility has led to increased anonymity of individual households, a decline of conviviality toward our neighbors, a less child-friendly environment, and the emergence of parental anxieties toward children's outdoor safety. His concerns are echoed by numerous studies that confirm a palpable sense of social isolation. Research surveys indicate that people now live farther away from relatives. Many of us barely know our neighbors and show little interest in their affairs. This indifference underlines the absence of communal affinity. We often live in neighborhoods without neighbors. The absence of an obvious network of support has important implications for how adults negotiate the task of child rearing.

The theme of social isolation is familiar to most parents. Mothers and fathers complain about an uneasy sense that they are "on their own." Many mothers, especially those who work, are preoccupied with what could go wrong with their child-care arrangements. When there are no relatives near, and you are not on first-name terms with your neighbors—who is to pick up your child when your meeting runs late? Who can stay home and nurse a child with chicken pox? The absence of an obvious backup, the tenuous quality of friendship networks, and the difficulty of gaining access to quality child care all create the feeling that life is one long struggle, increasing tensions within the household.

The fragmentation of family relations and the diminished sense of community have inevitably helped to make parents feel insecure. Not knowing where to turn in case of trouble can produce an intense sense of vulnerability—especially among single parents.

The isolation of parents is not simply physical. The erosion of adult solidarity transforms parenting into an intensely lonely affair. A climate of suspicion distances moms and dads from the world of adults. Parents become anxious and overreact—not just to the danger they see posed by strangers, but to every problem having to do with their youngsters' development. As we shall see, paranoid parenting now embraces almost every aspect of child rearing.

2

The Myth of the Vulnerable Child

Paranoid parenting is directly linked to the way our society regards children. Babies and infants are seen today as both intensely vulnerable and highly impressionable—above all to parental influences. They are said to be both greatly sensitive to the damaging effects of parental incompetence or neglect and responsive to parental nurturing and stimulation. The prevailing opinion conveyed in child-rearing manuals is that the long-term development of children is determined by their early experience, in which parents play a dominant and decisive role. It is claimed that if parental intervention during these early years is positive, children are destined to grow up to become intelligent and emotionally balanced adults. If it is negative, they are fated to become damaged individuals, condemned to personal failure. That is why adult failures are often represented as the consequence of problems encountered by children in their early years.

The interlocking myths of infant determinism, that is, the assumption that infant experience determines the course of future development, and parental determinism, the notion that parental intervention determines the future fate of a youngster, have come to have a major influence on relations between children and their parents. By grossly underestimating the resilience of children, they intensify parental anxiety and encourage excessive interference in children's lives; by grossly exaggerating the degree of parental intervention required to ensure normal development, they make the task of parenting impossibly burdensome.

The Denial of Resilience

Today we find it difficult to accept the fact that youngsters possess a formidable capacity for resilience. Hillary Rodham Clinton's folksy book on child rearing, *It Takes a Village*, begins with the sentence "Children are not rugged individualists." This statement —backed up by citations from well-known child experts—elevates vulnerability as childhood's defining condition. We often express this vulnerability through the phrase "children at risk." We think we understand the concept intuitively, even though it is rarely explained. When reporters allude to a child at risk, we rarely ask the obvious question: at risk of what? We don't ask because we already suspect that the reply would be: at risk of everything.

It is easy to overlook the fact that the concept of children at risk is a relatively recent invention. As I argue elsewhere, this way of imagining childhood involves a redefinition both of risk and of childhood.[1] Until recently, risks were not interpreted by definition as bad things. We used to talk about good, worthwhile risks as well as bad, foolish ones. Risks were seen as a challenging aspect of children's lives. Today, we are so afraid of risk that we have invented the concept of children at risk. A child that is at risk requires constant vigilance and adult supervision.

"Everywhere we look, children are under assault," claims Hillary Rodham Clinton. She believes children are under assault from "violence and neglect, from the breakup of families, from the temptation of alcohol, tobacco, sex and drug abuse, from greed, materialism, and spiritual emptiness." Here is a picture of a society that actively conspires to bring about the downfall of its children. Clinton concedes that these problems are not new but adds that, in our time, they have "skyrocketed."[2] Numerous other authors reaffirm the point that childhood has become more dangerous than ever before. Michele Elliot, author of *501 Ways to Be a Good Parent*, believes that previous generations of parents did not have to negotiate the worries that haunt mothers and fathers today. "It is no good asking our own mothers for advice," she writes. Why? Because "when they were bringing us up, they didn't seem to be hit by shocking news of yet another child murder."[3]

Every society has different ideas about the nature of childhood. Views about children change with fashion. Christina Hardyment, in her excellent study of the history of baby-care advice, shows how experts fluctuate between viewing children as little things that need hardening and toughening up or as vulnerable souls in need of constant love and attention. Since the end of World War II, the belief that children are fragile and vulnerable has gained strength. And since the 1980s, the belief that youngsters are inherently vulnerable and "at risk" has acquired the character of a cultural dogma. The experts have lost faith in children's resilience. They believe that children cannot cope with adverse experiences and that they are unlikely ever to recover from early traumatic episodes. Unpleasant encounters are said to scar children for life.

It is the exaggerated sense of children's vulnerability that justifies contemporary obsessions about their safety. Today, safety is no longer about taking sensible precautions. Parents are bombarded with advice that demands that they create a risk-free world. "Please keep your infant in your direct line of sight, even when you go to the bathroom," counsels a leaflet given to every new mother at Sibley Memorial Hospital in Washington, D.C. From the moment of birth, parents are directed to adopt a state of high alert.

The transformation of parks and playgrounds provides eloquent testimony to the fact that contemporary obsessions about children's vulnerability are reshaping everyday life. One accident in a playground can lead to its closure. In Greenwich, South East London, five playgrounds were permanently closed following an incident in which a child was injured.[4] As far as officials are concerned the best way of dealing with litigious parents and predatory lawyers is to close down playgrounds. The growing climate of litigation is clearly bad news for children.

Helen Brown fumed with rage when she received a letter from the headmaster of her child's school in Canterbury a few years ago. The school had just informed her that the playground for which Helen and other parents had spent months raising money was to be closed down because of concern about its safety. Helen's parent and teachers' association not only collected the money but also designed and did the physical work of building the playground. "This was a carefully constructed playground, and the children loved it," observed Helen. She conceded that the wood had rotted in one of the pieces of equipment and there was a danger that it could splinter. "But that could have been easily replaced and the playground kept open," she argued.

The experience of Helen Brown's PTA is not at all unusual. In the United States, the traditional playground is in danger of becoming a historic relic. California has become the first state to mandate compliance with safety recommendations. That means that many much-loved ground fixtures like monkey bars and merry-go-rounds are soon to be consigned to the museum. Other fixtures, such as swings, slides, and seesaws, have been scaled down and modified. According to playground designer Jay Beckwith, the equipment will be lowered to the ground. "Swings are going to be very scarce, and high swings are going to be gone." Even some schools have joined the antiplay crusade. In a trend that took off in Atlanta, elementary schools around the country are replacing recess with more structured activities. Consequently, many youngsters have never sat on a seesaw or played dodgeball during school hours. In a growing number of school districts in such states as Maine, Massachusetts, Texas, and Virginia, kids throwing balls at one another have been banned from gym class. Advocacy groups are campaigning to get rid of dodgeball on the ground that "it allows stronger kids to pick on and target weaker kids."[5]

In fact, there is no evidence that children face greater dangers outdoors today than in the past. Playgrounds are no more dangerous than they were twenty or forty years ago. What has changed is society's perception of children's resilience. Physical injury to children is no longer accepted as a fact of growing up. Zealous campaigners insist that parents should worry about "the high incidence of injuries to schoolchildren," and not intentional violence. Tripping and falling outside or in the school corridor are represented as major disasters.[6] Leaflets published by the Child Accident Prevention Trust note that in 1996 over half a million children under four years of age were injured as a result of an accident. It adds, "Many of these could be prevented." This is probably true, and naturally parents want to prevent as many accidents as possible. But accidents are a fact of life even for the most cautious parents. It is not possible to immunize children from physical injury. The attempt to construct an injury-free childhood can only inhibit children's development. Societies that still believe in children's resilience understand that the risk of a child injuring herself is worth taking in order to allow her the freedom to explore her environment. Priscilla Alderson has noted that children in Norway have a slightly higher accident rate than other European children, which "Norwegians consider is worth risking for the benefits of freely enjoying the countryside."[7]

Every parent must have experienced that nervous grab in the stomach as you watch your child balance to walk along a wall, or struggle to climb a tree. The words *Come down now!* are on your lips because you *know* that a fall will hurt, and you know that a fall is likely. But you also know that if your child doesn't fall, she will have demonstrated a new skill in physical agility, learned a new lesson, and gained a new sense of confidence. To let your child stretch her limits is not without risk, but thwarting her ambition has a risk, too. Getting the balance right is as difficult for the parent on the ground as it is for the child on the wall.

We are clearly not getting the balance right. A study written in conjunction with the University of Manchester found that a growing number of playgrounds are too safe. They are designed for anxious parents rather than for the developmental needs of youngsters. This survey of eighty-seven families found that apprehensions about children's safety often had the effect of restraining children from learning for themselves.[8]

Contemporary perceptions of children's fragility directly contradict available evidence. Children were far more vulnerable a century ago or even thirty years ago than they are today. Child mortality rates have been steadily dropping since the nineteenth century. Stillbirth and infant mortality have been substantially reduced during the past fifty years. Between 1960 and 1977, the U.S. infant mortality rate fell from 26 to 7.2 infant deaths per thousand live births. As a result, accidents continue to be the leading cause of death for children and youth ages one to nineteen, with car crashes being the most common fatal accidents. Death due to unintentional injury among children under age fourteen has declined 35 percent during the last decade. Accidental death to adolescents aged fifteen to nineteen has also fallen significantly since 1991. Even traffic accidents—one of the greatest sources of worry to parents—pose less of a risk to children than they did twenty-five years ago. Between 1987 and 1998, the pedestrian injury death rate among children ages fourteen and under was halved.[9]

A typical American child will never experience the horror of polio or spend time in an iron lung. She will not get tuberculosis from milk or rickets from vitamin D deficiency. She can go about her everyday life without worrying about smallpox or scurvy from vitamin C deficiency. On average, children can expect to live almost thirty years longer than their counterparts a century ago.

But this enormous improvement in children's physical health and safety tends to be ignored. Ironically, fears over physical safety are often accompanied by worry about emotional vulnerability as well. The emotionally damaged child has become the symbol of contemporary childhood. Increasingly, children's everyday problems tend to be interpreted as a manifestation of emotional damage. And since a damaged emotion, unlike a broken arm, can presumably never be put right, it must represent a graver danger to children's well-being than physical injury.

Many professionals involved in the fields of child care, education, and psychology believe that children are uniquely vulnerable to emotional damage. We have lost sight of the fact that frequently a child develops new strengths in the aftermath of an emotionally difficult encounter. Far from being resilient, children are portrayed as permanently subject to emotional distress. It is claimed that mental illness is a common condition of childhood. A growing number of young children are diagnosed as suffering from a psychiatric illness. An estimated 575,000 children nationwide were diagnosed with anxiety disorders during the year ending March 2002, including 136,000 under the age of ten. Doctors prescribed psychotropic medications—Zoloft, Paxil, and Prozac—to 390,000 children in 2001. Today, an estimated three million American children have been diagnosed with attention deficit hyperactivity disorder (ADHD). Increasingly, troublesome behavior among children is redefined as a mental health issue. Shyness has been turned into the pathology of social phobia. Shy children are offered Luvox, a brain-altering drug, in order to protect them from distress.[10]

There is something self-serving about the way that adults have seized upon childhood emotional problems to excuse their own behavior. Today, it is common for grown-ups to blame their personal problems on difficult childhood experiences. Public figures frequently try to avoid taking responsibility for their misdeeds by blaming distress suffered in childhood. Hillary Rodham Clinton clearly articulated this sentiment when she informed her interviewer that her husband's philandering was the outcome of the psychological abuse that he suffered as a child. "He was so young, barely four, when he was scarred by abuse," claimed Hillary Rodham Clinton during the summer of 1999.

The misconception that negative childhood experience constitutes a life sentence is justified on the ground that youngsters are uniquely vulnerable to damage to their emotions. Many observers contend that "invisible scars" inflicted on the psyche never heal and damage the victim for life. Unlike physical acts, which have a beginning and an end and are specific in nature, the realm of the emotions knows no boundaries. Emotional damage is invariably presented as an assault on a child's self-esteem. It is perpetually claimed that children who have faced such an assault are likely to lose their self-confidence, suffer from anxiety, and find it difficult to sustain close personal relationships. The term "emotional abuse" is sometimes used to convey the warning that even parents' insensitive remarks and criticisms can damage their child. Since children are fragile, they are easily traumatized and vulnerable to a wide variety of risks.

A characteristic expression of this approach was provided by reports around the time of the 1996 Olympic Games in Atlanta claiming that the rigors of competitive gymnastics amounted to child abuse. Such claims were backed up by a report in the *New England Journal of Medicine*.

According to the authors of the report, pushy parents and coaches were seeking to experience vicariously the success of the child, and this "achievement by proxy" could be seen as a "sort of child abuse."[11] Competition, particularly competitive sports, has been attacked because it is said to strike a blow at children's self-esteem. Contemporary guidance for protecting children in sports defines as emotional abuse what, in the past, would have been characterized as putting youngsters under pressure.

A recent report published by the Surgeon General insists that "the burden of suffering experienced by children with mental health needs and their families has created a health crisis." This study insists that one in ten children and adolescents suffers from mental illness severe enough to cause some level of impairment. Claims about the epidemic of mental illness afflicting children are fueled by a recent report of the World Health Organization (WHO), which predicted that by the year 2020, childhood neuropsychiatric disorders will rise by over 50 percent internationally to become one of the five most common causes of morbidity, mortality, and disability among children.[12]

The WHO's alarmist report relies on an ever-expanding definition of mental illness. Advocacy groups have been quick to embrace the WHO's approach. Take *Bright Futures*, the report of the British Mental Health Foundation. According to this report, at any one time, around 20 percent of children and adolescents are experiencing psychological problems ranging from anxiety and depression to psychotic and major developmental disorders. It claims that the rate of mental health problems among young people is on the increase and demands more funds for promoting their welfare. But this prediction follows from a definition that associates every significant childhood experience with the issue of mental health. "For a child, mental health means being able to grow and develop emotionally, intellectually, and spiritually in ways appropriate for that child's age," argues *Bright Futures*. Given its extremely broad definition of mental health, it's surprising that the proportion of children suffering from mental health problems is not nearer 100 percent. Dr. Jennifer Cunningham, a community pediatrician from Glasgow and a critic of the methodology used by *Bright Futures*, argues that "mental health is defined so widely that any child who has a normal reaction to adverse circumstances in his life is now assumed to have mental health problems."[13]

Moreover, experts continually indict poor parenting for children's emotional and behavior disorders.[14] Hippies in the sixties used to declare that "your parents screw you up." This flippant remark has now been converted into a significant risk factor for children. There is a danger that the contemporary obsession with children's mental health can turn into a self-fulfilling prophecy. If children are continually treated as if they are afflicted by a disease, they could quickly begin to perceive themselves as ill. Nothing is as powerful as a medical diagnosis to make children feel that they are indeed weak and vulnerable.

The Burden of Bonding

Society's exaggerated perception of children's vulnerability is most systematically expressed in the idea that emotional trauma and other negative experiences scar them for life. This fatalistic diagnosis assumes that once children have been emotionally hurt, they lack the resilience to repair the damage. Even as adults, the children will continue to be haunted by their early experiences. The American psychologist Jerome Kagan uses the term *infant determinism* to characterize this bleak view of the human condition.[15] According to Kagan, the doctrine of infant determinism has been around since the eighteenth century; Sigmund Freud is probably the most prominent thinker associated with it. But it is only in recent decades that infant determinism has been systematically deployed to terrify parents.

Child-rearing manuals and parenting magazines regularly convey the impression that since the experiences of the earliest years determine a person's future, the responsibility for an individual's fate lies in her parents' hands. The implication is that parenting, specifically parenting in early childhood, is the main variable influencing the fate of a child. The corollary of this argument is that incompetent parenting during the early years of children's lives can have long-term, devastating outcomes for them.

Contemporary arguments about infant determinism are based on ideas pioneered by psychologists such as John Bowlby and Eric Erikson, who believed that what happened to a child during the first hours, weeks, and months of his life had a profound influence on the entire course of the child's development. These arguments were further elaborated in the 1960s in Bowlby's theories of how children relate to their parents through attachment. Attachment theory claimed that the constant presence of a loving and responsive attachment figure—usually the mother—was the foundation for lifelong mental health. By the 1980s, it was even argued that a child's development would be put at risk if his mother failed to bond with him immediately after birth. Long-term personality disorders were frequently explained as a consequence of circumstances in which accessibility to a responsive attachment figure was denied.[16]

The idea of attachment has had a phenomenal impact on the Western imagination. New mothers who have just gone through painful labor are encouraged to bond with their baby. "After the umbilical cord is clamped, the nurse quickly lays the newborn child on its mother's belly to begin a magical process called *bonding*," comment Sandra Scarr and Judy Dunn, two child development psychologists critical of this ritual. Failure to bond has become one of the anxieties preoccupying expectant mothers. Some psychologists even go so far as to state that the failure to bond can lead to a condition they diagnose as attachment disorder. According to one hysterical account, "the numbers of unbonded children, who may become the victimizers of adults, parents, and other children, are growing and will continue to grow if the bonding problem is not addressed."[17] Scarr and Dunn continue, "if proper bonding does not occur, a child may become a 'child without conscience.'"[18] From the standpoint of infant determinism, failure to bond, substandard parenting, the absence of a stimulating environment, and any form of emotional injury will leave an indelible mark on a child for the rest of her life. When a news reporter informs us that a child has been traumatized through some terrible encounter, we all intuitively suspect that the poor soul will bear the burden of this episode forever.

Happily, infant determinism is more of a cultural myth than a scientific truth. Popular perceptions regarding children's vulnerability find little support in empirical research. Investigations of children who were subjected to negative experiences early in life but who subsequently were given an opportunity to thrive confirm that they possess the resilience to overcome adversity. One well-known study, of children reared in institutions from their early weeks in life and who remained there for periods ranging from two to seven years before they were adopted, showed that despite such adverse beginnings, with virtually no opportunity to form attachments to any one person during their early years, many of the children succeeded in adapting to their new environment.[19] Even proponents of attachment theory are forced to concede that there is little empirical evidence to sustain their thesis. When Bowlby attempted to test his theory, he was surprised to discover that youngsters proved to be far more resilient than he suspected. He found that children who were separated from their mothers for a prolonged period tended to behave in ways that were only marginally different from that of those who did not experience separation. Bowlby and his colleagues were forced to conclude: "Statements implying that children who are brought up in institutions or who suffer other forms of serious privation and deprivation in early life *commonly* develop psychopathic or affectionless characters are seen to be mistaken."[20]

Infant determinism seems plausible because it appeals to common sense. The proposition that in their early years children are impressionable seems self-evident. That traumatic events affect children for life has been accepted since Freud's psychological theories became current. During the past fifty years, his insights have been expanded to an extreme version of the argument that childhood experience of trauma or abuse has an irreversible impact on a person's life. It is now commonly believed that the experience of abuse continues to influence not only the abused but also the next generation. According to many proponents of infant determinism, abuse is an intergenerational disease. They contend that abusers were themselves abused when they were children and their victims are likely to manifest delinquent behavior in the future. Yet, like many of the propositions advanced by infant determinists, this too is open to doubt. There is considerable evidence that the best predictor of whether a child is likely to be an abuser is not whether she herself has been abused but whether she grew up in a disrupted and disadvantaged family.[21]

A major Danish study that sought to investigate the connection between early life trauma and the quality of life some thirty years later directly contradicts the thesis that children cannot overcome early traumatic experiences. The study found only a very small connection between quality of life as an adult and traumatic events in connection with pregnancy, birth, and the first year of life. The study looked at children who appeared to be unwanted, whose mothers suffered from mental illness, and who were placed in institutional children's homes. It even considered cases where children had been born despite attempts to abort them. Yet these early adverse circumstances appeared to have a "very small effect on the child as an adult." Their capacity to handle adverse circumstances suggests that children's resilience, along with positive support, can help neutralize the negative consequences of early trauma.[22] The same conclusion is suggested by an investigation of a group of children who had one parent that committed suicide. The investigators found that all the children were affected by this tragedy and experienced it as a major trauma. But when the children were followed up several years later, there was a noticeable difference in their long-term reaction. Some of the children were manifestly disturbed, yet others had managed to adapt and showed no symptoms of maladjustment. The investigators concluded that the explanation for this differential reaction was linked to the children's subsequent stability and quality of life. Studies of young children who had experienced natural disasters such as earthquakes, fires, floods, hurricanes, and volcanic disruptions also indicate that though these events had caused considerable upheaval at the time, they did not necessarily cause long-term damage.[23]

The American psychologist Emmy Werner studied a group of 689 children born on the Hawaiian Island of Kauai. Information was collected on this sample when they were two, ten, eighteen, and thirty-two years of age. A significant proportion of the children studied were raised under serious adversity. Prenatal complications, poverty, alcoholism in the family, family instability, and parental mental illness were some of the conditions they faced. Not surprisingly, many of these children developed serious behavioral problems. But about a third of them succeeded in overcoming their adverse circumstances and entered early adulthood unscathed. What the study suggested is that vulnerability is not a fixed phenomenon. It exists in an open-ended relationship with resilience. The best predictor of long-term psychological problems among these children was prolonged residence in an impoverished family combined with biological stress surrounding birth. However, even these factors were not strongly predictive. The authors concluded on an optimistic note: "As we watched these children grow from babyhood to adulthood, we could not help but respect the self-righting tendencies within them that produced normal development under all but the most persistently adverse circumstances."[24]

From his analysis of studies such as the one carried out in Kauai, psychologist Jerome Kagan concludes that the mother's social class, not differences in the medical or psychological treatment of the child, was the factor that most strongly influenced subsequent outcome. But while the impact of poverty on a child's development may be crucial, it is important not to accept a form of social determinism as an alternative to infant determinism, substituting one for the other. The long-term impact of early experiences is mediated through numerous events and relations. Depending on circumstances, youngsters can be either vulnerable or resilient. Moreover, reaction to one type of adversity tells us little about how a child might react to a different problem in the future. One leading psychologist argues that "vulnerable children can develop resilience; resilient children may become vulnerable." However, thankfully, positive experiences with supportive adults can provide a condition for overcoming the problems of early years.[25]

To question the assumptions of infant determinism is not to deny the special significance of early experience. What is at issue is how these early events affect a person. Infant determinism offers the one-sided, fatalistic view that the effects of early negative encounters will not be altered or eliminated by subsequent experiences. Early experience does not inevitably and directly determine adult life. It provides the point of departure for subsequent experience. For British psychologists Alan and Ann Clarke, the significance of early experience is that it sets the tone for future experience. One negative experience may lead to others. It can act as the first link in a chain of destructive behavior. But this outcome cannot be traced or reduced exclusively to the initial trauma: the entire chain of events determines the outcome. Moreover, there is no inexorable process that leads from one unfortunate event to another. According to the Clarkes, the chain can be broken and the effects of early trauma can be neutralized.[26]

Trauma expert Yvonne McEwan claims that children have a fantastic capacity for recovery—"much better than adults, because they don't understand the implications of what is happening." McEwan is a robust promoter of the idea that children's powers of recovery are phenomenal—and that includes children who are critically ill in hospitals, children involved in disasters, and children living in conflict zones and socially deprived areas. Her follow-up study on children after the Lockerbie tragedy indicates that they coped remarkably well. There was no difference between these children and others—"apart from an improvement in educational attainment."[27]

Proponents of infant determinism require extreme examples of child neglect to sustain their argument. A recent study of neglected, swaddled babies subjected to a life of misery in a Romanian orphanage concluded that a mother's touch is crucial for a baby's development. This study of extreme and by any standards exceptional neglect allowed Professor Mary Carlson of the Harvard Medical School to provide the "first hard evidence" that shows how the lack of physical affection can stunt physical stature and mental abilities.[28] But does this study prove anything? No doubt a child systematically neglected by a brutal regime in an orphanage or raised alone in a dark closet for thirty-six months is unlikely to emerge a normal, healthy three-year-old. However, such extreme examples offer little insight into understanding the general relationship of early experience to subsequent development. To associate the tragedies that emerge in extreme settings with the developmental problems confronting ordinary parents is to substitute scare tactics for reasoned argument.

Infant determinism is a powerful idea with which to frighten parents. If children are indeed so weak and fragile that they cannot overcome the negative experiences of their early years, then parents need to be permanently on guard. Fortunately, this powerful idea has little foundation in empirical evidence. Parents would do well to ignore these frequent appeals to what is in fact a display of cultural prejudice.

3 Parents as Gods

The corollary of assuming that children are innately vulnerable is that parenting has an overwhelming impact on a child's development. The tendency to downgrade children's internal resources, coping skills, and resilience has been paralleled by the rise of parental determinism. Time and again, mothers and fathers are informed that their behavior determines the experience of infancy that in turn determines their child's future. Omnipotent parenting is the other side of the coin of child vulnerability. Parental determinism not only diminishes the role of children, it also overlooks the influence of their peers and social circumstances in a child's development. By assuming that so much is at stake, it legitimizes a highly interventionist adult role in childhood. The widespread acceptance of this view helps to foster a climate of child protection and parental anxiety. The more vulnerable the child, the more her future depends on the actions of her parents.

Inflating the Impact of Parenting

Today, parenting has been transformed into an all-purpose independent variable that seems to explain everything about an infant's development. Parenting has been used as a main variable to explain the following childhood problems:

- *Risk of child abuse.* A new study by researchers at Oregon State University claims that how parents view their children is a critical variable for child abuse.[1]
- *The terrible twos.* An American research team claimed that parents are more to blame than their toddlers for temper tantrums and fits of obstinacy known as "the terrible twos." Parents who failed to work as a team and who were inept at managing a child's budding individuality created the conditions for violent tantrums.[2]
- *Student anxiety.* Don Davies, a British educational psychologist, believes that parents are responsible for the stress that A-level students experience prior to and during their exams. He claims that although parents were not entirely to blame, they made a "substantial contribution" to the problem. It appears that anxiety and panic are like an infection that students catch from their parents. Parents who worry simply transmit their fears to their children.[3]
- *Failure in school.* Numerous newspaper reports and two widely publicized television programs have claimed that children's academic achievement is compromised if their mother is employed full-time. One such report stated that such children are twice as likely to fail exams than if she stays at home. Mothers who work outside the home are also indicted for risking their child's psychological development.[4]
- *Depression.* Some studies report that a higher incidence of depression occurs in children with a parent or parents who suffer from the illness. Children of depressed parents experience significant cognitive and emotional delays and problems at school. Children with mothers who suffer from postnatal depression are said to be at a particular disadvantage. According to one account, infants whose mothers are depressed in their first year may not learn to modulate attention and emotion, resulting in permanently impaired cognitive ability.

- *Low IQs.* A controversial study carried out by Dr. Susan Pawlby and published in January 2000 argued that the sons of women who suffered from postnatal depression had notably lower IQs than their schoolmates. The study, published in the *Journal of Child Psychology and Psychiatry,* stated that babies suffer from the lack of attention they received in the first weeks of their new lives.[5]
- *Violent behavior.* In November 1999, the *Observer* reported on research claiming that children who were allowed to play with toy guns were likely to be violent in later life. According to Professor Pamela Orphinas of the University of Georgia, parental attitudes to play-fighting and aggression are the most important factors in shaping a child's future behavior.[6]
- *Psychological damage 1.* A report published by Parentline in April 2000 stated that thousands of parents are psychologically damaging their teenage children because of the way they speak to them.[7]
- *Psychological damage 2.* A report widely publicized in the press claimed that children are damaged by quality time. Researchers claimed that the brains of babies and toddlers could develop at a slower rate if they are overstimulated by parents in snatched moments of quality time.[8]
- *Eating disorders.* A study published in the *British Journal of Psychiatry* in February 2000 claims that anorexia nervosa among young girls may be caused by overprotective parents who deny their children independence. Despite being based on a small sample of forty families of girls with anorexia, the study was widely reported as authoritative by the media.[9]

This sample of child pathologies attributed to parental behavior represents a very small proportion of the conditions for which mothers and fathers are blamed. At one time or another, almost any childhood dysfunction is likely to be presented as the consequence of some parental act.

Although conventional wisdom dictates that parenting determines virtually every aspect of a child's future, this perception is a recent invention of society's imagination, developing along with the emergence of the nuclear family. Even today, many societies in Asia and Africa believe that it is not the action of parents but God or fate that determines the future of their children. The idea that adult life was predestined by factors outside parents' control was widely held in European societies until recent times. One reason for today's belief in parental determinism is that a child's reaction to a parent is easy to visualize. "We have seen children cry following a punishment, smile after a kiss, obey a gentle request, but disobey a harsh one," notes Kagan. These experiences appear to confirm a one-sided view of the parent-child relationship. The parent acts and the child merely reacts; thus parental initiative shapes the child. Kagan warns that since it is difficult to imagine a child's interpretation of her interaction with a parent, we mistakenly attribute a relation of cause and effect.[10]

In recent decades the view of extensive child vulnerability has encouraged some people to adopt an absolutist notion of parenting. The moment a child is born, the mother's behavior toward the infant is assumed to have profound long-term significance. Mothers must lovingly hold their baby in order to bond. In recent decades, fathers too have been encouraged to bond at this crucial stage. Failure to bond immediately after birth threatens to damage the mother-infant relationship. An infant's failure to thrive, neglect, even child abuse are said to be some of the outcomes when postpartum bonding does not occur.

After bonding comes the challenge of providing a baby with the right kind of stimulation and care. According to the doctrine of infant determinism, this is a critical period when child-rearing techniques can have a fundamental impact on the baby's long-term development. It is not good enough for parents to merely nourish and play with their babies. There is now an influential body of opinion that the earliest years of a child's life are critical for developing his brain. A special conference organized at the White House in 1997 gave official sanction to the view that the amount of time that caretakers spent talking to, reading to, and stimulating infants was the principal predictor of their long-term intellectual and psychological development. Proponents of this thesis claim that an adult's potential vocabulary is determined largely by the words filtered through the brain before the age of three. The publicity surrounding the White House Conference on Early Child Development provided a tremendous boost to advocates of infant determinism. Hillary Rodham Clinton offered a classic presentation of this doctrine. Her view was that the experiences of a child's first three years "can determine whether children will grow up to be peaceful or violent citizens, focused or undisciplined workers, attentive or detached parents themselves." The message was clear: parenting—especially during the first three years—is the principal variable that determines the outcome of a child's development.[11]

Linking a child's brain development with specific child-rearing practices greatly expands the significance of parenting. Parents are now advised that everything they do in these crucial early years really matters. As the lead article in *Newsweek* put it, "Every lullaby, every giggle and peek-a-boo, triggers a crackling in his neural pathways, laying the groundwork for what could someday be a love of art or a talent for soccer or a gift for making and keeping friends."[12] Gone are the days when parents could simply love and touch and enjoy their child for her own sake. Loving and stimulating are now mandatory child-rearing practices demanded by the new theory of early learning.

Today, numerous child-development experts claim that without proper parenting, emotional nurturing, diet, and stimulation, a child's brain development will be stunted. This alarmist claim is summed up by the following header in *Time* magazine: "Too many children today live in conditions that threaten their brain development."[13] According to this argument, the number of synapses between brain cells rapidly expands before a child's third birthday. However, if stimulating parenting does not reinforce these connections, they will shrink and disappear.

An industry of advice providers preys on parents' desperate hope that their children will turn out to be intelligent. When mothers and fathers are not lectured about the latest insights of brain research, they are told that breast-feeding makes for smarter babies. Bottle-fed babies will have lower IQs. "Love boosts brainpower," advises the child professional, going on to claim that babies who get lots of affection show better problem-solving skills at one year of age. Reading and playing classical music to babies are promoted as vital measures for ensuring children's intellectual development. Spurred on by psychologists who claim that teaching eight-month-old children sign language will boost their IQ, many parents have adopted the new fashion of baby signing.[14] In the United States, crime, teenage pregnancy, drug abuse, child abuse, homelessness, and welfare dependency are all blamed on parents' failure to nurture their children correctly during the first three years of life.[15]

Nutritionists claim that many parents are mistaken in the belief that a healthy diet for an adult is a healthy diet for children. It is claimed that babies and toddlers who receive normal adult fare are deprived of energy-dense food and therefore lack the right calorie intake. According to Dr. Jackie Stordy of the University of Surrey, this impedes children's mental and physical growth, placing them at risk of anemia, stunted growth, learning difficulties, diabetes, and heart disease.[16] Parents not only have to constantly monitor the food they give to their toddler, they also have to set the right example during meals. The May 2000 issue of *Mother & Baby* is categorical on this point: "With an increasing number of children—some as young as eight or nine years old—falling victim from eating disorders, it is worth considering the messages your own eating habits may be giving to your young baby or toddler." Parents are advised to desist from behaviors—dieting, not eating with children—that can give negative food messages to the child.[17] Mothers and fathers trying to cut down on their calorie intake now need to diet in secret in case their darlings receive the wrong signals about eating.

Parents who allow their children to use a pacifier supposedly risk undermining their children's intelligence. In the past, the anti-pacifier brigade raised the objection that "it did not look right" and that it exposed a child to dirt and infection. With today's emphasis on early learning, pacifiers are more likely to be indicted for delaying a child's speech development. Speech therapist Nadine Arditti argues that because pacifiers severely obstruct articulation, they can cause significant speech impediments. One British study carried out by the Medical Research Council has concluded that the use of a pacifier was the strongest predictor of reduced intelligence among young children. "Fact—sucking a dummy [pacifier] could delay her development," stated *Prima Baby* in no uncertain terms.[18]

And parents had better learn to be musical. The April 2000 issue of *Mother & Baby* asked its readers: "We all know music can soothe your baby, but did you know that it can also help him to grow?" Pity the poor child whose mother and father are tone-deaf. New research claims that music helps boost babies' brainpower.[19] But help is on the way. The national lottery has awarded one million pounds to an organization devoted to encouraging pregnant mothers to play and sing to their unborn children.[20] A study conducted by Zero to Three, a nonprofit research group, found that four out of five parents with a high school education or less were actively using flash cards, television, and computer games in order to stimulate their babies' brains.[21]

It is also claimed that children's intelligence is influenced by whether they are breast-fed or not. A number of studies have discovered a "small but still detectable" increase in cognitive development to an eight-point IQ difference between breast- and bottle-fed babies. In case you remain unconvinced, *Mother & Baby* offered another argument for the "breast way forward" (January 2000). It cites an Australian study of two thousand children, which purports to show that those who were breast-fed exclusively for four months were less likely to have asthma and other allergies by the age of six.

If parents are so irresponsible as to bottle-feed their baby, they better use milk supplemented with iron. According to *Parents* magazine, one hospital tested one hundred children aged up to twenty-four months and found that remedying iron deficiency led to improved language, motor, and social skills.[22]

Parents also have a duty to laugh on demand and stimulate their baby using the appropriate tone. A child expert in *Prima Baby* states that the time when babies first laugh "really depends entirely on what stimulation your baby is given." Unsmiling babies provide incontrovertible proof of unstimulating parenting.[23]

Listening is another skill that parents must perfect if they are to avoid causing damage to their children's well-being. "You can boost your baby's development and your child's confidence simply by listening to them," advises an expert in *Practical Parenting*. It also helps your baby to talk. The expert advice is to "practice listening so that it becomes automatic."

Parents must be constantly attentive to their babies' signals when they talk to them. In April 2000, *Practical Parenting* informed its readers that by the time of her second birthday, your toddler may know more than two hundred words, and you can teach her more if you are quick off the mark.

Why? Because when your baby points at something she wants you to name, "You have to be on the ball: even a 10-second delay before hearing the word may mean she'll forget what's being named." Parents who are slow on the uptake bear responsibility for the restricted vocabulary of their toddler.[24]

Parents must not only be quick off the mark and anticipate their toddler's next signal, they must insulate their children from television. "Kill your television," warns an expert in *Baby* magazine. It appears that babies and children under age three can easily get addicted to the visual aspect of television, and "this does nothing to help them learn and develop language."[25]

The educational value of laughing, singing, playing music, listening, and anticipating a baby's next signal pales in comparison to the impact that parents can have if they read books to their babies. It appears that it is never too early to read books to a baby for the magic to work. One leading proponent of this thesis, Professor Barrie Wade of Birmingham University, discovered that children whose families read to them from the age of nine months gained a head start in math when they got to school. Others have suggested that such children were on average 27 percent ahead in English and 22 percent ahead in number skills by the time they started school.[26]

The view that certain forms of parental behavior guarantee the development of certain character traits and educational outcomes has been around for the better part of two centuries. But claims made about the impact of parenting in the past dwindle into insignificance in relation to the bloated versions of today. Now almost every parenting act, even the most routine, is analyzed in minute detail, correlated with a negative or a positive outcome, and endowed with far-reaching implications for child development. It is not surprising that parents who are told that they possess this enormous power to do good and to do harm feel anxious and overwhelmed. John Bruer, in his powerful critique of the use of brain research to legitimize infant determinism, *The Myth of the First Three Years*, is concerned about the way that claims about early development incite a sense of guilt among parents. He quotes a parent who commented: "I have to admit when I first read the research, I felt as though I'd failed my three kids."[27]

The Myth of the Mozart Effect

An industry has been built around the doctrine of infant and parent determinism. Entrepreneurs prey on parents by offering them all kinds of gadgets to make sure that their children get the maximum amount of stimulation in their early years. The so-called Mozart effect—the idea that musical training and listening to classical music enhances a child's intelligence—has encouraged millions of American parents to purchase special videos or to send their toddlers to music class. A company called Baby Einstein has been particularly successful in marketing their series of videos titled *Baby Einstein, Baby Mozart, Baby Shakespeare,* and *Baby Bach.* Television commercials continually warn parents to buy these gadgets now, before the opportunity for improving their baby's brain is irrevocably lost.

The main effect of contemporary obsessions with early learning is to intimidate parents. Leading child psychologists Sandra Scarr and Judith Dunn believe that this myth provides the rationale for guilt-tripping parents. They argue that "the baby who needs to be taught and stimulated is, in our opinion, a creation of salesmen who profit from making parents feel that they are not doing enough for their children."[28]

Serious research questions the suggestion that infant development will be hindered without systematic parental intervention. For example, numerous studies attempting to measure the Mozart effect have failed to confirm Francine Rauscher's claim that listening to Mozart's music enhances a child's IQ or spatial-temporal abilities.[29]

Two leading American child psychologists and a leading authority on speech development have recently published a book warning that the demand to artificially stimulate children can actually do more harm than good. They question whether babies will become smarter if they are stimulated by flash cards, Mozart tapes, or other gadgets. They write: "Everything we know about babies suggests that these artificial interventions are at best useless and at worst distractions from the normal interaction between grown-ups and babies." Their sentiment is informed by a view of child development that understands that babies have important internal resources for interacting and learning from their experiences. According to Alison Gopnik, Andrew Meltzoff, and Patricia Kuhl, babies are already as smart as they can be, know what they need to know, and are rather good at getting the kinds of information they need. Babies thrive and learn about the real world by playing with things that surround them and "most of all by playing with the people who love them."[30]

The idea that a child's intellectual development is determined during the first three years of his life goes against much of what we know about learning. Children who are slow at learning to read at the age of six or seven often go on to master this skill three or four years later. Indeed, with proper instruction, teenagers and even adults can pick up reading skills later in life. According to John Bruer, most knowledge and skills are culturally transmitted rather than biologically determined. "Don't worry about cramming all those music, dance, and sports lessons into a child's early years," he advises. Bruer believes that as far as we know, "the windows of opportunity stay open much, much longer than that." According to the available neuroscientific data, the process of brain development is mainly under genetic and not environmental control. Bruer argues that the amount and quality of early stimulation "affects neither the timing nor the rate of synapse formation." There is nothing wrong with reading to, singing to, talking to, and cuddling your baby. These are pleasurable experiences that are worthwhile in their own right. But don't believe for one minute that they will do anything to boost your child's brainpower.[31]

In fact, children are hot-wired for developing. Steve Petersen, a neuroscientist at Washington University, argues: "At a minimum, development really wants to happen. It takes very impoverished environments to interfere with development." What does that mean? "Don't raise your children in a closet, starve them, or hit them on the head with a frying pan."[32] Children actually play an important role in influencing their development through their experiences in the environment they inhabit. It is only when they are confronted with an abusive and neglectful environment that this development can be compromised. What children require are protective and loving parents, responsible adults, and a surrounding community within which the child will be socialized. In the context of this normal environment, the impact of parenting is far less significant than we suspect. Child psychologist Sandra Scarr goes as far as to argue that good enough, ordinary parents probably have the same effect on their child's development as "culturally defined super-parents."[33]

Parents do have an important role to play in nurturing, stimulating, and socializing their children. And no doubt distinct parenting styles influence a child's subsequent development. Judith Rich Harris has written *The Nurture Assumption*, a stimulating critique of parent determinism. She believes that the impact of parenting is mainly restricted to how children behave at home. Harris adds that parents also supply knowledge and training that their children can take with them to the outside world. However, she contends, parents have little power to determine how their children will behave when they are not at home. According to Harris, children's behavior in the outside world is learned in their peer group.[34]

Arguments about what influences a child's development are far from resolved. There can be little doubt that important aspects of a child's personality are inherited. There is also considerable evidence that social circumstances and environment play a crucial role. No doubt Harris's thesis of peer influence also has considerable significance. The relationship of parenting to any particular outcomes is much more difficult to grasp. Parenting and family make an important contribution to a child's development—but they do not determine any particular outcome. As we argue in Chapter 7, we actually know very little about the impact of parenting. Serious research, unlike the plethora of parenting advice available through child-rearing manuals and parenting magazines, is very hesitant on this subject. Why? Because the contribution of parental practices to the development of a child's personality cannot be viewed in isolation from the wider social and cultural setting. Moreover, in some sense parental behavior is closely linked to that of a child, and through a complex process of interaction a unique parent-child relationship is forged.

So it is culture and not science that encourages parents to acquire an inflated sense of power over their children's destiny. It is culture and not science that stirs the public imagination to adopt an almost panic-stricken vision of children's vulnerability. Inflating the public's perception of parental impact promises influence and power but inevitably delivers disappointing results. Unfortunately, when this happens we don't discard the doctrine of parental determinism; we insist that mothers and fathers need to learn new parenting skills. Such pressures have led to a major redefinition of parenting. This redefinition, itself an important source of parental paranoia, is examined in the next chapter.

Parenting Before Children

Proponents of parental determinism continually expand the range of tasks demanded of fathers and mothers, who are continually forced to calculate the effect of their actions on their child's development. Parents are under pressure to adopt this approach long before the child is born. The idea that experiences of early life are decisive in influencing what happens in later years is increasingly interpreted to include the experience of pregnancy. Consequently, experts now warn parents to be vigilant about what they do and do not do while they are thinking of starting a family. In the United States, advocates of attachment parenting suggest that parental behavior during pregnancy directly determines that of their child. William Sears, the leading advocate of attachment parenting, teaches pregnant women to adopt a calm lifestyle for the sake of their child-to-be. "When mother is upset, baby is upset," writes Sears. He warns that "if your pregnancy is cluttered with emotional stress (especially the last three months), you have a higher risk of having a child who is anxious, and an anxious child has a high risk of being a difficult sleeper."[35]

Antenatal care is not a new concept. It has been a part of medicine from the turn of the century. As early as 1901, the Scottish obstetrician J. W. Ballantyne proposed a prematernity hospital where women could be cared for and doctors could study the pregnant state. Over the next three decades antenatal care became increasingly widespread, with 80 percent of women receiving some kind of antenatal care by 1935.[36] However, at that time and until recent decades, antenatal care concentrated on maintaining the health of the woman, rather than on the developing fetus. Little was known about what could and could not influence fetal development. In fact, it was not until the thalidomide tragedy in the late 1950s and early 1960s, when hundreds of women gave birth to severely disabled babies after taking the antinausea drug Distaval, that the medical profession realized that substances taken in medicine could harm the developing fetus. Until then it had been assumed that the placenta acted as a protective barrier between the maternal and fetal systems.

Since the sixties, much attention has been devoted to what can and cannot harm a developing pregnancy. Medical science has demonstrated that the health of a baby is not only affected by the actions of the mother while pregnant, but even, in some circumstances, by what she does before she conceives. Parental determinism has attached itself to this discovery, leading to a reorientation of the focus of modern antenatal and preconception care.

The modern pregnant woman is expected to adopt the lifestyle and behavior of a parent while she is pregnant and even before she becomes pregnant. There are some sound reasons why women might want to modify their behavior to maximize the chances of a healthy pregnancy and resulting child. A summary of expert evidence considered by the British Parliamentary Health Committee in 1991 identified certain factors known to influence the outcome of a pregnancy: smoking; alcohol intake; certain medicines and recreational drugs; diet; infections such as rubella, toxoplasmosis, and sexually transmitted infections; and exposure to environmental agents such as radiation and chemicals.[37] Consequently, women trying to conceive are advised to:

- Cut down on caffeine, as it is associated with a slight increase in the risk of early miscarriage.
- Ensure a balanced diet supplemented with folic acid from three months before attempted conception to three months after, to reduce risk of neural-tube defects such as spina bifida.
- Quit smoking, as smokers tend to have lower birth weight babies and smoking can affect the functioning of the placenta.
- Limit or avoid alcohol intake, as alcohol is thought to increase risk of miscarriage, and the intake of large quantities of alcohol has been linked to fetal malformation.
- Take a blood test to ensure immunity to rubella, and if necessary be vaccinated against it before conception.
- Be tested for infections such as chlamydia.

This advice is pretty much common sense, and it would be rash to take issue with it. But zealous health promoters insist on turning sensible advice into an obsessive concern with the lifestyles of pregnant women. Visibly pregnant women who flout healthy pregnancy advice by smoking or drinking or who fail to attend antenatal hospital checks are subject to disapproval and admonishment. This has reached absurd proportions in the United States, where it is common for bartenders to refuse alcohol to pregnant women, and users of recreational drugs have been subject to restraining orders.

Couples trying to conceive and parents-to-be are intensely vulnerable to the pressure they face from their professional advisors. Their insecurity is regularly exploited by experts who propose a variety of measures that can help babies become smarter or healthier. "Some babies will be brainier than others just because of their genes, but there are other ways to add extra points to your baby's IQ long before he is born," is the opinion of an expert in *Prima Baby*. How this feat is to be achieved is not explained; instead, parents-to-be are instructed to "start talking" to their tummies, so the baby learns to recognize his parents' voices. Getting parents used to the idea that what they do is decisive is the hidden agenda behind a lot of the advice. It has no scientific merit. Its main purpose is to inculcate its readers with the thesis of parental determinism. Getting parents to listen to the baby in the womb is a way of training them for their future role.

In recent years, a climate of fear has been created that leads many pregnant women to be neurotic about their behavior lest they inadvertently place their child at risk. David Paintin, Fellow of the Royal College of Obstetricians and Gynecologists and board member of the British Pregnancy Advisory Service, tells of how he has counseled women who have sought abortion advice because they are terrified that they have damaged their child-to-be by some action taken before they knew they were pregnant.

Advice to pregnant and pre-pregnant women stretches far beyond the boundaries of what has been proven. Women and their partners eagerly consume the output of a growing industry of books, magazines, and videos containing health-promotion advice about how to ensure that their child will have the best possible start in life. When Francesca Naish and Janette Roberts published their book *Healthy Parents, Better Babies: A Couple's Guide to Natural Preconception Care*, it took Australia by storm. The authors assert that by following their bible, women can maximize their chances of a "better" baby. The prologue contains two cautionary tales: one of a mother who followed their regimen, and one who did not. Predictably, the mother whose child was conceived before she had a chance to adopt the healthy lifestyle suffers a nightmare pregnancy, and after the birth she suffers all manner of infections and depression. The child is physically unhealthy, suffering diaper rash, eczema, and more. "When he starts school he finds it difficult to sit still, his attention span is short, he is disruptive and is diagnosed as having a learning problem. He has constant colds and develops glue ear. He continues to wet the bed." This sad creature is compared with the better baby born following a preconception care regimen: "He is particularly handsome and has a large perfectly shaped head, with broad, evenly spaced features. His skin glows with good health. He is alert but content . . . He never cries for longer than it takes his mother to attend to his needs. She seems to know instinctively what he wants and when he wants it." Much of the advice issued by Naish and Roberts flies in the face of published evidence—such as their assertion that the contraceptive pill damages fertility. Other advice is simply bizarre, such as the instruction to sit far from the television, avoid electrical gadgets in the bedroom, and avoid an overacidic diet (as this supposedly "increases your susceptibility to radiation and heavy metal toxicity").[39] However cynical we are about such advice, it is difficult to reject it out of hand. It is a strange parent who does not want a better baby.

In truth, from a health point of view it is doubtful that there is any particular advice necessary for pregnant women. For thousands of years, women have been giving birth to healthy babies without taking special precautions either before or after they conceived. Embryos and fetuses are remarkably well protected, as women who have tried to end their own pregnancies have found to their own cost. Before the legalization of abortion, women frequently damaged their own health with instruments or by taking substances thought to have abortion-inducing properties, only to deliver, eventually, a perfectly healthy baby.

The resilience of pregnancies is illustrated by the fact that things considered hazardous to pregnancy in our culture are perfectly acceptable, even recommended, in others. Sociologist Jacqueline Vincent Priya describes in her study of birth traditions how different societies recommend different diets to pregnant women. For instance, pregnant Yoruba women in Africa are not encouraged to eat protein foods such as meat or fish, the opposite of advice given to women in developed societies. In rural Bangladesh, pregnant women are encouraged not to eat too much so that their baby will be small and born without difficulty. A large baby that we would regard as healthy could spell disaster in a society without an obstetric service.

Even addictive drugs seem to pose less of a risk to the unborn than we tend to assume. For the past decade, researchers in the United States have tracked the neurological development of two hundred children from some of Philadelphia's poorest neighborhoods; half were exposed to cocaine during their mother's pregnancy, and half were not. But, despite fears in the late 1980s that a surge in crack babies—one in six born in city nurseries in 1989 had cocaine-using mothers—would lead to a whole class of children destined for neurological problems, the study turned up no evidence of a devastating cocaine effect. What it did turn up was that all the youngsters at age four, in both the crack and the control group, had underdeveloped intellectual performance compared to the U.S. average. The project concluded that social deprivation is the key indicator of children's performance—and that is not something that parents can resolve through good behavior and a pregnancy preparation plan.

An insidious effect of preconception and antenatal advice is that many women take to heart its message—that they are responsible for the healthy outcome of a pregnancy. Even if they reject the more bizarre instructions, few women feel sufficiently confident to shrug it all off. Most, during those endless, uncomfortable wakeful nights, worry about whether the baby will be OK. When a child arrives that is less than perfect—and around 2 percent of newborns are affected with an abnormality—most parents scrutinize their lives to discover if they could have "done anything" to cause the problem.

A fundamental problem with preconception advice is that it rests on the assumption that couples can and will prepare for conception, a myth in itself. When medical sociologist Anne Fleissig asked a number of women who had given birth six weeks earlier if their pregnancy was planned, she found that 31 percent of the pregnancies were not and subsequently concluded in a paper published by the *British Medical Journal* that almost a third of births in Britain could be the consequence of accidental pregnancies.[40] In such circumstances there is no chance for preconception care and possibly limited chance for antenatal care, and yet there is little evidence that birth outcomes of unintended pregnancies are significantly different from those of planned pregnancies.

Furthermore, even when babies are planned, they are rarely conceived in the circumstances that would please experts on maternal and child health. A survey for *Pregnancy and Birth* magazine horrified health correspondents by revealing that 73 percent of couples make no effort to get healthy before trying to conceive, and almost half of all babies are conceived while both parents have a blood alcohol level that, if they were breathalyzed, would probably win them a suspended license. Healthy babies, it seems, are born despite our behavior rather than because of it.

It is difficult to resist professional advice during pregnancy. This is a time when parents feel singularly dependent on professional support. That is why pregnant women are so frequently targeted by health professionals. During this period the present generation of parents is trained to become dependent on the expert. By the time the baby is born, the new fathers and mothers have already internalized the contemporary culture of parenting. If they believe that by singing and talking to the embryo they can help produce a clever baby, then they will believe just about anything that the experts will throw at them in subsequent years.

Parenting on Demand

A New Concept in Child Rearing

Many of parents' anxieties about their children are shaped by the changing expectations of society. The parenting role is no longer restricted to simply raising children. Parents are expected to do far more than that. Today's parents must pay attention to every moment of their child's day—ensuring that their lives are filled with appropriate activities. The roles of the modern parent stretch from that of a chauffeur, who transports the kids from one activity to another, to an educator, who supplements formal schooling.

Parents used to be deliberately excluded from some of the functions they are now expected to embrace. For example, in the past, teachers were often suspicious when parents intruded into their children's education. Parents who took too close an interest in what went on during the school day were regarded as interfering. Teaching your child to read was as likely to be treated with disapprobation as with praise. The parent was seen as the bumbling amateur who got in the way of the educational professional. But today, parents are exhorted to play an active role in education. Those who fail to get involved are stigmatized for letting their children down, dooming them to a life of failure. The cumulative effect of all these pressures is to expand the meaning of parenting. Parents are burdened with new and often unreasonable expectations.

Parental determinism expands the concept of parenting until it becomes an impossibly burdensome task. No normal father or mother can undertake responsibility for everything that affects their child. Moreover, even if this were possible, it would not be desirable. It complicates the task of child rearing and places an intolerable emotional load on the entire family. With so much at stake, no one can be a "good enough" parent.

Arguably, society loads so many expectations into what parents should do that parenting can no longer be carried out by two individuals, however hard they try. This is particularly true if both parents are employed. For a lone parent, the weight is even more difficult to bear. Parental determinism sets up all parents to fail by setting goals that cannot possibly be attained.

Contemporary ideas of children's vulnerability and infant determinism continually reinforce the notion that your child needs you. Consequently, what is often defined as child-centered parenting becomes in practice parenting on demand. Dr. Benjamin Spock's widely read *Baby and Child Care*, first published in 1946, played an important role in popularizing a child-centered view of parenting. Demand feeding, lenient toilet training, and constant attentiveness to a child's emotional development were the hallmarks of this approach. It is ironic that, although during the 1950s and 1960s Spock's approach was generally regarded as permissive, today his version of child-centered parenting appears positively authoritarian. He comes across as distinctly parent-centered when compared with the child-obsessed advice of today. Take one controversial issue: punishment and discipline. Most sources of contemporary advice are opposed to physical punishment of any sort. Many are hostile to the basic concept of punishment. Jan Parker and Jan Stimpson, in *Raising Happy Children*, argue that punishment is essentially a negative act because it involves making children suffer for their misbehavior. They distinguish discipline from punishment: discipline, for them, means teaching children what they have done wrong. From this perspective, Spock's approach appears callous, if not brutal.

Spock advised that the everyday job of the parent was to "keep the child on the right track by means of firmness." He believed that when firmness failed, it was appropriate for parents to apply some form of punishment. Spock was far more worried about emotional punishments that led a child to develop a heavy sense of guilt than he was about spanking. "I'm not particularly advocating spanking but I think it is less poisonous than lengthy disapproval, because it clears the air, for parent and child," he noted. Today's advice is hostile to punishment because current doctrine maintains that the problem is almost never bad children, but rather bad parenting. Children are not so much acting naughty as "seeking negative attention." The solution is to ignore misbehavior rather than to punish it. Instead of using firmness, parents are advised that they can never do too much for a child.

Although there is no longer a dominant child expert exercising the influence of Spock in the 1960s, Penelope Leach probably comes close to playing that role. She believes that a "gradual and gentle exposing of the child to the results of his own ill-advised actions is the only ultimate sanction you need." Parents are assigned the role of listening to the child and adapting their lives accordingly. Parents worried about spoiling a child are advised: "In fact there's no such thing as too much attention and comforting, play, talk and laughter; too many smiles and hugs."

Listening to a child and responding to his signals is a one-sided conception of child rearing that transforms parents into twenty-four-hour-a-day servants. Parenting on demand is based on an intensely deterministic view of the child-parent relationship. Leach warns parents that every aspect of a baby's development is in their hands. "You can help him develop and learn or you can hinder him by holding yourself aloof," she writes. And that's not all. Leach raises the stakes: "You can keep him happy and busy and learning fast, or leave him to be discontented, bored and learning more slowly."

Listening to children is something that sensible and sensitive parents do in any case. But the way that child professionals define listening gives it a very different meaning. It assumes that a toddler's every signal has an intrinsically profound significance that, if overlooked, can have a potentially negative consequence for her development. Contemporary experts dismiss Spock for being far too parent-centered. In her book *Three in a Bed: The Benefits of Sleeping with Your Baby*, Deborah Jackson takes issue with Spock's advice to mothers. According to Jackson, a baby left to cry at night is one who is forced to learn the "cruel lesson" that suffering is the human condition. By ignoring a baby's cry, she claims we are missing out on the potential "for small subtle, positive communication" between parent and child. Since so much value is invested in communication, the refusal to engage with a child's cry becomes irresponsible parenting.

Parenting on demand is systematically codified in manuals that advocate attachment parenting. Katie Allison Granju and Betsy Kennedy's *Attachment Parenting: Instinctive Care for Your Baby and Young Child* outlines a series of practices that transform mothers and to a lesser extent fathers into full-time servants. Granju and Kennedy advocate breastfeeding on cue rather than on a schedule, responding to every cry and not letting a baby cry it out, co-sleeping, and baby-wearing—that is, carrying a baby in a sling rather than placing her in a stroller or carriage.[1] This reorganization of adult life entirely around the alleged needs of the baby represents a culture of parenting that is historically unprecedented.

Parenting on demand is not confined to the interaction between mothers and fathers and their babies. The expansion of the terrain of parenting continues from childhood through adolescence. As noted in Chapter 8, policy makers and politicians of all parties see improved parenting as the one obvious solution to society's ills. This was the theme of the White House Summit on Early Childhood Cognitive Development in July 2001. Better parenting today means not only parenting on demand but also the assumption of new responsibilities. So what do we expect of the new parent? What are some of their new duties?

Parents as Full-Time Lovers

The principal demand that society makes of parents is to love their child. At first sight this seems like an entirely unexceptional request. The love of mothers and fathers for their children is one of the enduring themes of the human experience. Our culture and history are full of examples of the tremendous sacrifices that parents have made for their children. Mothers and fathers have been prepared to undergo great hardships in order to protect and improve the lives of their offspring. Of course, there are also stories of cold, aloof mothers and of uncaring, neglectful fathers. But such instances have always been seen as exceptions that violate the norm. Until recently, child-rearing manuals were concerned that parents were spoiling their children with too much love. A survey of child-rearing manuals published in the United States from 1915 to 1980 reveals that mothers were continually portrayed as tending to overreact emotionally, and their unrestrained passion was pathologized as harmful to both daughters and sons. Such ideas were constantly promoted right up to the 1970s.[2] So why do experts insist on instructing parents on the art of loving their children today?

In fact, the contemporary version of parental love has little to with the intense albeit indefinable state of feeling usually associated with the term. It is rarely presented as a spontaneous sentiment that arises from natural ties and manifests itself in warm affection. Instead, it has been transformed into a parental function or skill—the principal parental skill. It is the precondition for parenting on demand. That is why mothers and fathers are routinely advised to "enjoy their baby" and to give him "unconditional love." Penelope Leach goes so far as to state that if a working mother has only a limited time for her child, then her time would be better spent playing with her daughter than attending to her physical needs. "If you had to share your baby's total care with another person and you handed over all the physical tasks, using your limited time for loving and play, you would keep your prime role in the baby's life."[3] That loving and playing is elevated above, and separated from, the tasks of feeding and providing for the physical needs of a child is a testimony to the significance attached to the emotional side of parenting. Loving is not only elevated above the normal functions to do with physical survival, it is also isolated as an autonomous and distinct activity.

The separation of love into an independent activity and its association with play is a defining feature of a sentiment that actually means a call for unrestrained parental responsiveness to a child's emotional needs. Love is often used interchangeably with the term *attention*. Whereas parental love is defined to mean giving attention to children, a child's love is equated with a demand for attention. "Babies are born wanting to love their parents," writes the child psychologist Dr. Dorothy Rowe. To assert that biologically immature infants could want to love is to equate love with the instinctual drive for security. From the adult point of view, this instrumental and one-sided definition of love in effect means being nice to a child. According to Leach, playing and showing new things to babies are really what matters to them. "These are the things which make for love," she argues. Not surprisingly, the child's demand for nice things is unrestrained. Or to put it in Leach's words, "Love creates love." Love creates its own demand for a greater expenditure of loving. To ration love is dysfunctional, since through loving, parents discover a baby's need for . . . you guessed it, more love. In turn, loving programs parents to love even more. Deborah Jackson claims that "the more you hold a baby, the more you want to hold him."[4]

Advocates of unconditional loving ascribe powers to it that are almost magical. The authors of *Raising Happy Children* claim that if we "show our children that we love them unconditionally, that they and their feelings and wishes matter and that we value, acknowledge and care for them, we will boost their sense of self-worth." This in turn will set children up for life; they will become confident adults able to cope with everything that life can throw at them. There would be something endearing in this naïve belief if it were not promoted with the fervor of an intolerant ideology. The threat "love or pay the consequences" always lurks in the background of the discussion. That is why lectures on parental love have both a patronizing and an intimidating quality. They are patronizing because parents do not have to be told to enjoy their children. They are intimidating because failure to love on a child's terms is condemned as an act of parental malevolence. "Many parents do succeed in withering their children's love," writes Dorothy Rowe, ominously. Rowe seems to divide the world of parents into two types: those who love and those who try to control their children through fear. Rowe associates the failure to love with tragedies and dysfunctional behavior. There is always an underlying implication that the failure to love on demand is a precursor to abuse.

The exhortation to love on demand encourages adults to organize parenting around their children's demands for attention. Actually, most parents today spend far more time paying attention to their children than at any time in human history. Parents have internalized the exhortation to love and stimulate. The problem that many mothers and fathers face is that they can never meet their children's ever-increasing demand for their attention. Parental attentiveness is quite habit-forming. This is why many parents feel that they have become hostages to circumstances beyond their control. "My child has my undivided attention when I am at home" is a culturally sanctioned statement often repeated by working mothers. Child experts encourage this approach since they insist that listening, analyzing a child's words and signals, and stimulation will directly contribute to his development.

Yet it is far from evident that loving and giving attention for their own sake provide any real benefits for children. Children who are provided with attention on demand have little incentive to confront problems on their own. In particular, they have little incentive to learn to share their parents with others. They have little stimulus to explore the world by themselves, to learn to reflect on their experiences, or to engage in solitary play. Learning to be alone, away from the intrusive world of adults, is essential for the development of a child's imagination. Constant adult attentiveness tends to promote the self-centered child. Children can become addicted to parental attention. Youngsters who are trained to believe that parental attention and love on demand is their birthright are likely to find it difficult to cope with circumstances where they are not the focal point of everyone's attention.

Parents who provide attention on demand are not doing their children a favor. Constant attention is impossible to sustain, and mothers and fathers who go down this road soon exhaust themselves. As with any habit, attention on demand is likely to turn into an undiscriminating routine. Instead of leading, guiding, and inspiring, such parents are likely to spend too much of their time responding to their child's latest demand. Probably this ethos has the worst consequence for working fathers and mothers, who often report that they spend most of their time at home doing things for their child. The child, who only sees her parents doing things for and with her, rarely experiences them engaged in adult occupations. Yet adult-oriented activities are no less important for a child's development than the undivided attention of a parent.

Do parents always have to know what their children are feeling and thinking? Probably not. Sensitive mothers and fathers can strike a balance between seeking to understand their children and routinely responding to them. If everything that a child does is analyzed and reanalyzed, there is a danger of not seeing the woods for the trees. Not every signal is a portent of great significance, and not every word a child utters contains a profound hidden meaning. A child's development is not doomed if she is the daughter of an adult who has to divide her attention among many children. There is no evidence that parenting on demand does any good for children. But there is little doubt that reordering adult life around the child creates impossible expectations and fosters an atmosphere where parents—especially the ones who conscientiously try to act on contemporary advice—become doomed to a life of continual anxiety about the emotional welfare of their children. Despite good intentions, some parents actually end up trying to live their child's life in order to avoid failing to carry out their required duties.

Parents attempt to avoid failure by dragging their children from one source of stimulation to the next. If they can afford it, they chauffeur their children to music class before picking them up and taking them to a specially designed activity center. But still parents feel they are falling short. Unable to devote more time to their task, they seek to assuage their guilt by spending more money on children's gifts. Reports indicate that even relatively poor parents spend a disproportionate amount of their income on presents for a child.

But what is love? And why should love be associated with particular actions such as chauffering a child or buying him every toy he sees on television? As Jerome Kagan notes, the "invisible belief or feeling that one is loved is not dictated by any particular actions on the part of parent or child."[5] It is not at all clear what sort of acts convince children that they are loved. Children of authoritarian parents often acknowledge that they are certain that their mothers and fathers love them. And some children whose parents overdosed them with nonstop attention indicate that they are ambivalent about their parents' attitude toward them.

Love on demand becomes a parody of itself. The appeal that child professionals make for unconditional love superficially seems to make sense. After all, we quite rightly do not expect mothers and fathers to set conditions for the exercise of affection. However, this is not what the term *unconditional love* really means. It implies a sentiment that has no reference to anything outside itself. Parental love cannot be reduced to repeating the phrase "I love you." Love and affection are mediated through distinct actions. We express love through the way we nourish our child, through the way we reward or praise or question different forms of his behavior. Children become aware of their parents' love through the way that mothers and fathers encourage certain activities, discourage others, draw lines, and yes, even exercise authority. Loving a child is a wonderful, fulfilling experience. But loving on demand is an incitement to display an empty gesture. It introduces a dishonest ritual into the conduct of family life. Worse still, the compulsion to love trivializes authentic expressions of this most desirable sentiment.

Parents as Therapists and Healers

Today's fad of celebrating parental love is linked to the growth of the therapeutic ethos in society. As noted in the previous chapter, the all-pervasive sense of children's vulnerability has deep roots in the domain of the emotions. Advocates of unconditional parental love see it as a way of bringing parents emotionally closer to their children. This is a precondition for adults gaining emotional literacy, one of the essential skills demanded of today's parent.

Proponents of the doctrine of emotional literacy believe that lack of self-awareness and a reluctance to acknowledge one's true feelings are responsible for both individual distress and the problems facing society. Those who are emotionally illiterate are potentially destructive personalities who bear responsibility for many of the problems of childhood. This is eloquently expressed in Daniel Goleman's bestseller, *Emotional Intelligence: Why It Can Matter More than IQ*. Goleman takes the view that society faces a "collective emotional crisis." He sees "a growing calamity in our shared emotional life," which is expressed in marital violence, child abuse, rising juvenile delinquency, and the increasing incidence of depression and post-traumatic stress. American schoolchildren shooting their classmates, teenage pregnancy, bullying, drug abuse, and mental illness are some of the consequences of the public's refusal to attend to its emotional needs. The solution Goleman offers is more emotional education, which provides strategies for managing emotions and recognizing feelings.[6]

Texts on emotional intelligence and emotional literacy tend to be lightweight both theoretically and empirically. Most offer little more than homespun assertions in the language of psychobabble. In a roundabout way, what they describe is what was once represented as the quality of being sensitive. Parental sensitivity is not, of course, in and of itself objectionable. It is the obsession with emotional relations between parent and child, and the tendency to see them as problematic, that create difficulties.

It is no longer considered sufficient for parents to be able child caretakers. They need to be skilled therapists capable of getting in touch with their children's feelings. One of the most vociferous advocates of emotional parenting is Professor John Gottman. His manual, *The Heart of Parenting*, which received considerable publicity in the press, insists that good parenting requires more than intellect; it involves emotions. In the real world, parents are all too aware that managing emotions is an important component of their job. However, it is not the normal emotional engagements of family life that Gottman has in mind. He believes that parents have to be "emotional trainers" who use "emotional moments" to educate their kids in the art of emotional literacy. According to Gottman, love and positive parenting are insufficient by themselves for dealing with a child's negative emotions. It is a start, but mothers and fathers require additional skills in order to carry out their role as parents.[7]

There is considerable pressure on parents to fall in line with the therapeutic worldview. Most parents have probably never heard of Gottman and are unlikely to have submitted themselves to his "good parent test." But they might have heard government policy makers insist that the "quality of the emotional bond between parent and child is the key variable in the causation of delinquency." Child-rearing advice today, in all its forms, is saturated with the language of emotion and therapy. The management of feelings, learning how to interpret a child's emotions, and the art of listening feature prominently in manuals and advice columns. Tutors of parenting classes are trained to promote the therapeutic approach. A manual designed for such tutors by the NSPCC, titled *Positive Ways of Managing Children's Behavior*, informs group leaders that "most of the activities are designed to allow participants to think about their own feelings and the feelings of their children." Parenting magazines and manuals continually admonish parents that unless they learn communication and listening skills, they will lose touch with their children. "Without them, communication channels may begin to close—which is when problems can escalate beyond an easy point of return," warns *Raising Happy Children*.[8]

Therapeutic advice on parenting insists on complicating a child's feelings. Mothers and fathers are offered detailed advice about how to decode their baby's emotions. They are told how to go about praising their child and what words to use in response to negative behavior. Manuals explain in intricate detail how to acknowledge a child's emotion and provide practical tips on how to raise infants' self-esteem. It is not surprising that many parents who are daily bombarded by such advice agonize over the words they use to reprimand a son or daughter. "Is this going to undermine his confidence?" asked a friend, after showing disappointment at her son's refusal to go down the slide at the swimming pool. She must have been reading Dr. Michael Boulton, who informed the readership of *Mother & Baby* that reacting negatively to a child's failure "could actually hinder your child's self-confidence."[9]

The therapeutic approach presumes that parents can be on constant alert to interpret shifts and fluctuations in their child's feelings. And if they are not available for providing what child experts call "positive attention," then at the very least they can expect a gentle reprimand. "It's so tempting to carry on doing something with only half an ear to what your child is saying, but the fact is you're supposed to listen to her," insists Eileen Hayes in *Practical Parenting*. Hayes justifies mandatory listening on the grounds that you, the parent, are leading your child to the next stage of her development. A *Baby Power* article titled "Give Your Child Real Learning Power" tells busy parents that book sharing is "necessary" for their children's intellectual and emotional development. And if you are busy with housework— tough! "It's better to help build your child's future than to worry about chores all the time," counsel the authors.[10]

Parents are quite vulnerable to the charge that they lack the ability to understand their children. Many mothers and fathers are haunted by the fear that they might not be able to communicate with their children and might lose their love. Others are apprehensive about their ability to do what the books require at a particular stage of a child's development. Consequently, parents become captive to whatever is offered as the latest advice about how to get near to your child. Massaging your child is the latest fad offered to parents who are concerned about getting close to their children.

Massage now is regularly advocated for its alleged healing and therapeutic value. "Did you know," asks *Practical Parenting*, "baby massage is a wonderful way for you to get to know and bond with your baby, as well as helping with colic and sleeping?" According to *Prima Baby*, massaging your baby speeds up development, prevents skin problems, reduces stress, helps digestion, and boosts bonding. Apparently massaging has therapeutic value for the parent as well. Deborah Jackson, who believes that the "importance of sensory stimulation to the child may never be fully measured and appreciated," states that human contact has a "soothing effect on the adult as well as a child." And there are even more benefits, according to the video *In Your Hands: Baby Massage Therapy Techniques*. This video claims that baby massage improves sleeping, breathing, and digestive rhythms for both parents and babies. It provides enhanced physical and emotional development, alleviates postpartum depression, and boosts parental self-confidence.[11]

In the United States, according to *Time* magazine, "for today's upwardly mobile parents, baby massage is becoming what Lamaze was to the previous generation." The University of Miami's Touch Research Institute—coincidentally funded by Johnson & Johnson—regularly publishes research that promotes the therapeutic value of baby massage. Johnson's baby oil sponsors a Web site that offers parents tips on how to massage their baby. It informs the reader that "babies need to know they're adored"—not just loved but adored—and reassures parents that if they follow the instructions, the baby will know that "she means the world to you." Parents desperate to get close to their child are more than willing to give it a try.[12]

Physical contact between parent and child is a worthwhile, enjoyable experience in its own right. However, by assigning an all-powerful therapeutic significance to the power of touching, the fad of baby massage provides a convenient pretext for mystifying yet another aspect of the parent-infant relationship. Like loving, talking, and listening, touching is transformed into a complicated skill that parents need to learn in order to perform their function. When parental touching is transformed into the ritual of baby massage, it turns physical contact into an instrumental act devoid of spontaneity.

Ironically, the compulsion on parents to adopt the role of a therapist actually undermines the expression of genuine emotions. Parents who feel obliged to feign constant interest in their child's every word are likely to become desensitized about real new developments. Back in the eighties, the psychiatrist Stella Chess warned about the constant pressure on mothers to woo their babies. She was alarmed by the tendency of infant psychiatrists "to pressure mothers to be constantly on the alert for any sign that they or their babies are deviating from the prescribed ideal." During the time that has elapsed since this warning, the pressure to which Chess alludes has become far more intrusive. Tragically, the very obsession with a child's feelings and emotions has fostered a climate where mothers and fathers feel less able to handle many aspects of their relationship with their children.[13]

Back in 1977, in a prescient study of family life, the American social commentator Christopher Lasch warned about the emotional overloading of the parent-child connection. A quarter of a century later, the emotional load has become far more onerous. An exaggerated perception of an infant's emotional vulnerability has helped to reinforce the view that children are by definition at risk. In the realm of the emotions, certainties give way to doubt and confusion. Parents have tried to respond to this state of affairs by spending more "quality" time with their children. But, as we shall see later in this chapter, they still get criticized for not giving enough quality time.[14]

The problem with therapeutic parenting is not that it focuses attention on emotion. In modern societies, successful child rearing is invariably founded on the establishment of a firm relationship of emotional intimacy. Effective mothers and fathers need to show sensitivity and flexibility in response to a child's development. The real problem with the privileged status accorded to emotional parenting is that it complicates family relations and undermines the effectiveness of mothers and fathers. The therapeutic ethos promotes parental obsession about a child's momentary feelings, creating parents who cannot intervene in children's emotional lives in a discriminating and decisive manner. Worse still, the preoccupation with a child's momentary feelings is likely to provide an incentive for attention-seeking behavior. It is also likely to distract children from the effort that is required to deal with their own emotions.

Promoters of therapeutic child rearing continually treat mothers and fathers as insensitive people who lack the capacity to understand children's feelings. It is often argued that parents are uniquely illiterate when it comes to their emotional relationship with their children. "We find children's emotional lives difficult to respond to because we are habituated to ignoring, suppressing, disregarding our own," states the psychotherapist Susie Orbach. Parents are often accused of being terrified of their emotions. What terrifies parents is not emotions but the obligation to deal with children's momentary feelings. Actually, a parent's emotional relationship to a child is more complex than depicted by advocates of the therapeutic ethos. Most parents are able to show a remarkable degree of flexibility in responding to the individual needs of their infants. Parents spend a lot of time trying to figure out their kids and on reflecting on their own motives. But emotional encounters mediated through intimacy appear very different when placed under public scrutiny. Intimate emotions are not designed for public display. It is exposure to this scrutiny that puts fathers and mothers on the defensive. Parents' perception of being judged on personal and intimate details is unlikely to contribute to confident parenting.

Parents as Teachers

The main consequence of the therapeutic approach to child rearing is to put tremendous emotional pressure on parents. "I always worry that I am not doing nearly enough for Jessica and Angus," was how one father put it. John works as a software designer. He spends most of his free time with his two children and outwardly presents the image of a confident father. Yet, after a short conversation about fatherhood, it becomes evident that he harbors profound anxieties about letting his two kids down. Like many other fathers, he worries about disappointing his children and not doing enough to give them a good start in this world. Nor are these concerns confined to the comfortably off, university-educated, middle-class parent who has carefully studied child-rearing literature.

I was talking to a group of fathers at the swimming pool. They had brought their children for their regular Sunday swim, and while they kept one eye on the pool, the conversation soon turned to an exchange of opinions about parenting. Most of them were worried about money and about their own ability to manage their child's life in what they perceived to be a challenging and complex world. Money was a problem because they felt obliged to provide their children with the latest toys and clothes regardless of whether they could afford it. But their main preoccupation was not family finance. Pete the mechanic expressed the common dilemma most clearly: "I know that there is nothing I can do to make sure that my son is going to get a decent education."

Words of doubt exchanged at a public swimming pool are repeated time and again when you talk to parents. Moms and dads who feel insecure about whether they're doing enough to stimulate their children are particularly exposed to new social pressures to do more for their children's education. Parental responsibility for child development has been expanded so that mothers and fathers are expected to play a direct role in their children's education. As far as parents are concerned, it is not only the children who are judged and assessed by school authorities.

Since the 1980s, there has been a steady expansion of the claims that schools make on parents' time. No one can assume the title of a good parent unless she takes an active interest in not just the education of her child but the affairs of her child's school. It is no longer simply the ambitious mother and father who regularly attend parent-teacher meetings. There was a time when parental involvement meant baking pies for school picnics and serving punch at Christmas parties. Not so today. "Today, it's moms and dads answering phones, decorating bulletin boards, rewiring computers, building playgrounds and just generally offering their time and energy to help their children's schools," writes a reporter for the *Charleston Daily Mail*.[15] "You've got no choice but to give your time," says Judith Hill, a thirty-six-year-old Boston-based consultant, before adding, "Time is the one thing I haven't got."

Politicians, educators, and child-rearing experts constantly pile on the pressure, continually informing mothers and fathers that students perform better academically when their parents are part of the learning process. Schools regularly produce home-school agreements that set out the new role of parents in monitoring their children's attendance, discipline, and homework. Nor is this role simply restricted to a monitoring function. The term in vogue is *supporting a child's learning*. This means that parents play an active pedagogic role in the educational life of their children. Numerous schemes have been introduced to train parents to directly participate in their children's homework.

With so much emphasis on the role of parents in their children's education, it is not surprising that many mothers and fathers have concluded that they ought to take entire responsibility for it. Many parents are now homeschooling their children. The transformation of parents into full-time teachers is easy to justify as just another form of hands-on parenting.[16]

The new role of parent as teacher is particularly burdensome. Unlike many of the new functions assigned to mothers and fathers, this one is directly exposed to continuous public scrutiny. The behavior and performance of schoolchildren is now seen to be a direct reflection of the quality of support they receive from their fathers and mothers. This is not surprising, since homework is no longer what schoolchildren do when they get home—it has become a joint enterprise with their parents. In a very literal sense, homework has become an instrument for assessing parental behavior.

Parental responsibility for homework and their children's progress in school is a source of tremendous consternation to many mothers and fathers. Since the contemporary definition of what constitutes a "good" parent depends so much on effectively managing this responsibility, moms and dads feel powerless to complain. A survey published in March 2000 indicated that instead of complaining, many mothers and fathers are struggling to live up to the expectation that society has of them. The survey of 1,200 parents reported that many fathers and mothers were experiencing great difficulty in trying to assist their children—especially in subjects such as math and science. Since these subjects are taught differently than in the past, many of the respondents were confused about how to guide their children. Parents sought to compensate for this problem by putting long hours into their children's homework. The survey claimed that on average parents spent seven hours a week on homework. In effect, parents were spending more time on after-school studies than the official five-hours-a-week guideline for eleven-year-old children.[17]

Not every parent has seven hours a week to spend on homework. And some parents have the confidence to draw the line and not accept that it is their responsibility to play the role of surrogate teacher. However, the normalization of this new parental role has become an accomplished fact. There has been virtually no public debate on the implications of this development for parent and child alike. And parents struggling over their children's math assignment have internalized the role to such an extent that they see the problem as a reflection of their own weaknesses.

Not so long ago, it was sufficient to send the kids to school clean, rested, well fed, and well clothed. Teachers assumed that they would do their job and the parents would do theirs. They and not parents were responsible for the educational progress of students. School was for children and children alone. Homework was seen as what children did out of school, not as the direct or indirect product of a parent's output. And parents who "helped" their children with homework sometimes felt ambivalent about where to draw the line between helping and cheating.

Today, in a desperate attempt to improve standards of education, parents' concern for their children is manipulated to draw them in as unpaid teachers. In the process, schooling has become an informal instrument for monitoring parental behavior. Parents are going back to school—whether they like it or not. One school I visited offered at least five evening classes concerned with "helping your child to read" or "helping your child with math" or "helping your child through English." Some schools provide special evening classes for parents to train them for their new role.

The expansion of parental responsibility in children's schooling represents a major claim on their time and energies. But adding yet another load on the backs of parents is unlikely to improve the quality of their children's education. Parents can play a valuable role by providing a stimulating environment for their children and plenty of positive encouragement. Sometimes this involves discussions of issues and problems raised in school. But too much involvement discourages children from making the effort to stretch and challenge themselves and can act as an obstacle to their developing self-sufficiency and maturity.

Nor do parents make the best teachers for their own children. As Elizabeth Newson noted in her study of the parental role, "a good parent-child relationship is in fact very unlike a good teacher-child relationship." The deep and intimate emotional ties between parent and child makes it difficult for mothers and fathers to have the distance necessary for effective teaching. That is why so many parents have so naturally adopted the role of their child's advocate in their dealings with teachers. Predictably, teachers have reacted with the complaint that greater parental involvement has led to an increase in violent and abusive behavior toward school staff. The erosion of the line of demarcation between parent and teacher contains a recipe for conflict and mutual recrimination. It's not good for the parent, not good for the teacher, and certainly not good for schoolchildren.[18]

5 Parenting Turned into an Ordeal

The expanding definition of parenting in relation to child rearing at home is more than matched by the increase in the amount of time fathers and mothers spend monitoring the activities of their children out of doors. To a considerable extent this increase is motivated by concern for their physical safety. Parents are not only worried about not doing enough for their child's education, they also feel the need to do more to protect their child from a world they perceive as threatening. However, their concerns are not limited to physical dangers such as drugs, bullies, drunk drivers, or child abductors. Parents are expected to stimulate and educate their children not only when they are at home but also when they are outdoors. This pressure means that parents can never have enough time to do what is expected of them.

Is There a Parenting Time Famine?

In recent years, numerous commentators have claimed that mothers and fathers are disabled by the heavy demands their employers make on their time. According to this argument, since the eighties there has been an increase in work pressure. It is claimed that men and women are expected to work longer hours than previously, and as a result they have little time to devote to their family responsibilities. Hewlett and West have characterized this as a *parental time famine*. Concern about the time that parents are able to spend with their children is widespread. At a White House conference, Raising Responsible and Resourceful Youth, in May 2000, parents were urged to spend more time with their teens. The Denver-based Rocky Mountain Family Council claims that the amount of total contact parents have with their children has dropped 40 percent during the last twenty-five years. And indeed, many parents believe that they are not able to spend enough time with their children due to the pressure of work. A recent *New York Times* poll found that 83 percent of employed mothers and 72 percent of employed fathers say that they are torn by conflict between their jobs and the desire to spend more time with their families.[1] The view that long hours of work have made parenting a difficult if not impossible task has become a regular subject of discussion in the pages of parenting magazines. Calls for flexible work arrangements are often presented as a potential solution to the crisis of parenting.

Parents are indeed busy, and in some cases, *really* busy. The entry of millions of mothers into the labor market has placed new strains on the management of family life. The association of the time famine that confronts many parents with the demands placed on them by work is understandable. It is easy to draw the conclusion that time spent at work is directly responsible for the pressure that parents face in managing their family life. After all, the expansion of maternal employment is a highly visible process. In contrast, the expansion of parenting time takes place behind the scenes and is rarely debated in public. Yet it is this invisible increase in the demands placed on parents' time that represents the greatest pressure on their lives.

Millions of mothers and fathers experience the pressure of time as a relentless everyday problem. Many parents who feel that they do not have adequate time to spend with their children feel guilty and anxious about this state of affairs. The "time famine" helps to intensify and shape parental paranoia. But is it really the case that our problems are caused by an impossibly long working week?

The discussion about the long-hours culture and its impact on parenting actually says more about what is expected of parents than about a loss of time. The working week in the United States today is not particularly more onerous than the norm experienced by societies a century ago. Mothers and fathers worked long hours before and during World War II. They certainly did not like it, but they experienced their condition as a general lack of time rather than as a parental time famine. They not only managed to raise their offspring in difficult circumstances but also did it well.

It is far from evident why the amount of time fathers and mothers spend at work should, in and of itself, have catastrophic outcomes for child rearing. In the course of both world wars there were dramatic shifts of women into and out of the labor force, but these did not result in fears of damaging consequences for children. Others claim that the problem is men's long working day. It is suggested that they come home too exhausted to perform their fathering role adequately. However, the relatively minimal increase in working hours during the nineties follows more than a half a century of reductions: up to World War I, the average working week was over fifty hours—and for most, that meant arduous manual labor that few now have to endure. It is difficult to believe that when our grandfathers staggered home from twelve-hour shifts in factories they were any less exhausted than the computer programmer is when he gets in from the office. Yet with far less time available to them, parents managed to raise their children.

It is difficult to avoid the conclusion that the problem is not to be found in the place of work. It is not the culture of long working hours but the culture of parenting on demand that exacerbates many of the problems faced by mothers and fathers. As long as society continues to expand the role of parenting, mothers and fathers will never have time to be good enough parents. Parental paranoia is not simply excessive worry about the well-being of a child but a gnawing doubt about having the time to be able to perform the job expected of mothers and fathers.

The real issue is the way that society regards parenting. The newly invented concept of quality time is based on the belief that children need a specific period of undivided attention from their parents. Quality time is founded on the conviction that it is not good enough for children to be around their parents or other adults but that their development requires special treatment. Today, some experts claim that even quality time does not meet the needs of children. "Millions of working parents cling to the belief that 'quality time' with their children makes up for frequent absences from home," warns one newspaper headline, before adding that "research suggests this is a myth."[2] Numerous child professionals accuse parents that devotion to their career means that they are neglecting the welfare of their children. "I think quality time is just a way of deluding ourselves into short-changing our children," says Ronal Levant, a psychologist at Harvard Medical School. He claims that children need "vast amounts of parental time and attention."[3]

The continuous pressure to expand energies and time on child rearing accounts for the widely held view that employment imposes a singular burden upon working mothers and fathers. It is always legitimate to raise questions about whether there are more creative ways to organize the world of work. There is always room for introducing more flexible arrangements that could help make life easier for parents. But it is also worth asking questions about the "long hours" that society expects mothers and fathers to devote to their children.

Lack of time is not the cause but a symptom of parental paranoia. Concern about children's safety, welfare, and development requires that parents spend more time on the specific job of child care than at any other time in history. Blaming a new ethos of long working hours overlooks the significant expansion of energy devoted by mothers and fathers to child rearing. As long as parents feel that they can never devote enough time to their children, any claim on their time by their employer can be experienced as unreasonable. Conversations with full-time mothers indicate that extra time at home does not buy them immunity from the fears and anxieties that haunt working parents. Anthea, a twenty-nine-year-old full-time mother, gave up her job as a graphic designer in order to have enough time with Maddie, her four-year-old daughter. Far from being relaxed, she is intensely concerned about Maddie's development. Maddie is an only child, and Anthea is worried because she is shy and does not make friends easily. Because of this anxiety, Anthea has embarked on a mission to find friends for Maddie. She takes her child to play groups, swimming, adventure playgrounds, and the houses of potential friends. Anthea is entirely sincere when she reports that she is rushed off her feet.

Can Never Do Enough

Child-rearing experts continually advise parents not to lose any opportunity to communicate with and stimulate their children. The advice that it is never too early to start is repeated with monotonous regularity. "If you want your child to speak another language fluently, start early," advises one educationalist. For the enlightened upwardly mobile parent, nonpurposeful children's activity is wasted time. In the United States, hyperparenting has become a way of life. Books like *Baby Signs: How to Talk to Your Baby Before Your Baby Can Talk*; *Super Baby*; *Brain Games for Toddlers and Twos*; and *Releasing Your Child's Potential* are readily embraced by caretakers committed to parental determinism. Parents who are trained by a manual titled *How to Multiply Your Baby's Intelligence* are unlikely to abandon this crusade when their children turn four or five. Many parents are eager to get their infants started on music and language lessons, sports, and other stimulating activities so they will be ready for the next stage of development.

Hothouse children are the inevitable product of contemporary culture's preoccupation with constant infant stimulation. Many parents who intuitively draw back from this obsessive behavior nevertheless feel pressure from family and friends to keep up with the superdads and supermoms on the amount of enrichment they provide their children. Clever entrepreneurs have realized that there is money to be made from parents desperate to give their children a head start. The catchphrase "It is never too early to start" is used as a sales gimmick to market early learning products. Organized, structured activities for children have become a boom industry. They have also turned parents into permanent chaperones forced to spend even more time carrying out their responsibilities.[4]

The constant demand on parents to entertain and supervise their children takes its toll. During the summer months, when children are not in school, parents are under relentless pressure to reorganize their lives around the task of entertaining their child. Parents have been coerced into accepting the view that their children need to have something to do since they could not be left on their own to play outside or simply mess about. Many parents, whose carefully balanced child-care arrangements can easily come unstuck by the extra claim on their time during school breaks, dread holidays.[5] Amanda, a thirty-six-year-old physiotherapist, went part-time when her daughter Nicky started her school holiday last year. She loves her job and is angry about having to give up a promising career. "I could not face another summer of begging people to help me with child care," she told me.

Despite the fact that the proportion of mothers who work has increased dramatically, from 27 percent in 1955 to 65 percent today, they still manage to spend more time with their children than in the past. Both working and stay-at-home mothers spend more time caring for their children than their mothers did. Suzanne Bianchi, a University of Maryland researcher and family demographer, found that both mothers and fathers devote more time to child rearing than was the case in the past.[6] At a time when the deadbeat dad has emerged as a widely held stereotype, it is important to realize that today's American father spends far more time with his children than did his father and grandfather. The New York–based Families and Work Institute estimates that fathers spend 75 percent of the time that their wives do on domestic chores, whereas in the seventies, this figure was only 30 percent.[7]

One consequence of parents spending more time with their children is that the time children spend together or alone without the company of adults has fallen. This is particularly true of free time outdoors. A major study carried out by the University of Michigan showed that between 1981 and 1997, the amount of free time available to children dropped by 16 percent. Time spent playing fell by 25 percent, and outdoor activities such as walking and hiking declined by a staggering 50 percent. Conversely, children's involvement in organized, adult-supervised activities has shot up.[8]

This survey suggests that there has been a noticeable increase in the amount of time that children spend on scheduled activities. It points to two important findings: children's free time has declined, and free time is increasingly structured. The major cause is the increased amount of time children spend in school, which rose from twenty-one to twenty-nine hours weekly. Children spend less time playing and more time going places. Sadly, this development encroaches on children's freedom to play. It also reduces the amount of time family members spend just sitting around, talking, and not doing anything in particular. In turn, parents spend more time organizing and driving children from one stimulating activity to the next.[9]

The belief that mothers and fathers can never spend too much time with their children fuels the belief that society faces an exceptional era of a parental time famine. Recent research by the University of Michigan shows that American children spend four to six more hours per week with their parents than they did in 1981. Both working and nonworking mothers contributed to this significant increase in time devoted to child care.[10] Surveys of parents clearly demonstrate this upswing. One published in August 2001 indicated that nearly two-thirds of the respondents felt that they "spent more time playing with their preschooler than their parents spent with them when they were kids."[11]

The expansion of parenting time in the United States is part of an international phenomenon. A recent British survey published in March 2000 confirmed that the amount of time invested by parents in their children's upbringing has more than trebled over the past three decades. According to this study, carried out by the Future Foundation, British parents are now devoting an average of eighty-five minutes per day to each child compared with a mere twenty-five minutes a day in the mid-seventies. Interviewers talked to three generations of families to find out the difference in time each cohort spent on child rearing. In every key aspect of parenting and family life investigated by the researchers, the vast majority of the respondents indicated that they spent more time with their children than their parents did. On the basis of this study, the Future Foundation predicted that by 2010 the amount of time that parents spend with their children would increase from eighty-five minutes to one hundred minutes a day.[12]

The Future Foundation's report provides compelling evidence of a fundamental reorganization of parenting time. It notes that a variety of developments, some negative (growing concerns about children's safety and well-being) and some positive (increasing desire for creative involvement in children's lives), means that "parenting takes more time, more consideration and more emotional energy." This augmentation of time is driven by the belief that children need to be supervised more extensively than was the case in the past. That is why parents interviewed by *Complicated Lives* felt that they spent more time with their children than their parents did with them. The conclusion of the report was: "Parenting is going to take up even more time and energy in the future as the desire to be an accomplished parent increases." Michael Willmott of the Future Foundation predicts that "if society continues to blame a range of problems on the perceived failings of parents, parental neurosis and stress could increase."[13]

Complicated Lives is one of the few authoritative sources to acknowledge how the redefinition of parenting has led to a massive increase in the amount of time parents concentrate on child care. This rise from twenty-five minutes a day in the mid-1970s to eighty-five minutes a day in the 1990s represents a dramatic statement about the changing character of child rearing. The redefinition of parenting and the perception that self-centered mothers and fathers shortchange children constitutes an important influence in the shaping of parental anxieties.

The relentless pressure to expand parenting time inevitably forces mothers and fathers on the defensive. Even outwardly confident career women spoke about their guilt. Tracey, who works as a consultant, recounted a lecture she received from her son's teacher after she was ten minutes late picking up her child from after-school care. "It was one of the most humiliating experiences in my life," she said. "No one in my line of work would dare use that tone of voice with me—but everyone believes they have the authority to lecture working mothers."

No matter how parents organize their time, there is always an expert to remind them of the inadequacy of their arrangements. So-called quality time is the latest target of expert criticism. Numerous experts have lined up to criticize parents for trying to pack their child-rearing duties into quality time. Mothers who work in paid employment come in for special criticism. A controversial study by the American sociologist Arlie Russell Hochschild accuses parents of deliberately staying behind in the office because they would rather be there than at home. Some studies place the onus on errant fathers who refuse to play an equal role in child care.[14] Others criticize not so much the parents but a long-hours work culture for the alleged neglect of American children. Hundreds of articles have been written advocating just about everything—a revolution in work culture, more involvement from fathers, and more support for parents to stay at home. Advice on how to balance home and work is liberally offered by what-to-do columns. What the debate about the Great Balancing Act overlooks is that the real issue is not time in the abstract but the culturally endorsed redefinition of parenting time.

Parenting as an Ordeal

Mothers and fathers have never had an easy time. The demands of family life have always posed difficult challenges. In the past, most sensible people realized that child rearing involved a lot of grind and hard work, but it was embraced by most, if with various degrees of enthusiasm. People were prepared to make sacrifices for their children partly because society expected it of them. But child rearing wasn't seen merely as a duty. Until recently, most Western societies were subject to cultural influences that represented family life in glowing terms as the institution through which self-realization took place. The family was hyped up, celebrated, and romanticized. Probably many adults who had bought into this dream of family were disappointed and left wondering what they were missing out on.

Today, when parenting is continually linked to a perception of crisis, it is difficult to sustain the promise of family bliss. If anything, society insists on inflating the problem of child rearing so much that the prevailing vision of family life is likely to deter prospective candidates from going down the parenting road. Society has rightly rejected the myth of domestic bliss of the 1950s, but in so doing it has swung in the opposite direction. The myth of the naturally competent parent who finds fulfillment in family life has given way to a myth of parenting as an ordeal. The same trends that led toward parental determinism and the expansion of the role of mother and father also give rise to the view that child rearing is an extremely complicated and difficult job. Parenting is no longer assumed to be an activity that adults can spontaneously carry out. On the contrary, the assumption is that many people are simply not up to the job, and society would be better off if they did not have babies. Some authoritarian-minded experts in the United States have even proposed a system of licensing parents. Jack Westman, a professor of psychiatry at the University of Wisconsin who is the author of this scheme, claims that since "incompetent parents gravely endanger society," they need to be weeded out through a system of screening.

Parenting programs go out of their way to prepare prospective parents for the ordeal they are likely to face—such as toddlers' temper tantrums—because many experts believe that such situations are enough to send them flying out of control. Child-rearing advice has also adopted a somber, downbeat tone. It often has the character of a letter written by someone who has been through hell and who now wants to share the experience with the soon-to-be-defeated reader. Christina Hardyment's study of the changing emphasis of baby-care advice draws attention to this new trend: "Researchers are now saying that the advent of a baby is likely to be the most disruptive thing that can happen to a marriage." Susan Maushart's *The Mask of Motherhood* is devoted to exposing past myths about the unproblematic joys of this experience. Unfortunately, she not only succeeds in acknowledging the difficulties of motherhood but also turns it into a pathological experience. According to Maushart, motherhood "can be and often is dangerous" to women's mental health. The bearing of a first child is represented as the source of a "psychic crisis" to the mother. The blurb on the back of Susan Jeffers's *I'm Okay, You're a Brat!* claims that this "fearlessly honest book breaks the conspiracy of silence" and pulls no punches about how "difficult parenthood is for many." It seems that virtually the entire child-advice industry is in the business of fearlessly breaking the conspiracy of silence. Anyone leafing through recently published child-rearing manuals is unlikely to find any examples of a conspiracy of silence. On the contrary, he will encounter advice that is realistic in its portrayal of the difficulties faced by parents, sometimes brutally so. He will also find material on the bookshelves that is downright scary. Jeffers's fearless exposé of the perils of parenthood actually represents a new genre of advice designed to reconcile parents to the lowest possible expectation.[15]

The representation of parenting as an ordeal is fueled by strong social pressures that continually inflate the problems associated with it. Parent-scaring has become so deeply embedded in our culture that sometimes commentators wonder how anyone can enjoy the experience of child rearing. A report published in December 1999 by Johnson & Johnson promotes the message of somber realism. Commenting on the report, Maureen Marks, a psychologist, remarks that given "the inherent difficulties of childbearing and child rearing," it is "surprising that the euphoria and immense joy of becoming a mother, and the sense of achievement and fulfillment it brings, is so widely reported."[16] Other reports paint a far more dismal picture. A survey carried out in Britain in November 1999 reports that the words used to describe child rearing by the overwhelming majority of parents are *demanding, thankless,* and *exhausting.* Sixty-one percent of the respondents found caring for their children difficult or very difficult, and 71 percent stated that they were "rushed off their feet."[17]

Negative perceptions about child rearing mean that a significant and growing proportion of the adult population is opting not to have children. Child-free adults do not constitute an insignificant minority. They are the fastest-growing demographic group in industrial societies such as Britain, Japan, and the United States. One reason why some women have decided not to have children is the perception that parenthood is an intolerable responsibility, a life of sacrifice and of risk. The inflation of parenting time is one significant factor shaping this perception. Although there are many good reasons why adults make sensible decisions about not having children, it seems that paranoia about parenting has also become a factor influencing some people's calculations.

The transformation of parenting into an ordeal is inseparable from the culture of parent-scaring. It is not child rearing as such but the tendency to expand parental responsibility that distorts and destabilizes the lives of mothers and fathers. The more we complicate child rearing and the more we insist on inflating the tasks facing mothers and fathers, the more we ensure that paranoia will dominate the style of contemporary parenting.

6 Why Parents Confuse Their Problems with Those of Their Children

Policy debates about children are dominated by individuals claiming to give voice to children's needs. We frequently hear that children need this or children want that. Invariably, these claims—however well-meaning— are based on grown-up interpretations of children's minds and behavior. It is easy to forget that the way we regard childhood depends on adults' perception of that experience. It is not children who write books and newspaper articles about the meaning of childhood. It is not children who produce television programs about their requirements, or who make pronouncements about their emotional needs. Even the demand for children's rights has been formulated by adults. It is not children who are desperately shouting that they are afraid of the risks they face. The image of a child at risk is the product of current adult sensibilities and imagination. Ideas about childhood are invariably filtered through the adult imagination and say as much about the world of grown-ups as that of children.

Throughout history, children have been portrayed in many different ways—as savages, selfish little animals, objects of spiritual veneration, resilient, or, today, permanently at risk. These changes in perception are primarily the outcome of tensions that permeate the adult imagination and have had a great impact on how children experience their lives. Indeed, children learn about the world through interacting with and internalizing adult values and expectations. Cognitive skills—thinking, conceptualizing, problem solving—are assimilated through interaction with competent adults before they come under a child's control. The initiation of a child into the wider social world takes place through the guidance of adults. How children think is inseparable from how adults imagine childhood.

In recent decades the adult world has become interested in the voices of children. It has become fashionable to advocate children's rights and to consult children on a variety of topics. Books are written to explore what children think and what adults can learn from their messages. Ellen Galinsky's *Ask the Children: What American Children Really Think About Working Parents* sought to find out what children thought of their parents and in particular, what their reaction was to their parents working. This sensitive account—well received on both sides of the Atlantic—argued that from a child's perspective what mattered was not whether a mother worked or not but how good she was at parenting. *Ask the Children* provides important insights into the dynamic of the parent-child relationship. But it is important not to overlook the fact that what children think about their parents is inseparable from how adults define appropriate forms of family life and child rearing. Galinsky's findings can be interpreted as a portrait not merely of children's feelings but of contemporary adult expectations regarding maternal paid employment. Children's reactions to their mother's paid employment is to a considerable extent scripted through the stories that adults tell about it. If working mothers were more highly stigmatized by society, there is little doubt that children's reactions would have been far more negative. And in that case, the negative response would have been used as proof of the thesis that mothers who work outside of the home are failing in their responsibilities.[1]

Many of the issues we associate with childhood are defined by adults interpreting children's lives through the medium of their own experience.

Adults have always lived their lives through their children. From the moment of birth, when arguments break out about whether a baby resembles the mother or the father, adults never cease to discover themselves through their offspring. And too often, especially at times of uncertainty, parents find it difficult to avoid the temptation of seeing their children from the point of view of their own insecurity. The main point of this chapter is to outline how parental paranoia expresses adult anxieties in the guise of concern over children.

Parent Identity

Child rearing is not the same as parenting. In most human societies there is no distinct activity that today we associate with the term *parenting*. In agricultural societies, children are expected to participate in the work and routine of the community and are not regarded as requiring special parenting attention or care. In our agrarian past, they were perceived as little people, not yet fully formed. There was not very much concern or interest in their cognitive or physical development because it was assumed that these biologically immature people would eventually mature on their own accord. Compared to today, this relative absence of adult interest in children is striking. Allowing nature to take its course assigned a minor and passive role to adults in the process of child rearing.

The belief that children require special care and attention evolved alongside the conviction that what adults did mattered to their development. These sentiments gained strength and began to influence public opinion in the nineteenth century. The work of mothering and fathering was now endowed with profound importance. It became defined as a distinct skill that could assure the development of character traits necessary for a successful life. Alternatively, the absence of this skill—poor nurturing—could deprive a child of a positive future. This view of parenting is closely linked to the decline of large households and the rise of more individualized nuclear family arrangements. Once children are seen as the responsibility of a mother and father rather than of a larger community, the modern view of parenting acquires salience.

The social recognition accorded to parenting ensured that this role began to influence the way that mothers and fathers viewed themselves. Throughout most of human history, parents have claimed a special relationship with their children. But once children were perceived as the more or less direct product of parenting, the status enjoyed by mothers and fathers became more intimately linked with the development of their children. For parents, children provide proof of competence. With the growing influence of parental determinism, children also come to embody a moral statement about their mothers and fathers. A child's behavior, skill, intelligence, and character traits serve as testimony to parenting virtues or faults. Not surprisingly, parenting exercises an important influence on the self-image of adults. Successful parenting enhances the identity of adults. It becomes an important constituent of the identity through which adults make sense of the world. Parenting is not merely about how adults react to children—it is also about how grown-ups make a statement about themselves through their children.

So parenting is not simply child rearing. It is also how adults construct their lives through and in interaction with their children. Adults do not simply live their lives through children but, in part, develop their identity through them. When expectant fathers and mothers debate what name to give to a child, it is often obvious that they are using the occasion to express themselves. A "cool" name for a newborn invites the conclusion that the parents are also "cool." An unusual name provides a hint that the parents are exceptionally clever. Parents who play classical music to their baby may do so because it reflects their agenda and not necessarily that of the child. Parents who pierce their infant's ears, dress them like little adults, or insist that they become vegetarians are in part making statements about themselves. Through raising children, parents are also inventing themselves.

In most discussions the problem of parenting is perceived as the difficulty that adults have in managing their children. But there is another side to the parenting problem—that of how adults ought to behave in order to carry out their functions as child caretakers responsibly and effectively. That parenting is to a surprising degree about adult behavior can be seen from even a cursory review of parenting literature during the past century.

Such books offer lots of helpful hints about what fathers and mothers ought to do with their children in a wide variety of circumstances. But they also contain guidance about how mothers and fathers should behave, especially in front of the children. A recently published manual, *Change Your Child's Behavior by Changing Yours*, provides an explicit formulation of this approach.[2]

During the past two decades the focus of parenting advice has shifted even more toward targeting the behavior of parents. This shift is not surprising, since the continuous expansion of the parenting role demands that greater attention be paid to the conduct of child caretakers. Hardyment's review of the history of baby-care advice confirms the significance of this shift of emphasis. She believes that the "single most striking new emphasis" in recent parenting advice is a change "from a concentration on the child to concern for its parents."[3] Our own review of child-advice manuals suggests that not only has there been a shift of focus toward the parent but this literature can best be defined by its goal of altering adult behavior. Advice promoted as child-centered is often aimed at the behavior of the parent. The opportunistic targeting of insecure parental identities has become a central part of the repertoire of child professionals. Children become the vehicles through which parents are instructed about how they should act in general. That is why a chapter titled "Your Relationship" has become a regular fixture in most recently published parenting manuals.

Parenting advice is often predicated on the assumption that unless guided and educated, parental behavior represents a risk to children. An article titled "Advice Aims to Stop Parents Behaving Badly" in the London *Times* sums up the approach. The article reported on the publication of an advice booklet that sought to reduce the stresses of new parenthood in order to minimize the harm done to children. Parent training programs also adopt the approach of altering adult behavior.

Helping stressed-out parents cope with life is another theme in the parenting literature. Chapters titled "When It All Gets to Be Too Much" advise mothers and fathers to take a relaxing bath or to find some other way of switching off. Special breathing techniques are promoted for parents who feel trapped and exhausted. Many adopt an understanding tone toward the stressed parent: "Keeping healthy, feeling all right about yourself and your life, being you as a person as well as a parent, are all very important," is the often-repeated refrain. Typically, parents are counseled to spend "some recharging time—doing the special things that you especially like"—since if "you are feeling good, you are more likely to have the energy to help your child and be a good role model."4 This approach is the explicit theme of Paul Zucker's *Loving Our Children, Loving Ourselves.*

One important way that parenting literature tries to alter parent conduct is by attempting to give meaning to adult life through experience with children. Parent identity represents a powerful bid to adult self-image. At its most basic level, parents are advised that the more you love your child, the more he will love you in turn. This instrumental call for love is carefully directed toward the parent's hunger for status and recognition. Penelope Leach's *Your Baby and Child* is paradigmatic in this respect. Leach informs mothers that "babies fall in love with people who mother them emotionally." Appealing to a mother's desire for affirmation, Leach promises that "the baby flatters you with his special attentions, making you feel unique, beloved, irreplaceable."5 The pledge of a special and uniquely fulfilling relation is offered to the parent who is prepared to adopt the prescribed behavior.

Appeals to parent identity are often directed at the self-preoccupation of the adult caregiver. *Parents Who Think Too Much*, Anne Cassidy's provocative critique of today's parenting culture, draws attention to the growing phenomenon of publications ostensibly about child care but really about the emotional problems confronting adult identity.6 Books like *Mothering the New Mother; The Shock of Motherhood; Coaching for Fatherhood; The Gift of Fatherhood: How Men's Lives Are Transformed by Their Children; Growing Up Again: Parenting Ourselves, Parenting Our Children;* and *The Inner Parent: Raising Ourselves, Raising Our Children* aim to alter adult behavior through engaging with tensions contained within parent identity. Books like *How Love Works: How to Stay in Love as a Couple* and *Be True to Yourself . . . Even with Kids*, by child-care guru Steve Biddulph, provide guidance to the emotionally confused parent. Parents are offered advice about how to survive and keep their marriage going after having children. In some cases, child rearing is represented as a form of therapy through which the adult embarks on a voyage of self-discovery. "Many older fathers speak of a 'deepening' of their lives, or an 'opening out,' or 'loosening up,' conveying a sense of recognizing something new in themselves," writes Jeremy Hamand with reassuring authority in *Father Over Forty*.[7] Psychiatrist Frank Pittman writes in *Man Enough* that "fathering is not something perfect men do, but something that perfects the man." In case the reader is confused by what fathering is about, Pittman remarks that the "end product of child raising is not the child but the parent."[8]

Anne Cassidy takes the view that the fact that child rearing is now called parenting is not an accident. The term shifts the focus on parents rather than children. One reason for this shift, she believes, is that adulthood has become more self-absorbed and that it has become culturally acceptable to use "our children's childhood" as the vehicle for adults' own psychic transformation.[9] Using children as a vehicle to discover adult identity is actively promoted in books like Elizabeth Fishel's *Family Mirrors: What Our Children's Lives Reveal About Ourselves*. Cassidy has a point, but as we shall see later in the chapter, there are other influences that shape contemporary adult identity. The shift in terminology does raise one particularly interesting paradox: in the era where all aspects of family life are declared to be child-centered, many adults seem to have lost the ability to distinguish their own concerns from the issues that affect their children. Too often, child development is interpreted through the parenting agenda. This may mean that many of the concerns that society raises about parenting may have less to do with children than we are led to believe.

Emotional Investment in Children

Adult preoccupation with their identity as parents does not mean that mothers and fathers do not love their children. Children have never been so much loved by their mothers and fathers as today. In a world that is more and more dominated by instrumental calculation, the parent-child relationship stands out as a unique example of an interaction that is primarily guided by sentiment and even altruism. The child has become a unique object of love and sometimes of veneration. This celebration of children has been characterized as the "sacralization" of childhood. This term refers

to the important historical process through which contemporary childhood has come to be invested with sentimental or even religious meaning.

The term *sacralization* emerges out of an important study by the American sociologist Viviana Zelizer titled *Pricing the Priceless Child*. Zelizer's
text explores the profound alteration that took place in the economic and
sentimental value of children in the United States during the period
between the 1870s and 1930s. At the beginning of this period, children were
still mainly valued because of the economic contribution they made to the
family. However, important changes in economic and social life ensured
that child labor diminished in significance. With the passing of time, children were less likely to be valued for their productive role and became more
and more objects of sentiment. Zelizer argues that the expulsion of children from economic life at around the turn of the twentieth century was
paralleled by the cultural process of sacralization of children's lives. She
believes that this process provides the platform on which the subsequent
veneration of childhood has been constructed. She writes that the "emergence of this economically 'worthless' but emotionally 'priceless' child has
created an essential condition for contemporary childhood." The normal
pragmatic economic calculations that adults make about most aspects of
life have little bearing on their decision to have children. Having a child in
an industrialized society is primarily emotionally motivated.[10]

The sacred child of the modern era is an object of sentiment and veneration. This new conception of children as intrinsically precious and an
unequivocal source of love evolved alongside the new domestic role
assumed by nonemployed middle-class women. The American historian
Carl Degler believes that changing the value of children served women's
interest: "Exalting the child went hand-in-hand with exalting the domestic role of women; each reinforced the other while together they raised
domesticity within the family to a new and higher level of respectability."[11]
The exaltation of childhood and by implication the role of caring continues to influence parental ideology to this day. Through the care that adults
provide to precious children, parenting acquired a new moral significance.
Although the exaltation of childhood might have been initially restricted
to a relatively small group of nineteenth-century middle-class mothers, it

gradually spread to wider sections of society. Today it gives definition to the ideology of parenting. That is why parents who fail to provide the best care for their children are judged to be immoral.

Parental identity is also shaped by the expanding influence of parental determinism. The idea that the well-nurtured child is the product of the skills of his caretakers has proved attractive to many caretakers. However, the belief that parents bear so much responsibility for the development of their children also creates anxieties. With so much at stake, parents have considerable moral incentive to implement the most up-to-date child-rearing practices as early as possible. As a result, the parent has become dependent on the information and advice offered by professional child specialists.

In recent decades, the exaltation of children has acquired far greater significance than at any time in the past. In most Western societies, children are less and less brought into this world as a matter of routine. Increasingly, the timing of a child's birth is carefully planned. In contrast to the pre–contraceptive pill era, many women have a real choice about when to have children, if at all. Greater control over fertility has led to a marked reduction in the size of families. From conception, children are far more likely to be "wanted," and from the outset they are objects of enormous emotional investment. In short, greater control over human reproduction makes every new child more priceless to parent and society alike. It also enhances the moral responsibility of the adult for guaranteeing the well-being of the precious child.

The immense emotional investment in children that society now expects of their caretakers is almost always readily accepted by parents. The status that is granted to the good child-raiser is a source of both moral authority and of parental identity. Many parents who positively embrace this status are also aware that every new stage in their child's development raises new questions about their skill and competence. With so much emotional investment at stake, parents are often seriously preoccupied with how their performance is judged in public. Parents are remarkably vulnerable to the many busybodies that continually instruct and advise them about their role. Since the identity of parents develops through public affirmation, mothers and fathers can never be indifferent to the way that others view them. Part of this identity is constituted through demonstrating competence in the skills of child rearing. That is why advice that is oriented toward altering the behavior of parents is so rarely contested by mature adults. A sense of performing for an audience is liable to weaken the confidence of even the most self-sufficient adult. Mothers and fathers who are not entirely confident about their performance as child caretakers are therefore very vulnerable to external pressure and influence. Consequently, they listen to and in many cases seek out advice from individuals who bear the mantle of expert authority.

Parents also anxiously watch one another and compare their performances. Few can resist the pressure to keep up or at least not to be seen to be falling down on their duty. This aspect of today's parenting culture is rarely debated, and yet it places an enormous burden on the lives of caretakers. Mothers and fathers who feel that they are under constant scrutiny cannot help but perform for others. Parents who are distracted by the need to perform can sometimes lose sight of what child rearing should be about. Competitive parents often end up being pushy mothers and fathers. In recent years, there has been an outcry that many parents are going over the top, in effect hothousing their youngsters. Alvin Rosenfeld and Nicole Wise claim that "the most competitive adult sport is no longer golf" but "parenting."[12] There is considerable truth in this observation. However, there is now a risk that the rise of the competitive parent will provide a new opportunity for experts to discover new reasons for bashing mothers and fathers. Well-to-do middle-class parents who push their offspring hard to learn new skills at far too early an age are often accused of placing their children's mental health at risk. This phenomenon of hyperparenting is prevalent in the United States.

The pervasive impact of hyperparenting has been extensively explored by the child psychiatrist Alvin Rosenfeld. Rosenfeld believes that the intense scheduling of children's lives is not only a waste of time but actually harmful. Rosenfeld's work provides an important antidote to the pernicious idea that children's time should be organized around worthy goal-oriented objectives.[13] He is concerned that overscheduled children who "busily rush from activity, to endless homework, to tutors who help them excel at high school subjects" are denied time to "veg out" and to imagine through play and through learning to cope with boredom.[14] The impact that Rosenfeld's book has had on public debate indicates growing concern about the pressures to which children are subjected by competitive parents.

Hyperparenting is often one-sidedly blamed on insecure and ambitious parents. In his classic account of this form of parental pressure, *The Hurried Child*, David Elkind pointed the finger at self-obsessed caretakers who are insensitive to the feelings and needs of their children.[15] Such accusation is not without foundation. The parent identity does little to discourage adults from living through their children, and as we note later in this chapter, this trend has become more noticeable in recent years. But there is more to hyperparenting than the archetypal pushy parent. The roots of hyperparenting are found in the culture of parent-scaring. Many of the trends previously outlined—perceptions of childhood vulnerability, infant determinism, the expanded definition of parenting—work as mutually reinforcing influences on the worldview of mothers and fathers. The constant exhortation "You can never do too much for your children" has had the unfortunate consequence of fostering a climate in which parents do too much for their children. For many individual mothers and fathers, this approach is not a matter of choice. "Sophie was the only one among the girls her age that did not take ballet lessons," explained her mother, Ruth. Ruth was made to feel that she was cheating her four-and-a-half-year-old daughter by depriving her of this valuable activity as well as the company of her friends. "Sophie felt excluded, and I got fed up with her friends' mothers wanting to know why she didn't take ballet," says Ruth with a hint of resignation, "And yes, after four weeks we gave in." Even some parents who cannot financially afford to "give in" still do.

Hyperparenting reveals just how far the insecurities contained with the identity of parenthood can contradict the real needs of children. The most obvious response to the pressure for parenting on demand is to overparent. Unfortunately, such a response has little to do with improving the quality of the child-parent relationship. It simply implies a quantitative increase in the range of "stimulating" activities and possessions made available to children. This is a classic example of how the expansion of parenting time has little to do with child rearing as such. After-school activities take up a lot of parenting time. Their contribution to improving child rearing is debatable. Hyperparenting is generally criticized for placing too much pressure on young children. But hyperparenting can also be seen as depriving children of precisely the kind of pressures they need. One of the most stimulating activities for young children is unsupervised play with others their age. Learning from and through other children encourages the acquisition of coping and communication skills and the habit of independence. But allowing children to be children is perceived as far too much of a risk by adults who have been trained to believe that they can never do too much for their children. Hyperparenting is merely a logical extension of parental determinism.

The Emptying Out of Adult Identity

The emotional investment that adults make in children is far greater today than in the early days of the sacralization of childhood. Our culture today is probably child-obsessed rather than child-centered. The continuous rise in the demands imposed on parents is fueled by the steady elevation of the moral status of children. The reason has little to do with new insights into the lives of children. Current concern with the position of children is sometimes interpreted as the consequence of a more enlightened and caring society. But our culture's preoccupation with the child is inseparable from the problems that afflict adults. It is the uncertainties that surround adult identities that motivate many parents to put so much of their emotional capital into their children.

That today's world is one of uncertain identities is something of a truism. It is widely recognized that we live in a time of insecure attachments. Many of us have serious difficulties with offering more than a provisional answer to the question of "Who am I?" It is generally appreciated that the identities that served previous generations fit rather uncomfortably with the demands of life today. The sense of belonging that we derive from being connected to others has in recent decades been undermined through important changes in the way we live and organize our lives. Take the role of work. Work has traditionally been an important source of collective experience that connected people to one another. It was and still remains an important part of an individual's identity. When people ask, "Who is he?" they expect an answer bound up with work. "He is a mechanic," "She is a nurse" are not just statements about people's jobs but also about their identities. An individual's personality and status is in some sense inextricably linked to her job. However, work today has a less permanent and identity-forming role than during most of the last century. In an era when the idea of a job for life is dismissed as an illusion and people are expected to train to be flexible and responsive to the changing needs of the labor market, people's sense of who they are becomes more ambiguous. *Corrosion of Character*, by sociologist Richard Sennett, provides a powerful account of the consequences of work insecurity on how employees regard themselves. The experience of insecurity makes it difficult for many workers to achieve a sense of moral identity, breeding detachment and a sense of estrangement from others. Finding fulfillment through work becomes difficult for those who are unable to identify with their jobs. He claims that the question "Who needs me?" has become difficult to answer in modern capitalism. According to Sennett, a system that "radiates indifference" generates personal confusion and confers a profound sense of personal isolation.[16]

The insecurities that many people experience in relation to the realm of work are also felt in other spheres of everyday life. The satisfaction we derive from being connected to others is radically challenged by uncertainties about our communities. What does it mean to be an American? At a time when every aspect of life appears to be subject to debate, the answer to this question is not self-evident. Lack of clarity about national, ethnic, and even community affiliations tests people's sense of belonging. Debates about national identity, gender, religion, and the effect of globalization also reflect concerns about the human desire for recognition. When we fail to recognize ourselves through work or feel detached from others and have a weak feeling of community, then our very identity becomes unclear.

Weakening of Durable Relations

Nor is the question of who we are restricted to work and community issues. The cumulative effect of social and cultural change has had a major impact on the way we conduct our affairs as men and women. Relations within the family and between people are generally experienced as unstable and transient. Something like one out of two first marriages end in divorce.

Today, a growing proportion of adults is opting to cohabit, either before or instead of marriage. In the United States, 56 percent of all marriages between 1990 and 1994 were preceded by cohabitation. From 1987 to 1995, the number of women in their late thirties who reported having cohabited rose to 48 percent from 30 percent. A study published in 2000 by the Institute for Social Research at the University of Michigan reported that about two in five children will spend at least some time living with their mother and her unmarried partner.

The number of first marriages in the United States has decreased significantly since 1970; annual marriage rates continue to decline. The median duration of an American marriage is 7.2 years. The decline of marriage and the rise of cohabitation and divorce have led to important variations in family life. Since the seventies, there has been a steady increase in the proportion of births outside marriage. By the late nineties, almost a third of all children under eighteen were living in a single-parent household. The growing instability of adult relations—married and unmarried—means that a growing number of children are brought up in lone-parent families and in stepfamilies.

The instability that surrounds family relations in part reflects and in part consolidates the emptying out of adult identity, a process whereby men and women find it difficult to derive a secure sense of affirmation through their relations with one another and with other adults. Other sources of adult affirmation—vocation, career, work, and community—have also become less reliable means of conferring stable identities.

We feel our uncertainties about adult identity most intensely in our intimate encounters. At a time of changing gender roles, certainty about the meaning of being a man or a woman sometimes proves to be elusive. Even the ties of passion and love are experienced in peculiarly short-term and insecure ways. The emotions that adults invest in one another are tempered by expectations of impermanence. In everyday life, love between men and women is often treated in a calculating and pragmatic fashion. There is a heightened public awareness regarding marital breakdown and the fluidity of intimate relationships.

For many, the emptying out of adult identity is experienced through a sense of estrangement from other people. In such circumstances, people's relations to one another is guided more by calculation and less by sentiment. Our very ability to make emotional investments in one another is restrained by a public mood that stresses the difficulties inherent in human relations. The growing popularity of binding prenuptial agreements illustrates the temper of our times. The aim of a prenuptial agreement is to settle the division of property if and when a marriage breaks up. From the standpoint of legal and business calculation, it makes perfect sense. However, such an agreement assumes that the marriage could break up and end in divorce—that marriages cannot be expected to work and so provision should be made for individuals in the event of failure. For some, this assumption represents a realistic appraisal of social trends. However, the expectation of failure necessarily endows marriage with a different meaning than if it is seen as an unquestioned commitment for life. At the very least, the expectation of impermanence is likely to limit the emotional investment that the two contracting parties make in one another. "Self-protection and closing the deal are paramount" for mistrustful adults, notes Candace Bushnell in Sex in the City.[17]

It is ironic that precisely at a time when personal relationships have been freed from many of their traditional constraints, they are often represented as more tortuous and problematic than ever before. Even intimate friendships are portrayed as institutions of a bygone era. Some academics claim that people today fear intimacy because they have become more individualistic, more self-protective and cynical. This was the thesis of Dr. Robert Firestone's study The Fear of Intimacy.[18] Numerous researchers who argue that there is a trend for the middle classes to have less emotionally demanding friendships have echoed this California clinical psychologist's verdict. The sociologist Ann Swidler believes that the trend is an outcome of the conflict between a preoccupation with the individual and the idea of love.[19]

Although most people still long for durable romantic attachments, contemporary culture appears to encourage a skeptical stance toward long-term emotional commitment. Such attitudes are also reinforced by a popular culture that continually highlights problems associated with family life.

The romantic notion that love can conquer all has been laid to rest, condemned as naïve idealism that never works in practice. Instead there is a growing wariness about love and romantic attachments, where individuals are encouraged to adopt a self-centered, calculating, and short-term attitude to their emotional commitments and not to invest too much in anybody other than themselves. As Swidler argues, "permanence becomes almost a sign of failure" in a world where personal growth acquires a privileged status.[20]

The cultivation of the self continually fostered by contemporary culture has a destructive impact on adult relations. It is not that individuals have become selfish people devoid of any interest in the welfare of others. Rather, present-day culture finds it difficult to provide men and women with both the meaning and the focus for their commitment. The failure to situate intimate relationships within a wider, culturally sanctioned web of meaning is most striking in relation to the contemporary narrative of love. Love today finds it difficult to say anything plausible about attachment, self-sacrifice, or lifelong commitment. The story of love is about me— finding myself, self-actualization, autonomy, and personal growth. Ultimately, the orientation toward the self erodes the foundation for intimate relationships. Self-interest unmediated by wider cultural meanings encourages a withdrawal from the pursuit of intimacy.

Intimacy cannot thrive in a terrain where relationships lack shared meaning, clarity, and context. Without any obvious answer to the question of what a relationship is, its conduct becomes arbitrary. Commitment that has no external point of reference simply cannot stand up to the pressures of everyday life.

The difficulties that people experience in finding a focus for their emotional commitment has the effect of consolidating anxieties about intimate relationships. Not surprisingly, it is now common for people to approach their private relations with a heightened sense of emotional risk. One strategy for dealing with emotional risk is to distance the self from the potential source of disappointment. Detachment from others appears to offer a measure of protection from emotional pain. At the very least, men and women are encouraged to manage the expanding levels of perceived risks associated with intimate relationships. A variety of tactics—from prenuptial agreements to cultivating the virtues of solo living—are used to manage the risks associated with self-fulfillment.

The reinterpretation of personal commitment as a risk represents a warning to anyone foolish enough to desire passionate engagement. One pragmatic response is to declare that our expectations of intimate relationships are unrealistic. "Be careful—you may get hurt!" is a message that reflects the temper of our time. Disengagement from commitment is thus fueled by the dictates of risk management.

The elusive character of romantic love is not in doubt. However, this focus for adult passion and emotional attachment has not been replaced by any plausible alternative. Jane Lewis's study *Individualism and Commitment in Cohabitation and Marriage* claims that what has happened is an increase of individualism in relation to personal relations and that selfishness has "undermined the commitment of men and women to each other and their children." It is far from evident why individualism should lead to a fear of commitment. Nor is it evident that people have become more selfish. The problem of commitment is inextricably bound up with the emptying out of adult identity. Today, many of us find it difficult to know what we can be committed to. The sense of confusion about who we are makes it difficult to establish durable ties to one another. As a result, our expectations of relationships diminish and sometimes our ability to forge bonds of intimacy becomes weaker.

The moral significance of the child today is directly linked to the emptying out of adult identity. When the desire for recognition lacks an obvious outlet, the validation of the sense of self through one's child acquires a new importance. When in previous eras adults lived through their children, they did so as members of at least outwardly relatively stable families and communities. The child was used as a means of self-realization and sometimes as an instrument of family advancement. Today, the child has been transformed into a far more formidable medium for the validation of the adult self. At a time when very few human relations can be taken for granted, the child appears as a unique emotional partner. "The trust that was previously anticipated from marriage, partnership, friendship, class solidarity and so on, is now invested more generally in the child," writes sociologist Christopher Jenks.[21] Unlike marriage or friendship, the bond that links a parent to a child cannot be broken. It is a bond that stands out as the exception to the rule that relationships cannot be expected to last forever.

The general perception of transient relations between men and women stands in sharp contrast to the distinctly durable bonds that bind a parent to a child. The short-term view of marriage does not extend to the emotional commitment of a parent to a child. The difference was widely commented on in a series of articles on the attitudes of female youth icons. One commentator contrasted the pragmatic orientation of British media personality Zoë Ball toward her marriage with the sense of permanence she expressed toward a future child. She remarked that both she and her husband "were quite realistic" about marriage. She added, "Things aren't always going to be forever, but he really is a lovely man and he will be lovely to my kids, no matter what happens between us."[22] Zoë Ball's comment that things don't last forever reveals low expectations about relations of intimacy. Such a vision does not aspire to permanent commitment between two adults but of adults to their children. Marriage partners and lovers can come and go, but what must remain is commitment to the offspring of the relationship.

This reorientation is invariably accompanied by a rise in the emotional capital invested in the child, a development well expressed by German sociologist Ulrich Beck: "Partners come and go, but the child stays. Everything one vainly hoped to find in the relationship with one's partner is sought in or directed to a child. . . . The child becomes the final alternative to loneliness, a bastion against the vanishing chances of loving and being loved."[23] Of course, most people have not abandoned the hope of finding fulfilling intimate relationships. But the desire for long-term commitments coexists with a heightened wariness. Children offer a sense of permanence that in other situations appears to elude adults attempting to forge secure attachments.

In an uncertain adult universe, there is a formidable incentive to expand emotional investment in children. Excessive affection and concern for children results from regarding them as one of the few permanent facts in people's lives. Mothers and fathers can lose their jobs and the status that is attached to it. Divorce and separation have become so common that many men and women are conscious of the prospect of future disappointment. Lovers, husbands, and wives come and go. But whatever happens with adult relations, a parent's daughter or son will always be his child. Children provide a sense of permanence in an otherwise fluid world. That is why mothers and fathers invest so much of their emotion in them.

Uncertain Attachments

One of the consequences of uncertain attachments in the workplace, community, and family is to elevate the role of parent identity. In many cases, emotional investment in children becomes so encompassing that parents' social and moral identities become inseparable from their parenting identities. Ideas about parenting and child development reflect the adult quest for secure attachment. Jerome Kagan has drawn attention to the way in which current concern with an infant's attachment to her parent is linked to anxieties about people's connectedness to their community. "The sacredness of the mother-infant bond and therefore the psychological significance of the attachment of a baby to its mother are among the sturdiest of our dwindling set of unsullied ethical beliefs," writes Kagan.[24] In a world of transient encounters, the promise of permanent attachment through bonding endows the mother-infant relationship with deep meaning.

Parenting strategies that are based on an all-consuming emotional focus on one's own child are paradoxically often indifferent to children in general. There is little that is altruistic about adults' emotional investment in children. Adults who greatly value their own children and lavish them with attention can feel little responsibility for other people's children. There is an important divergence between the private and public value of children. As Viviana Zelizer notes, the sentimentalization of childhood often stops at the family's doorstep.[25] The deep emotion that parents direct toward their own children in the privacy of their home stands in sharp contrast to the lack of responsibility that they feel toward other people's children. Other children make noise in restaurants, howl and yell in supermarkets, compete for scarce places in the schools of our choice, or bully our own sons and daughters.

The reluctance to take responsibility for children in general makes an important statement about the quality of parental altruism. Emotional investment is often inseparable from validating the self through one's own children. Cultural pressures to love on demand reaffirm this orientation and make it difficult for adults to distinguish their own private preoccupations from wider issues concerning children. It would be wrong to imply that parents have become peculiarly selfish or self-absorbed. The emptying out of adult identities reinforced by parental determinism has fostered a climate in which the search for the self has become bound up with the relation to children. With so much at stake in this relationship, adults are sometimes prepared to alter their conduct to fall in line with conventional norms regarding parenting identity.

I Could Not Live with Myself If . . .

Many parents know that their concern with their children borders on the obsessive. But they believe they need to be this way for their children's sake. Almost every parent that I talked to about their views on child rearing referred to the external dangers facing their children. "There never used to be so many drug dealers hassling young kids," said a thirty-six-year-old father of two children aged seven and nine. A mother of a thirteen-year-old who does not allow her daughter to walk to school seven hundred yards down the road complains that there have never been so many pedophiles on the streets as today. Larry lives in a peaceful leafy suburb, outwardly just the sort of place where parents ought to feel relaxed about letting children to wander around. Yet neither his eleven- nor his thirteen-year-old son is allowed to go outside to play on his own. These reactions are regularly confirmed by surveys and opinion polls. The report of the Future Foundation noted: "Parents are increasingly reluctant to compromise their children's safety by leaving them unsupervised." [26]

Although parental overreaction to statistically insignificant risks is widely reported, its relationship to the way that adults perceive their roles as parents is seldom considered. And yet the inexorable rise of parental fears should not be seen as simply an overreaction or irrational response to external developments. In conversations, most parents are prepared to concede that the likelihood of their child being abducted is minimal. Most parents have a reasonably good grasp of the specific threats faced by their offspring and have no problem discussing it in a rational and balanced manner. However, such good common sense does not prevent the very same parents from feeling burdened by a general sense of external danger. Nor does it prevent parents from feeling extremely concerned when they hear a news report of a tragic incident involving a child. It is not so much the case that parents overreact all the time but that they have a disposition to do so in a variety of circumstances.

Parental paranoia is symptomatic of the concerns that caretakers have of their own sense of self as parents. Parental perceptions of the risks facing their children are grounded in a tension that many mothers and fathers experience between their identity as parents and a lack of confidence in their ability to live up to that identity. Many parents who derive considerable affirmation through their role of nurturing and protecting their children also feel that they have insufficient moral and psychological resources to effectively discharge these responsibilities. Sometimes the external world is perceived to be a threat precisely because it is external to the parent-child relationship. It is difficult to reconcile the comfortable feeling of certainty promised by this unique relationship with the sense of uncertainty that prevails in the external world. For some parents, the question is not simply the threat to one's child but also to this unique relationship.

From talking to parents about their fears, I have concluded that the concept of children at risk mainly conveys the diffuse insecurity that many adults feel regarding their identity as parents. When parents talk about their fears for their children, one phrase keeps recurring. This frequently repeated statement, "I could not live with myself if something happened to my child," provides an important insight about the meaning of parental anxieties today. The phrase refers not so much to the vulnerability of children but of adults; it expresses an adult consciousness of insecurity. With so much emotional investment in a child, it is difficult to take risks. Parents' fear of losing the defining relationship of their identity encourages a heightened sensitivity to the troubles of childhood. Sadly, being able to live with oneself—a key issue confronting adult identity—has become a burden on children's lives.

7 Confusions About Facing Up to Adulthood

Parents don't just confuse their problems with those of their children, sometimes they are unsure about where to draw the line between adulthood and childhood. When adults perceive their identity through their children, the parent-child relationship becomes confused. In contemporary society, this confusion has been compounded by cultural trends that dispute adult authority. Since the 1960s glorification of youth culture, many parents have felt uncomfortable with their role as responsible adults. Today, it is common for adults to cling to a youthful identity, insist that they still have a lot more growing to do, and shamelessly copy the fashions of the younger generation. For some time now, parents, teachers, and other adults involved with children have gone out of their way to cross the generational divide and become young people's friends rather than their mentors. This changing perception of adulthood—an unconscious process of infantilization—both reflects and reinforces the weakening of adult authority.

Uncertainties about adulthood are invariably linked to changing ideas about childhood. Adults who sometimes behave like children are just as likely to treat children as adults. Maturity is disparaged as being "past it," and older generations are seen as having no special claim to wisdom. The corollary has been the promotion of the concepts of children's rights and autonomy. As a result, many mothers and fathers find it difficult to act decisively with their children.

The Depreciation of Adulthood

In a world where a parent's word is not law, a sense of powerlessness and the fear of losing control haunt most parents. Mothers and fathers often react by doing whatever they can to make home life as attractive as possible. Since the 1930s, child experts have encouraged parents to adopt a more open and playful relationship with their children. Historians of family life have noted the crucial role played by the caring professions in convincing parents to abandon their old-fashioned authoritarian ways for more fun-loving interactions. Lisa Jacobson's study of the modernization of the American home points out that "child experts urged parents to adapt its language of salesmanship, persuasion, and enticement and to forsake harsh discipline for understanding companionship." These new authorities insisted that the ideal father should be a friend, an enjoyable companion rather than a policeman. A new conception of middle-class motherhood and fatherhood emerged, based on the belief that parental authority was most effectively exercised through play and friendship rather than obedience and discipline. The ideal parent was someone who was with it, learned his children's slang, and adapted to their world. By the fifties, what Martha Wolfenstein characterized as "fun morality" became a dominant influence on American parenting styles. A decade later, it also emerged as the norm in Britain and parts of western Europe.[1]

Playing and having fun is an important part of any lively parent-child relationship. An easygoing atmosphere makes for greater openness and flexibility in family life. Fun morality can be problematic, however. Often parents have hard choices to make. We need to insist on forms of behavior that a child will experience as anything but fun. Sometimes fathers and mothers have to adopt a policing role and demand the unquestioned obedience of their child. For many parents, the shift from the role of a friend to that of a disciplining authority is difficult. Fathers who have become their children's friends often have trouble exercising authority when they must act firmly or decisively. The difficulty of reconciling these apparently conflicting roles means that parents often cannot make or enforce decisions.

Parents complain that their authority is continually weakened by outside pressures. They say that it is difficult to make their children toe the line when the rest of the world encourages lax behavior. Children can tap into this uncertainty and manipulate it. Children are good at finding contradictions between their parents' instructions and standards of behavior endorsed by other adults. They complain that their friends are not subjected to such unreasonable demands as having to be home by suppertime. Of course, parents sometimes find it easy to blame others for their failure to get their child to comply. But it is true that mothers and fathers receive virtually no public support or encouragement in the exercise of parental authority. Instead of reassuring us that holding the line serves children's best interest, contemporary culture signals that parental authority should be viewed with suspicion. For example, discipline is often presented as harsh, authoritarian, and sometimes a form of abuse.

Everywhere we look, parents appear in an unattractive light. Popular culture portrays parents as out-of-touch deadbeats who are insensitive to their children's needs. In contrast, children are represented as essentially smart, streetwise, and resourceful. In particular, parents who try to discipline their children are treated as objects of derision. This depreciation of adulthood and the elevation of the child are strikingly conveyed through television and popular films. Children are regularly featured as morally superior to grown-ups, while their parents and other adults are depicted as craven fools. Angelica, the three-year-old star of *Rugrats*, manipulates and dominates her foolish father. Young Ricky Fitts is the cleverest character in the Oscar-winning film *American Beauty*. The middle-aged Lester Burnham looks to him as an inspiration for his new life model. The highly acclaimed *Sixth Sense* is emblematic of the theme of dumb parent and resourceful child. The youngster, Cole Sear, is the smartest person in the film. His mother doesn't believe that he sees dead people, but he does. The boy also appears to understand the behavior of grown-ups better than the adults. *Parent Trap* sees two clever twin daughters of separated parents conspire to get them back together again. The sisters succeed, showing up adults who are hopeless in managing their emotional affairs. The *Simpsons* provides the definitive portrayal of adult dysfunctionality. Lisa is the smartest individual in the family. All the rest are dumb—really dumb. Repellent images of parents are also conveyed in blockbuster films like *Home Alone, House Arrest,* and *Honey, I Shrunk the Kids.* More "thoughtful" films like the award-winning *Shine* present parents as obsessed child abusers.

Parents are really bad news. At least that seems to be the verdict of the popular media. Sylvia Ann Hewlett and Cornell West have condemned what they characterize as "a poisonous popular culture" in the United States for continually denigrating parental authority. During the summer of 1997 they monitored daytime talk shows to see how they treated parents. The conclusion they came to was that parents tended to be portrayed as either "irresponsible fools or in-your-face monsters." Hewlett and West contend that talk shows have no monopoly over negative stereotypes of moms and dads.[2]

This negative stereotyping flows from a culture that regards adulthood with mixed emotions. The crisis of adult identity and the special moral status accorded to children has encouraged a cultural process that can best be described as a flight from adulthood. Popular television programs like *Ally McBeal* portray immature adults as an indisputable fact of life. Many of the leading comedy series—*Frasier, Friends, Absolutely Fabulous*—feature grown-up men and women living a life of extended adolescence.

Not surprisingly, some parents do not want their children simply to like them, they also want to be like them. Everyone knows a forty-something father who feels that he has a lot more living to do. They make a virtue of identifying with their sons and daughters and want to be treated as their equals. Of course, they insist that their children's friends call them by their first names. They possess a curiously up-to-date knowledge of the music scene, and when you visit them, they ostentatiously flaunt the latest indie CD. The advertising industry even has a special name—kidult—to describe the growing number of Peter Pan adults.

Andrew Calcutt's *Arrested Development* offers a compelling account of the erosion of adulthood in popular culture. Calcutt claims that what was once the exclusive preserve of youth—youth culture—is now popular culture, which commands the allegiance of the majority of the population under sixty. For its part, this culture promotes a forever-young Peter Pan–like aspiration to immaturity. Such influences make it difficult for many adults to accept the facts of life. There are few kudos attached to being a grown-up. The world of advertising understands that there is little point in appealing to the experience of middle-aged men and women. Calcutt cites one executive of a leading advertising agency who explains: "If all advertising seems to be directed at the young it's because we've found the most effective way to appeal to everyone is to make commercials which embody attitudes associated with youth."[3]

The depreciation of adulthood and the current obsession with youth have important implications for the exercise of parental authority. Adults who behave like children are unlikely to enjoy the authority essential for parenting. Curiously enough, the idea of infant determinism that we encountered earlier has provided the intellectual underpinnings for a diminished sense of adulthood. The proposition that the experience of early childhood directly determines future character traits and behavior transforms the adult experience into the mere playing-out of a script written decades previously. Adults damaged during childhood simply can't help it. Such a vision of the helpless adult is by no means confined to the margins of our culture. Therapeutic professionals often claim that childhood experience does not merely influence but unequivocally determines adult identity.

The importance attached to childhood experience results in a diminished version of adulthood that suggests that grown-up men and women are incapable of controlling their lives. That is why in therapeutic literature the line that divides children from adults is difficult to discern. The term *adult child* expresses this infantilized version of the self. The notion that adults are merely acting out a script set in motion during their childhood has encouraged people to look for clues about their lives in the past, in the belief that the key to understanding the adult self lies somewhere in childhood or before. Primal therapy and past-life therapy attempt to extract existential meaning through a process of moral archaeology. The recovered-memory movement never fails to discover acts of deep significance in childhood, which are said to account for the adult's predicament. According to one version of the therapeutic ethos, self-identity is formed less by what people do and know about themselves than by what they can no longer remember. Hence, the privileged role assigned to therapy for uncovering the lost identity of the self. The importance attached to the character-forming role of childhood and even pre-childhood experience is based on a highly deterministic view of the human condition. The many experiences we have as adults pale into insignificance compared to the trials we experience as children. As in a Greek tragedy, throughout our lives we are doomed to realize a predestined existence. People are encouraged to see themselves as victims of their childhood rather than as self-determining agents. This coincides with a dramatic redefinition of the adult as weak or diminished, disassociated from many of the characteristics historically linked to adulthood: moral autonomy, maturity, and responsibility.

The depreciation of adulthood coincides with the idealization of childhood and childishness, positing adults as morally inferior. In a secular variant of the religious theme of humanity's fall from grace, innocent children are said to be ruined by toxic parents in a toxic society. Campaigners promoting the idea of stranger danger contribute to a climate where the stranger—that is, the vast majority of adults inhabiting this planet—is not worthy of a child's trust.

The weakening of the association between moral maturity and adulthood is by no means complete or irreversible. Most of us do our best to act as mature adults despite the cultural pressures that question our role. These pressures can best be understood as a manifestation of the crisis of adult identity discussed in the previous chapter. Often what is described as the search for identity turns into a journey back to childhood. Most of the time, this psychological retreat from maturity is a temporary episode in the larger project of making sense of who we are. But at a time when uncertainties are framed through the cultural interrogation of adulthood, it is easy to become confused about the line that divides grown-ups from children.

The future of every community depends on the successful socialization of its children. Every society needs to work out a solution to the problem of transforming children into adults. Parenting is the principal medium for realizing this goal. When parents try to act as their child's equal, it is far from evident what they are teaching their charges to be. Are they socializing them into mature adults, uncertain adults, or adults who would like to go back to being children? Confusions about how to face up to the responsibilities of adulthood place an extra burden on parents' shoulders. They contribute to the weakening of adult solidarity and increase tensions over the exercise of parental authority.

8

The Problem of Holding the Line

How do we get our children to behave themselves? Parents know that children cannot be properly socialized unless they learn to draw lines, respect certain rules, and gradually acquire the habit of self-control. Unfortunately, there is no obvious guide as to how to gain the compliance of a child.

Testing boundaries is part of a child's development. Young children live for the moment; they want instantaneous attention and find it hard to accept that they should not watch more television or should go to bed at the prescribed time. Some aspects of a child's defiance of parental authority can be creative expressions of his developing personality. Others, however, are positively dangerous. For a parent, knowing when to hold the line and when to overlook bad behavior is a difficult problem to negotiate. Although we all try to be consistent, in practice it is impossible always to get things right. Mothers and fathers sometimes overreact and sometimes, for the sake of an easy life, tolerate behavior that could create problems for the future. It is not surprising that discipline is at the top of the list of issues raised with child professionals and providers of parenting advice. A look back at parenting publications shows that discipline has been their readers' chief concern for most of the past century.

In recent times, the question of discipline has been complicated by the fact that family life is no longer governed by unquestioned rules enforced by the head—usually the patriarch—of the family. Modern families tend to rely on reason and negotiation to sort out their affairs; or at least, they try to. The democratization of family life has been driven by a more enlightened appreciation of human behavior. The contemporary family accords individuals more freedom and choice and gives children more status and respect. The decline of an authoritarian style of parenting means that mothers and fathers have adopted more open, sensitive, and responsive tactics for managing their children's behavior. This has been a positive and welcome development.

The question of discipline is further complicated by the ambiguities that many grown-ups feel about their own identity. Taking disciplinary action invites rejection, or even the withdrawal of a child's love. One of the recurring themes in the drama of parenting is the fear that firm discipline might drive children away from their parents. Parents are particularly concerned about how to exercise control over what their children are doing in the outside world. Just saying "no" may mean losing a child to the wrong crowd. Parents who fear that disciplinary measures could turn their children against them will resort to bribery, selective amnesia, or just simply giving in.

The uncertainties that adults experience about knowing when and how to draw the line have helped to consolidate parental paranoia. Mothers and fathers have always felt unsure about what to do when their child said "no." Today, some are not only unclear about how to control their children but uncertain whether they should even try to do so.

Drawing the Line

Where do we draw the line between adulthood and childhood? The lack of clarity on this issue poses big problems. Children are often cast into the role of "little adults" who are deemed capable of making informed choices. At its most extreme, children are presented as equal decision makers within the family. A particularly absurd expression of this is the ongoing discussion about whether children should be endowed with the right formally to divorce their parents. The assumption that children are capable of bearing the responsibilities that attend having "adult rights" is a prime example of failure of nerve when it comes to drawing lines between a child and an adult. Such confusions can only undermine the ability of parents to guide and discipline their children.

Children these days seem to be victims of a split-personality syndrome. On one hand they are depicted as vulnerable creatures in need of constant supervision. On the other, they are often represented as competent to make informed and responsible choices about their lives. Today, adults are advised to consult and negotiate rather than to act, or make decisions, on their children's behalf. These widespread sentiments are codified in the doctrine of children's rights. According to its proponents, children have the right to participate in making the decisions that influence their lives.

In reality, even the most radical supporters of children's rights have to concede that children cannot exercise such rights. One leading advocate of this cause, Bob Franklin, states, "Children have been excluded from participation in formal decision making for so long, that it seems unlikely that they could enter this arena without the initial support and advocacy of adults." Priscilla Alderson gets around the objection that children lack the resources to speak the language of rights by arguing that children have their own way of demanding that their voices be heard.[1]

There is a lot to be said for adults being sensitive to children's voices. Children make sense of the world in their own way and develop illuminating insights about their experience. But to equate a child's voice with the deliberations of an experienced and reasoning adult is to confuse the potential for mature reflection with the actuality of it. Many parents operate on the assumption that their children are their equals—"my best friends," as one put it to me—and so should be treated the same as other adults. Superficially, this response appears as child-centered and child friendly. However, treating children the same as adults can have profoundly disorienting consequences. Children have the potential to become the equals of adults. But for this potential to be realized they need to be treated differently than if they were already thirty-year-olds. The very act of nurturing depends on being able to distinguish the potential to grow up from maturity itself.

As our understanding of childhood has developed, we have come to understand that children have their own unique feelings, aspirations, dreams, and fantasies and that they see the world differently than adults. Acknowledging the special way that children feel and understand has been key to gaining important insights into the process of child development. We now know that children do not simply know less but that they also know differently than adults. Of course the worlds of children and of adults overlap, and children develop through the interaction between the two. The moral and intellectual universe of a child is not the same as that of an adult, nor are they simply different. It is difficult to get the balance right. Sometimes adults imagine children as their polar opposites. At other times they lose sight of what distinguishes themselves from their offspring.

When mature adults talk to each other, they do not simply issue orders or directives. Because they regard one another as equals, they expect to arrive at a decision through reasoned negotiation. Intelligent parents are also likely to seek to explain, reason, and negotiate with their children. This makes sense because one wants to teach children what to consider in making decisions. Unfortunately, today's parenting culture seeks to turn this teaching device into an absolute principle of the child-parent relationship. This approach was vociferously promoted in the seventies in Thomas Gordon's million-copy-plus bestseller, *Parent Effectiveness Training*, which advised parents to stop punishing their children and start treating them "much as we treat a friend or a spouse." Since the seventies, this outlook has been restated time and again. Penelope Leach is critical of parents who think their child impudent for refusing to obey them; she objects that parents believe that they "have the right to tell him what to do" but "they don't want to concede him the same."

The view that children should be treated like adults within the family informs the argument that they should have a say in all decisions affecting them. In *The Family Question*, Professor Stein Ringen proposed that children could be given a veto to stop their parents from divorcing or to prevent their mother from having an abortion. Such ideas might seem bizarre to some of us. But once the tactic of negotiation becomes a principle governing family life, giving children a veto over their parents' actions is not a maverick idea. Nor is there any logical reason why, once conceded, a child's right of veto over her mother and father should be restricted to abortion or divorce. Why should children not have the right to prevent their mother from going back to work? How about moving to a new house or a different part of the country? Who makes the final decisions about holiday destinations?[2]

There is a big difference between a sensible attitude of give and take and giving children the right to override parental decisions. Negotiation is a valuable way to educate children about making choices and dealing with the consequences. When used effectively, it can help children to participate in making informal rules and to gain an appreciation of the limits on their actions. But this interaction should not be confused with the negotiation between two equal parties. Rather, it is a child-rearing tool based on the understanding that an adult and a child are not equals. If children are genuinely treated as equal negotiating partners, knowing where to draw the line becomes a permanent source of anxiety.

The belief that parents should adopt the same standard of behavior toward children as they do toward adults is also behind the controversy about spanking. Opponents of spanking argue that behavior that is unacceptable among adults should not be used against children. They decry the fact that if a man hits another adult, it is called assault, but if he spanks his child, it is called discipline. They believe that the defense of reasonable chastisement legitimizes behavior that would be "illegal when directed at an adult." These propositions have profound implications for the whole process of child rearing. They are really saying that we should renounce any attempt to impose parental will on children.

But parents have to do things to their children that they would not do to another adult. From the moment of conception, mothers and fathers continually impose their will on their babies. Parents who would never dream of telling another adult it was time to go to bed have no problem demanding that their child should go to sleep on the dot at seven o'clock. Parents who check that their child's bottom is clean are unlikely to do the same to people their own age. Whenever they wash them, feed them, or read to them in bed, mothers and fathers unthinkingly treat their children as children and not as adults. We may wish to negotiate over how these things are done, but only toward a nonnegotiable end, such as making sure that our child is clean.

In reality, the notion that parents should treat children like adults is wholly impracticable. This point is implicitly recognized even by the advocates of children's rights, who use the argument inconsistently. For instance, the fashionable idea of parental determinism, with its one-sided stress on the power of nurturing, is based on the premise of treating children very differently than adults. The two conflicting assumptions of parental determinism and the treatment of children as adults are rarely reflected on by professionals, who uphold both arguments simultaneously. Some demand that parents should treat children as adults in one breath, while insisting in the next that children are vulnerable creatures who are permanently at risk. This confusion about negotiation expresses a deeper unease about the exercise of parental authority.

Some insist on the principle of negotiation because they want to limit parental authority, seeing the power that parents possess as potentially damaging to children. This sentiment informs the thinking of children's rights advocates. Bob Franklin writes that "being a child continues to express more about power relationships than chronology." While there is little doubt that parents have considerable power over their children, it is far from evident why this should be perceived as a problem. It only becomes a problem in practice if there is a fundamental conflict of interest between them. Unfortunately, that is increasingly the way that the relationship between parent and child is represented. Stein Ringen's proposal to grant children the right of veto over their parents' right to divorce is based on the premise that such a conflict of interest exists. He also believes that children's interests cannot be represented adequately by their parents in elections and that therefore the voting age should be reduced to sixteen, while those who are younger than sixteen should also have a vote administered by their mothers, presumably at the child's diktat.[3]

Most advocates of restraining parental authority through negotiation do not go as far as Ringen. However, they all believe that children have distinct interests separate from and often contradictory to those of their parents. Parenting manuals continually contrast the parents' needs with the child's needs. Parenting professionals often adopt the posture of umpire or mediator. They talk about getting both sides to understand each other's needs. The tone resembles that of marriage counseling, conveying the impression that the conflict of needs is of the same order as that between husband and wife. This model of the parent-child relationship can have damaging consequences for everyone concerned. Counterbalancing the interests of the adult to those of the child can weaken the very relationship through which nurturing thrives. If a relationship based on affection and sentiment becomes subject to narrow calculations of self-interest, it will have unpredictable consequences for parent and child alike.

The caring professions thrive on alleged conflicts of interest between members of a family. Such conflicts justify their existence and provide them with plenty of work. The conflict-oriented model of family life makes professionals indispensable to the resolution of parenting problems.

Assumptions about the conflict model of family life are rarely spelled out forcefully. In the end, society requires adults to nurture and socialize the young. Too strong a representation of parents as self-serving, selfish individuals would contradict the demand for mothers and fathers to behave as altruistic nurturers. That is why parenting is still so highly esteemed. But while the idea of parenting is acclaimed by politician and child professional alike, support for parental authority is conspicuously absent. It appears that our culture wants devoted adults to parent on demand but also to refrain from exercising their authority. One of the ironies of the present era is that while politicians complain that parents don't control their children, powerful voices also decry the exercise of strong parental authority. We tend to believe that strict parental discipline is repressive and makes for a dysfunctional childhood. Even the term *discipline* now carries connotations of an abuse of power. Predictably, most parents have internalized the confusion that surrounds the exercise of authority, and it is hardly surprising that they feel insecure about their ability to control their children. Sometimes they are uncertain whether it is even right to try to impose their will, and they worry about the consequences of whatever course of action they adopt.

Discipline

Many parents report that the attempt to gain their child's compliance is a twenty-four-hour-a-day struggle. Most of us find it difficult to simply say no. Parents spend an inordinate amount of time weighing up different options. Should I make an issue out of this now, or wait until we are alone? Should I pretend not to notice that she has ignored me yet again—or come down on her firmly? Child caretakers agonize over every reprimand they issue and often go on to relive the experience. Should I have used different words? Should I have waited until I was less angry? Routine anxieties about everyday disciplinary issues are reinforced by more intense apprehensions about losing control altogether. A national poll for the Children's Institute International in 1999 revealed that the majority of adults believe that children sometimes need a good, hard spanking. The survey found that 82 percent of adults surveyed were spanked as children and that 55 percent believe spanking is necessary. Anyone who mixes with other parents would not be surprised by these findings.

It would be wrong to suggest that discipline is a unique problem of our times. Parents have always faced the challenge of dealing with their toddler's defiance and with adolescent rebellion. This age-old issue is inextricably bound up with the parent-child relationship. Today, however, the problem has become even more complicated and far more difficult to tackle because of changing cultural attitudes toward adulthood, parental authority, and the exercise of discipline. It seems that the widely held expectation of treating children the same as adults makes the task of maintaining discipline a very difficult if not impossible task.

For all its hundreds of manuals and periodicals, the parenting industry avoids confronting this huge problem. Parenting manuals often provide a bag of tricks for anxious parents and hint that the compliance of a child can be gained through clever psychological maneuvers. Some of the advice is sensible and may help a father who has tried everything and has still not managed to get his son to put his toys away. Unfortunately, there are no foolproof techniques for gaining compliance. Managing a child's behavior requires drawing a line, insisting that children respect rules, and also enforcing them.

Parenting manuals counsel us to be firm, to be consistent, and to draw boundaries for our child. Unfortunately, such good advice is linked to disciplinary techniques that evade the question of punishing negative behavior. Disciplinary techniques based on reasoning, positive reinforcements, and negotiation can play a useful role in managing a child's behavior. But such techniques are unlikely to be effective in all circumstances, and other more assertive methods are sometimes required to discourage a child from negative behavior.

In an ideal world, parental authority could be discharged through the power of reason. In the real world, matters are quite different. Any mother or father who is prepared to renounce entirely the use of punishment also risks having to abandon the claim to parental authority. Parents recognize that they need a wide range of sanctions to carry out their role, which is why we continue—albeit reluctantly—to punish disobedient children. This intuitive response to circumstances now faces a challenge from influential voices in the parenting industry.

The new wisdom is that discipline is actually a teaching tool through which children learn how to negotiate the world they face. From this standpoint, discipline is about teaching children what they have done wrong, the consequences of their behavior, and how they can go about modifying it. Discipline as an enlightened teaching tool is favorably contrasted with punishment, which those who see discipline as a teaching tool portray as an inferior tactic that aims to "shame, frighten or otherwise force children into compliance without them understanding why." This redefinition of discipline assumes that punishment is inappropriate for the enlightened parent. Some psychologists oppose all forms of punishment. The American psychologist Joan McCord takes this attitude, on the grounds that it means "giving physical or mental pain to others."[4] Opposition to punishment is predicated on the belief that it must damage children. The leading American child psychologist, T. Berry Brazelton, thinks that punishment can promote aggression and discourage children from cooperating with others.

There are considerable problems with redefining discipline to mean enlightened teaching. It could be argued that everything that caretakers do with children contains an important element of teaching. But there is teaching and teaching. Teaching children about different shapes or colors or how to cross the street is not the same as disciplining them. Whether we like it or not, on occasion parents need to demand unqualified obedience—we have to assert control over a child's behavior and punish the transgression of an important rule. We have to do this not because discipline has an intrinsic educational value but because the child needs to be stopped from doing what could harm herself and others.

As it happens, discipline can have an important educational value. A child learns that his actions have consequences, and that certain forms of behavior are so unacceptable that they invite serious sanctions. Diana Baumrind, one of the foremost American authorities on parenting, argues that the "judicious and limited use of power-assertive methods, including punishment" helps children to internalize their parents' values.[5] Although the primary aim of punishment is not teaching, it can constitute an important learning experience for children. A disciplining strategy that is based entirely on reasoning is likely to be neither effective nor a particularly valuable teaching tool. A discussion over a troublesome episode may teach a child very little unless the child understands that it has important consequences. When discipline is equated with teaching, it becomes neither a teaching nor a disciplining experience for a child.

Effective parenting requires a judicious mix of disciplinary tactics that encourage positive behavior and power-assertive sanctions that punish negative ones. Effective discipline depends on parents praising good behavior and punishing that which they deem unacceptable. Both of these tactics play an important role in encouraging good behavior. But they are unlikely to be enough. Parents also need to explain the point of discipline, so that a child learns why he has been praised or punished. It is at this point that reasoning becomes significant. Explaining a parental action helps a child to generalize from a specific act what will be expected in other, similar circumstances. Effective discipline links reasoning, punishing, praising, and communication. Punishing unwelcome behavior is part of this system, not its polar opposite.

Child professionals who stigmatize punishment work on the assumption that parental discipline constitutes a danger to the child. Parenting guides continually warn mothers and fathers to reflect on why they want to punish their child. "Ask the members of the group to think about what makes them snap," advises an NSPCC manual written for tutors of parenting classes. Tutors are advised to guide parents to think about their feelings so that they can learn to defuse their anger. Throughout the manual there is a clear subtext that the real issue is the behavior of parents rather than children. As Kay Hymowitz argues, "Experts repeatedly warn adults of the dangers of their authority, or, as it is termed, their 'power.' "[6] It seems that every form of disciplinary tactic used by parents can be interpreted as a positive danger to children. The very exercise of parental initiative is often represented as damaging to children's development. The authors of *What to Expect the First Year* take the view that adult guidance deprives the baby of a sense of control.

Those who want to sidestep the issue of punishment tend to play down the significance of a child's bad behavior. Parents are consistently advised to analyze their child's behavior and to understand what caused it. Once these causes are understood, children's bad behavior can be reinterpreted as "difficult" or even as a "normal" response to a particular experience. "It's just a stage" is the stock answer offered by editorials in parenting publications. Such publications regularly rehearse the argument that children's defiance of parental authority is quite normal. They rightly claim that youngsters need to explore, to test the boundaries of what is acceptable and what is not acceptable, and to assert their independence. But instead of encouraging parents to work out an appropriate response to acts of defiance and to maintain the boundary of acceptable behavior, parents are advised not to overreact. "Children can be astonishingly unresponsive to requests from their parents, especially when deeply absorbed in pretend play," reports Professor Thomas G. Power of the University of Houston. Power's assurance that a child's naughty behavior is quite normal encourages parents to evade the issue of how to curb normal but antisocial behavior. When he states that defiance is often "really nothing more than the difficulty a child experiences making the mental switch from one activity to another," Power offers an argument for avoiding the issue of discipline.

The proposition that it is just a stage in a child's development rather than an expression of negative behavior is a call to inaction.[7]

Children's disobedient behavior is rendered acceptable not only through the "it's just a stage" argument but also by the tendency to treat misbehavior as a medical condition. In recent years we have witnessed the discovery of a variety of hidden syndromes that are reported to afflict children. Attention deficit hyperactivity disorder (ADHD) is only the most recent childhood syndrome to be highlighted in the media. ADHD is characterized by many of the traits that would, in the absence of a medical definition, be frowned upon as bad behavior: inability to concentrate, lack of application, unruliness. For some parents, it seems, the discovery of new childhood disorders provides a welcome explanation for their children's bad behavior or poor performance in school: "She isn't naughty, she's ill." There has been a phenomenal upsurge in the number of parents who demand that their children be labeled as suffering from ADHD or some other disorder. In some parts of the United States, 50 to 75 percent of children newly referred to child neurologists and behavioral pediatricians are diagnosed with ADHD. It is claimed that 10 to 20 percent of children of school age in the United States are affected by this disorder. It is evident that in the United States, large numbers of parents and their children are using ADHD as an excuse for poor school performance. Failure to finish homework, inability to focus on class discussion, and boredom in school are regularly blamed on ADHD.

The readiness with which parents accept medical labels for their children's bad habits and behavior suggests that few mothers and fathers need to be lectured about the pitfalls of harsh discipline. Most parents have assimilated the "fun morality" advocated by childhood specialists in the middle of the last century. To a surprising degree, parents have also internalized the stricture to negotiate and to use reason instead of punishment. We all want to rear our children in an atmosphere that is free of intimidation. But parents are far from certain about what to do when the child refuses to obey reasonable demands. "Hold the line" is the sensible answer offered by most child-care manuals. Unfortunately, it is difficult to hold the line without the assertion of parental authority. And parents are rarely encouraged to be tough. Parents are told to control their children but are warned not to rely on punishment. No wonder many parents feel not in but out of control.

The Spanking Debate—Evading the Issue

The rights and wrongs of physically punishing children is the most controversial subject in the field of parenting. The debate about spanking excites formidable passions among child professionals and parents alike. Its opponents portray it as a form of child abuse that is likely to stimulate long-term violent behavior. Among child professionals, the campaign against corporal punishment has assumed the character of a moral crusade. They have organized lobby groups to push for a ban on parents spanking a child. This campaign has proved remarkably effective in influencing opinion makers and politicians. In general, the media reflect the sentiments of the anti-spanking crusade and frame their stories according to a script that defines spanking as outdated and brutal.

There are very few robust defenders of spanking. Most of its proponents strike a defensive chord and fear being castigated as apologists for child abuse. The only obstacle that stands in the way of the anti-spanking crusade is the behavior of the great majority of parents. Surveys carried out on both sides of the Atlantic indicate that a significant majority of parents continue to use physical punishment to regulate their children's behavior. Campaigners against spanking recognize that their main job is to alter the behavior of parents. An editorial in the *British Medical Journal* has called for a "public education campaign" to teach parents not to spank.[8] Campaigners use parenting education programs as a vehicle for changing attitudes on spanking.

On closer examination, the campaign against the physical punishment of children is not simply about the appropriateness of spanking. Some leading opponents of spanking are actually against all forms of punishment. They believe that parents who rely on the withdrawal of affection as an alternative to spanking may cause even more damage to a child. They claim that punishments designed to make children feel stupid or undignified are just as ineffective and emotionally dangerous as the physical kind.

"Withdrawal of affection is often used as an alternative to spanking, but in the opinion of many psychologists, this can be more damaging than corporal punishment," comments Frances Hamcock in *Nursery World*.[9] Such concern about emotional punishment suggests that all power-assertive methods are liable to be criticized for the damage they inflict on children. However, since it is not realistic to campaign against the right of parents to punish as such, spanking provides the crusaders with an emotive target. Anti-spanking campaigners are often motivated by animosity to all forms of tough parenting. Their opposition to the physical punishment of children is linked to a wider hostility to what they perceive as authoritarian parenting styles.

The implicit objective of the campaign against spanking is to restrain the exercise of parental authority. As noted previously, this project is inspired by the conviction that parent and child have contradictory interests. Penelope Leach eloquently expresses this view when she advises her readers to stop thinking about a child's behavior in terms of "obedience" and "disobedience." Leach thinks that what parents interpret as acts of disobedience are actually manifestations of a child's separate and distinct interest. If a child refuses to go to bed, "it is not his disobedience that is causing trouble, it is a simple conflict of interest."[10] From this perspective, the way forward is always to negotiate a compromise and never to punish.

The debate on spanking is actually a product of our confusion about what it means to be an adult and a parent. It raises questions about the boundary that separates childhood from adulthood and the legitimacy of parental authority. Unfortunately, the debate evades these wider questions and unhelpfully places the spotlight on a single disciplinary technique. This has led to a simplistic debate that has polarized opinion between those who condemn and those who support spanking. In such a debate, there is always a temptation to adopt one-sided and misleading arguments. In the United States, Gary and Anne Marie Ezzo have published several books that recommend spanking for toddlers as young as eighteen months for being naughty. They believe that physical punishment has inherent virtues for raising children. Opponents of spanking, who represent the mainstream of the parenting profession, take a diametrically opposite stance.[11]

Such sharply polarized opinions have helped create an atmosphere where hysteria and moral outrage make it difficult for parents to work out their own rules for disciplining their children.

So what do we actually know about the consequences of spanking children? Opponents of spanking claim that scientific research conclusively demonstrates that spanking has long-term negative effects on the behavior of children. They continually appeal to research to justify their indictment of "violence to children." One of the most robust claims is to be found in a recent publication by Penelope Leach, *The Physical Punishment of Children: Some Input from Recent Research.* Leach writes that "respected research tells us that the more children are hit, the more aggressive, disruptive and anti-social they are." She claims that research provides evidence that spanking can even lead to criminal behavior in adolescence and adulthood. To support her argument, Leach repeatedly refers to research carried out by Murray Strauss, a veteran American campaigner against corporal punishment. Yet Strauss's work is far less clear-cut than the claims made by Leach on its behalf. Strauss concedes that the case against spanking is "not truly conclusive" and raises the question of "whether advising parents to spank is ethical and responsible." Strauss believes that it is not— not on the grounds of scientific research but on moral ones.[12]

There are good arguments for opposing the spanking of children, but they are not to be found in the realm of scientific research. Despite dozens of studies on this subject, nobody has established a causal relationship between spanking and negative behavior. A recent anti-spanking editorial in the *British Medical Journal* concedes that there is a lack of evidence supporting its position. Nevertheless, the *BMJ* insists it is possible to "apply good judgment" to this issue. Once again, the rejection of spanking is based on moral judgment rather than scientific fact.

American opponents of spanking are often disarmingly open about the need to mount research that will prove their point and convince parents to abandon this practice. At a 1996 meeting of the American Academy of Pediatrics, Irwin Hyman proposed a campaign of what he called "advocacy research," using bits of research as propaganda to change public policy. His colleague, Leonard Eron, urged the audience to have the courage of their conviction regardless of the state of current research. "How much evidence must we have and how incontrovertible must this evidence be before we can act?" he pleaded. Other doctors attending this conference managed to retain a measure of objectivity. After hearing the evidence, or the lack of it, this meeting of doctors and psychologists refused to condemn spanking.[13]

No study has managed to prove that spanking leads to child abuse and long-term violent behavior. The experience of Sweden, often used as a test case by anti-spanking campaigners, has not provided them with any new ammunition. After Sweden outlawed spanking by parents in 1979, reports of serious child abuse actually increased by 400 percent over ten years. The Swedish experience does not prove that banning spanking leads to an increase of abuse, but it clearly suggests that it does not have the effect of lowering the rate.[14]

There is also some evidence that suggests that in certain situations, spanking can be an effective disciplinary tool. In 1996, the psychologist Robert Larzelere published a major review of the existing research on the subject. Focusing on the thirty-five most rigorous empirical studies, he concluded that there was no convincing evidence that the nonabusive spanking typically used by parents damaged children. Larzelere's review also concluded that no other disciplinary technique—including time-outs and withdrawal of privileges—was more effective than spanking for gaining the compliance of children under thirteen. Larzelere's review is confirmed by the work of psychologist Diana Baumrind of the University of California, Berkeley. Baumrind, the innovator of the concept of authoritative parenting, believes that the spanking debate wrongly polarizes punishment and reasoning. She claims that authoritative parents are warm, firm, and responsive, and that in this context, the occasional smack will have no long-term damaging effect.[15]

Baumrind's approach offers a useful antidote to the narrow clash of opinions on spanking. The main merit of her work is that she continually underlines the *context* within which disciplining takes place. Her argument is that disciplinary methods are mediated by children's perception of their legitimacy. In the context of a warm and responsive relationship, children can understand the imposition of authority, even the occasional smack. Any form of punishment can have unexpected negative consequences. But such an outcome has less to do with the form of punishment than with the nature of the particular parent-child relationship. The outcome of an act of discipline is closely bound up with how a child experiences that relationship. That is why the mother and father are in the best position to work out what form of punishment is appropriate for their child.

Unfortunately, in the zealous climate that surrounds this issue, Baumrind's sensible approach tends to get overlooked. The terms in which the debate is framed militate against a reasoned exchange of views. Campaigners define spanking as violence against children. They then contend that violence can only lead to more violence and that therefore it should be stopped. The argument that violence breeds more violence is a powerful one. Who can stand up and extol the virtues of violence? However, the equation of spanking with violence is a verbal trick designed to associate this form of punishment with abuse. Parents who occasionally spank their children are not behaving violently. Violence is physical force intended to injure or abuse. Caring parents who administer a smack in response to a child's act of willful defiance with the objective of discouraging unacceptable behavior are not behaving violently.

The inability to distinguish violence from caring discipline exercised by loving parents says more about the outlook of anti-spanking campaigners than about real-life mothers and fathers. It is an outlook that assumes parental abuse is the norm rather than a rare exception. Such a harsh view of parental behavior also extends to a suspicion of other forms of punishment. But it makes better PR to confine hostility to punishment to the easy and evocative target of spanking. Spanking serves as a symbol for a campaign that believes that the exercise of parental authority is potentially damaging to children.

An Invitation to Overreact

Whatever the outcome of the debate on spanking, its impact on the parent-child relationship will be unhelpful. At a time when parents are already apprehensive about exercising discipline, the debate is likely to undermine their confidence further by strengthening the association between punishment and abuse. It will enhance the pressure on the exercise of parental authority.

With all the publicity that surrounds the spanking debate, it is easy to overlook the real issues facing the vast majority of parents. For most parents the real question is not spanking, but discipline. They understand that their role is to guide their children's development, but they are far from clear about how to realize this objective. Parents are continually told what is wrong with different disciplinary methods, but they are at a loss to know what is right. We are urged to adopt techniques of positive parenting. But these turn out to be banal exhortations to be consistent and sensitive. The techniques promoted by advocates of positive parenting are based on the assumption that the effective alternative to punishing children is to reward children who do right. In theory this advice seems sensible. Praising children for their good behavior is an important part of sensitive parenting. But it provides no help to parents who want to know what to do when their child behaves badly. Real children behave in a variety of ways. Sometimes the model well-behaved child turns into a destructive little monster who needs to be contained for her own good. There is a time for rewarding and a time for punishing. The one-dimensional approach of the disciplinary strategy based on positive reinforcements leaves parents with no resources for coping with bad behavior.

"Pick your battles." "It is only a stage." "It is your problem, not your child's." "Your child's defiance is only a call for attention." "It is better to ignore bad behavior than to reward it with attention." "Compromise." "Communicate your feelings." Most advice these days provides a ready-made excuse for not holding the line and for avoiding the exercise of parental authority. Mothers and fathers, who in any case are worried about losing the affection of their children, are often happy to postpone making hard decisions. There is very little public support for any other option.

Parents often lead a schizophrenic existence. They are worried about the effects of disciplining their children and also feel uneasy about losing control if they don't punish them. Lack of confidence about knowing when to hold the line encourages an unhelpful style of over-parenting. Parents who are reluctant to say no have sought other means for controlling their children's lives that avoid conflicts. Many of the characteristic features of paranoid parenting—using surveillance technology to keep an eye on children, preventing them from participating in outdoor unstructured activities, relying on constant adult supervision—represent forms of control that serve as an alternative to parental discipline. In this way the issue of discipline is displaced and reposed as a question of safety. Parents who feel uncomfortable about refusing yet another piece of chocolate are much more relaxed about imposing their will by preventing their son from playing in the park with his friends. Regulating children's lives on the grounds of safety is accepted without question as good parenting. Overreacting to the risks faced by children allows parents to maintain a semblance of control without exercising too much authority. Keeping children under constant adult supervision creates the illusion of retaining control without having to confront the issue of discipline. These excessive restraints on the experience of childhood are the price that children pay for the problems of grown-ups who have not come to terms with their role as parents.

Unclear Rules

Prejudice Masquerading as Research

Practical ideas about child rearing are inseparable from moral outlook. Today's lack of consensus on the right approach to parenting is reflected in continual debates about the pros and cons of family values, marriage, cohabitation, and single parenthood. Customs and traditions that in past generations could be taken for granted seem to have lost their relevance in a world haunted by uncertainty and self-doubt. Many mothers and fathers think that what their own parents did has few lessons for child rearing today. Changes in the status of women and gender relations have also broken some old habits. The changing contours of family life create new complications for everyone concerned, adding to the already considerable burden borne by parents.

Everything about parenting seems open to question; nothing is certain, nothing can be taken for granted. Yet controversy is the last thing busy fathers and mothers need when they are struggling with the day-to-day pressures of family life. So much public attention is focused on parenting issues that parents feel they are under constant scrutiny, continually forced to account for and justify their actions to teachers, health visitors, doctors, and other professionals. Not surprisingly, parents who feel so exposed feel less than confident about their ability to do what is right. Parents try to resolve these ambiguities by conforming to the demands of experts and professionals. Unfortunately, experts turn out to be no less confused than parents. Their "off-the-peg" advice does little to arm parents with the guidance they yearn for.

Starting from Scratch

For the past two centuries, ideas about child rearing have been in a continuous state of flux. New beliefs about nutrition, infant health, and education, along with changing moral values about the family and the status of its members, have led to a rolling revolution in the way we think about parenting. Geographical and social mobility have also generated novel approaches. A significant number of new parents live far away from their own families. Unlike previous generations, they are not subject to relatives' unrelenting free advice. Consequently, they are less likely to uncritically copy their own parents' approach to child rearing. Some young parents actively welcome the absence of nosy family members. But many mothers and fathers wish that they had access to a reliable source of sensible advice. In any case, mothers and fathers living away from their families are compelled to work out their own rules.

According to historians of the family, the expansion of the education system and the availability of higher education to a significant proportion of the population have had an important influence on the way that young men, and particularly young women, regard their future roles as parents. Young educated adults frequently believe that they know more about the world than do their own fathers and mothers. They often draw the conclusion that the old folks have old-fashioned ideas, whereas they themselves understand the ways of the modern world. At a time of change, when many fields of knowledge develop at a rapid rate, intellectual and emotional distance develops between the generations. This is inevitable, and as long as people are prepared to learn from the experience of the past, change will usually be for the better.

Reacting against the old way of doing things does not have to mean dismissing family advice about child rearing. The notion that family advice was inherently flawed was the invention of a new group of professional experts that emerged at the start of the twentieth century. They claimed that parenting was a science that was too important to be left to ignorant mothers and fathers. Although parents had managed to bring up children for tens of thousands of years without the help of experts, professionals claimed that their science would provide a far more enlightened and effective approach to child rearing. Writing in 1929, Susan Isaacs was delighted that "mothers and nurses" had "begun to turn away from mere custom and blind tradition to science." She insisted that "many practices that had been taken for granted for centuries have been found to be false guides when carefully tested." Baby rearing was now to be based on proven "scientific knowledge about food and sleep and clothing, the effects of light and air, and ways of preventing disease."[1]

The influence of people like Susan Isaacs was reflected in the growing volume of literature telling parents how to bring up their children. By the 1950s, the industry of parenting advice was well established and reflected an important shift in family culture. Since it was assumed that parenting practices would change alongside new discoveries about child rearing, the role of the previous generation of mothers and fathers as a valuable resource diminished. "American parents, for instance, do not expect to bring up their children in the way they were brought up, any more than they would want to live in the house in which they were raised or to drive around in the family car of their childhood," observed Martha Wolfenstein in 1955.[2]

However, in the 1950s, the reaction of young adults to the child-rearing practices of their parents rarely touched on fundamental issues of values and moral principles. By and large they accepted the moral universe of their fathers and mothers but sought to do a better job of parenting than the previous generation. "They hope to bring up their children better than they were brought up themselves," is how Martha Wolfenstein put it.[3] During this postwar period of relative economic prosperity, educational opportunity, and optimism about the future, many young people believed that they could offer a life to their children far superior to the one they had experienced.

Today, however, young adults are encouraged not so much to bring up their children better than they were brought up themselves but to bring them up differently. The emotional distance between generations has widened until it can no longer be taken for granted that they share the same values and rules governing family life. Current culture continually encourages the expansion of the emotional distance that separates generations. Films, television documentaries, fiction, and other forms of popular culture ceaselessly dwell on the so-called dark side of the family. Previous generations of parents are often depicted as emotional illiterates who consciously or inadvertently damaged their children. It is increasingly rare to encounter public tributes to the wise parent. And there is a veritable genre of confessional writing devoted to exposing the destructive practices of brutal parents. Negative stereotypes of traditional child-rearing practices are widespread in parenting magazines and heavily influence the practice and thinking of professionals.

Whenever any child-rearing problem is under scrutiny, it is invariably treated as a hangover from the bad habits of previous generations. Opponents of corporal punishment advance a standard argument that parents hit their children because their parents hit them. "Why do we spank at all?," asks a feature in *Parenting*. "It makes sense to spank because we'd seen the generation before us do so, when spanking was considered acceptable."[4] Unacceptable behavior toward children is routinely attributed to copying one's parents. The argument is rarely extended to positive forms of behavior. We don't ask the question "Why do we love our children?" in order to invite the answer "Because we have seen our parents smother us with love." Positive parenting is usually attributed to the effects of our enlightened society, while negative parenting is blamed on the poor nurturing of our parents.

Professional thinking on child rearing is permeated by the premise that parenting practices from the past should be avoided like the plague. Though rarely acknowledged, this represents the point of departure for today's child-rearing philosophy. Previous generations rarely serve as role models. Parenting education programs and publications continually encourage their target audience to react against the model provided by their incompetent mothers and fathers. In some instances, such publications appear to subscribe to an unconscious agenda of encouraging the reader to distance herself from her parents. A magazine titled *Get Ready!*, part of the birth pack distributed to pregnant women in the United Kingdom, never loses an opportunity to distance the reader from her family and even from her friends. "Trusted friends and family are probably your first port of call when help and advice is needed, but times change and it's useful to work out your own ideas about being a parent and to have a fresh approach to raising each new generation," it notes. This exhortation for adopting a fresh approach—parenting from scratch—actually represents a call for ignoring the counsel of your friends in order to absorb the arguments contained in *Get Ready!*[5]

The appeal to "work out your own ideas" is quickly followed up by the first of many reminders as to why new ideas are needed. "If you feel your own mom or dad didn't do such a great job bringing you up, you might feel worried about making the same mistakes." This euphemistic reminder of parental incompetence is a prelude to more ominous hints. "Having a baby can bring back strong memories of childhood," warns *Get Ready!*, with the implication that such memories are likely to be negative. In a rhetorical aside, it concedes that for most people childhood memories are happy ones, before getting to the point. "If they are not happy, it's essential to get support and find a trusted, sympathetic listening ear." In case you are too dense and missed the point, you are advised to "think about whether you now agree with everything in the way you were brought up." Such advice inevitably leads to only one conclusion—no—since no one can possibly agree with everything her parents did. After doing its best to emotionally distance the pregnant reader from her family, *Get Ready!* is happy to concede that her parents did not act entirely out of malevolent motives. "Remember, parenting styles have changed, and your parents probably did the best they could," it patronizingly notes, before suggesting, "If possible, talk to them to see if any of this can be worked out."

This crude approach is rooted in the assumption that negative experiences with a mother or father account for adult problems in rearing children. Parenting education programs systematically attempt to influence their clients to think critically of their parents' behavior and to avoid the bad habits they learned from their parents. One of their key objectives is to help parents to reflect on their own experiences of being parented so that they can adopt new more enlightened practices and avoid repeating the child-rearing model of the previous generation. Child-rearing manuals now regularly adopt this approach. "Think back to the way you communicated with your own parents," counsels *Raising Happy Children*. "Did you feel that they listened to you and that you were able to express anything that worried, concerned or even interested you?"[6] This question is followed by seven similar ones, all rhetorically framed so as to invite a negative response.

The indictment of yesteryear's parenting style represents a powerful theme in current culture. Its practical consequences are difficult to define. Most mothers and fathers continue to borrow and adapt insights and practices from their parents. But more than ever before, they feel that the past provides them with little guidance about how to carry out their responsibilities as up-to-date, enlightened parents. They have lots and lots of questions and very few obvious answers. Of course mothers and fathers talk to friends and peers and share views and experiences. They also consult professionals and read a lot of material on child rearing. Some of this information is useful and helps parents make informed decisions. But expert advice is not a substitute for guidance based on commonly accepted rules and values. In the absence of such consensus, advice itself is liable to be contested. Instead of providing certainty, expert advice may well become the source of further doubt and confusion.

Unclear Rules—Conflicting Advice

Parenting and child-care advice is shaped by the prevailing moral and cultural values of the time. Anyone who cares to read the numerous editions of Dr. Spock's *Baby and Child Care* will be struck by just how closely this authority reflects shifting moral moods. In the sixties, Spock wrote in disapproving terms about mothers who went out to work. By the seventies, when there was greater acceptance of maternal employment, Spock adopted a more positive attitude. In 1991 Spock became a vegan. His next edition reflected this shift: "We now know that there are harmful effects of a meaty diet," he observed, "I no longer recommend dairy products after the age of two years."[7]

Lack of consensus about rules and values governing family life means that advice offered to parents can be highly unstable. When my wife gave birth in 1995, I faced considerable pressure to be present during her labor. I was told that this was an essential experience that would bring me closer to my baby and to my partner. A few years later, one of the world's leading childbirth gurus, Michel Odent, spoke out against this practice, asserting that men impede women from getting on with the business of giving birth. The National Childbirth Trust, which had previously actively encouraged men to attend the birth of their child, indicated that "there may be something" in what Odent argued.[8]

Child-care advice has always changed with the times. But today, advice offered with the authority of science can be called into question within a matter of months. For example, in May 1999, parents were informed that young children who sleep with the light on are much more likely to be nearsighted when they grow up. According to research published in *Nature*, long periods of darkness are essential for the healthy development of the eye. Parents were advised to get rid of nightlights in their children's nurseries. This new source of worry for mothers and fathers was refuted by new research published in March 2000 claiming that it was perfectly all right to leave a nursery light on since it did not harm an infant's sight.[9] In October 1999, the press widely publicized research that claimed children were less likely to develop allergies, asthma, and eczema if they were exposed to farmyard animals and plenty of muck. It was claimed that even one visit to a farm could make a big difference. A few months later, after it was revealed that a child contracted an E. coli infection during a school trip to a farm, some experts took it upon themselves to warn parents about the risks facing children visiting farmyards. The alleged health benefits of a school visit to a farm were swiftly forgotten as it came to be depicted as an ominous source of contagion.[10]

When I started working on this book, the consensus among child professionals was that parents should do whatever they could to raise their child's self-esteem. This was promoted as an all-purpose solution to virtually every childhood problem. Some elementary schools displayed posters saying "Praise every child every day." In recent years, apprehensions regarding self-centered children, stimulated by high-profile cases of school violence, have led numerous experts to question the emphasis on self-esteem. "Praising every time lowers a child's motivation," argues Dr. Ron Taffel, a Manhattan psychologist and author of *Nurturing Good Children Now.*[11] One well-known author, John Rosemond, goes a step further and claims that "high self-esteem is bad" for children.[12] Dr. Roy F. Baumeister, a social scientist based at Case Western Reserve University, claims that people with high self-esteem are likely to respond aggressively when their inflated view of themselves is threatened by criticism or perceived insult.[13]

Thus, advice that is offered at one time with great authority is a few years later seen to be not only redundant but also positively dangerous. Burning old parenting manuals is now one of the tasks of a responsible librarian. "Parenting titles that do not discuss or even acknowledge contemporary conditions, current scientific information, and up-to-date additional readings have lost much of their value and should be weeded from working collections," warns Kathryn Carpenter in an article in *Library Journal.* Some advice in older texts—such as giving honey to infants or allowing babies to cry it out rather than attending immediately to their needs—might be "harmful to life and well-being."[14]

Lack of consensus about rules and values is reflected in the absence of a recognized authoritative voice on parenting. Today parents are much more likely to turn for advice to someone who reflects their particular values and lifestyle. William Sears and Martha Sears's *The Attachment Parenting Book* often suits anxious, self-consciously responsible parents. Parents wedded to traditional values may find John Rosemond's *Parent Power* more to their liking. Every constituency—ambitious hothousing parent, lone mother, single father, green parent—is able to find manuals that reflect its outlook.

Leading authorities continually changing their minds about child-rearing problems sometimes publicly clash with one another. When Spock advised parents to not let their children eat meat and dairy products,

T. Berry Brazelton informed the *New York Times* that these guidelines were "absolutely insane" and that children needed the protein and calcium of meat and milk. Penelope Leach has publicly attacked Gary and Anne-Marie Ezzo for recommending what she considers to be harsh child-rearing techniques. She called them "very dangerous people" whose program constitutes a form of child abuse. The Ezzos in turn have blamed Leach for her "immoral" influence on family life. Public arguments about toilet training, child-care arrangements, early learning, and quality time indicate that child-rearing advice is itself a source of controversy. Clashes between experts sometimes mean little more than competition for status and authority. But often their contrasting opinions express important ideological and moral differences.

Consider advice on the rights and wrongs of maternal employment. During the past century, opposition to maternal employment has been fueled by fears about its impact on family life. Some traditionalists regard maternal employment as the cause of family breakdown and neglect. From their standpoint, mothers who work undermine relations between husband and wife and fail in their duty as mothers. This belief is based on the assumption that a woman's primary role is nurturer and housewife. But instead of openly promoting this view, many child experts hide behind research and advice that claim it is wrong for mothers to work outside the home.

Throughout most of the 1950s and 1960s, child-rearing professionals promoted the idea that children under three need the continuous presence of their mothers. Dr. Spock led the way in declaring that maternal employment before the child had reached this age was likely to be harmful to his development. Fears were expressed that children exposed to day care would be emotionally damaged and deprived of stimulation. Mothers were also warned that care by others would weaken their baby's relation to them. It was suggested that parents would be deprived of their baby's love and that their baby would grow up feeling unloved by his parents. This approach, which Scarr and Dunn have dubbed "psychology to keep mothers at home," dominated the parenting literature until the late 1970s. The steady growth of female paid employment made it difficult to sustain such a one-sided condemnation. As public opinion shifted in the 1970s, more liberal and feminist child-rearing experts began to offer their own advice, asserting that maternal employment had considerable benefits for family life. And even writers who had previously condemned the practice modified their criticisms. Spock acknowledged his earlier prejudices and wrote that "both parents had an equal right to a career if they want one." Kathryn Young's review of received wisdom published in *Parents* magazine confirms this reorientation from hostility to acquiescence. By the late 1970s, its feature articles were advising that the quality of mother-infant interaction plays an important but not exclusive role in the subsequent emotional health of their infant.[15]

The pragmatic acceptance of maternal employment meant that traditional family morality could no longer be advocated in an undiluted form. Instead, opponents leveled a variety of fresh charges, appealing to the authority of science and research to suggest that children in day care end up with lower IQs and perform worse in school than those who are looked after by their parents. Opponents of maternal employment continue to insist that day care is damaging for children. "If your concern is the development of babies and toddlers into healthy, capable, well adjusted, and productive adults, substitute child care is not only inferior, but damaging to human potential," claims Allan Carlson, a critic of what he calls the "Trojan horse of day care." Carlson believes that putting children into day care can lead to the destruction of family life, but instead of boldly upholding his ideological standpoint, he hides behind child-rearing advice and research.[16]

Unfortunately, supporters of maternal employment tend to imitate their opponents' approach. Instead of arguing the case for the right of women to pursue careers on equal terms with men, they justify their cause through the medium of child welfare, arguing that quality child care will benefit children. They cite studies that purport to show that in the United States, children who went to day care are five times less likely to become delinquent than others. Some feminists attempt to divert attention from the absent mother by pointing the finger at the absent father. Many experts now advise that the quality of a father's parenting has a significant impact on his child's intellectual and emotional development. "What and how often boys read is influenced by what their fathers read at home," claims one expert in *Parents*. The NSPCC publication *Baby's First Year* makes the startling assertion that babies smile more quickly, smile more, and "as they grow into children, they have fewer problems if their dads are involved." Advice promoting the father's involvement in child care today is a mirror image of the approach that demanded continuous maternal attention thirty years ago. Parent-blaming has shifted its focus from maternal to paternal deprivation. Mothers are still expected to be the primary caretakers, but dads have also been dragged into the frame. The shifting contours of advice say far more about the cultural and moral expectations of our time than about the needs of children.

There is nothing objectionable about an open and intelligent debate on the moral issues pertaining to family life or the role of fathers and mothers. But when moral statements are recycled through the medium of child-care advice to hide an unacknowledged ideological agenda, they transform a practical parenting issue into a source of anxiety for mothers and fathers. When ideological and practical matters are confused, even the most banal issue can become ammunition in an undeclared moral crusade. Take the current discussion on breast-feeding. Breast-feeding involves a lot of practical issues, especially for working mothers. But the transformation of breast-feeding into a crusade makes it almost impossible to make an informed choice about whether to breast- or bottle-feed.

Throughout most of the twentieth century, breast-feeding was promoted on the ground that it was essential for maternal bonding and for the emotional well-being of the child. It was claimed that breast-feeding was the natural way of nurturing, and therefore the breast represented the center of a child's emotional life. Pragmatic considerations concerning the growth of maternal employment led to the modification of this position. By the 1970s, experts conceded that either method of feeding would work; however, their preference was still for the breast because of its alleged emotional benefits for the child. Since then, many mothers have opted for bottle-feeding, though sometimes feeling guilty that they may be acting unnaturally.[17]

In recent times, cultural concern about the environment, food safety, and anything that appears unnatural has boosted the appeal of breast-feeding. Parenting experts also regard breast-feeding as an important experience for bringing mothers closer to their children. There are good health arguments for this option, at least during the first three months of a child's life. Unfortunately, the health benefits associated with breast-feeding have become so politicized that it has become difficult to discuss it as merely a practical feeding issue.

Whatever the merits of the arguments, the crusade promoting breast-feeding has acquired an intimidating and even authoritarian tone. Child-care publications continually promote the same message. The article might be titled "Breast or Bottle?"—but instead of providing women with an informed choice, the message is that bottle-feeding is an inferior option chosen by irresponsible mothers. "Only you can decide how you want to feed your baby," states an expert in *Baby* magazine, before pointing out that the "benefits of breast milk are obvious." Another "Breast or Bottle" feature in *Mother & Baby* published in May 2000 turns into a celebration of the fact that most of the women it has surveyed breast-feed their babies: "The great news is that 72 percent of you breast-feed." Turning to the other 28 percent, who bottle-feed, the article notes that not all is lost since most of these women—68 percent—"did try to get to grips with breast-feeding first." Like smokers who tried to give up the habit but failed, these unsuccessful breast-feeders are offered a measure of recognition.[18]

Women who have chosen to bottle-feed their baby face a barrage of propaganda. "What's stopping you breast-feeding?" asks *Prima Baby* in disbelief. It complains that "It's perfectly natural and will help protect your baby from many illnesses from asthma to diabetes, but despite that, most moms still don't breast-feed." *Prima Baby* also has a clear message for any women who are tempted to abandon breast-feeding: "Keep going if you can—persevere and both you and your baby will benefit." Advocates of breast-feeding continually discover new reasons that legitimize their cause. They have seized upon a New Zealand study published in 1998 that suggests that children who have been breast-fed are more intelligent than those who have not. Throughout the summer of 1999, *Prima Baby* published material that linked having a "brainy baby" to breast-feeding. "Breast-feeding will help add even more points to your baby's IQ because breast milk contains more long chain fatty acids than standard formula milk," revealed this publication. And *Parents* stated that breast-feeding "may help reduce the risk of childhood deafness in the first two years of life." It has been argued that breast-fed babies are less likely to be crib death victims. Breast-feeding is also recommended on the ground that it is the best remedy for teething as it provides maximum comfort for the baby. The positive advocacy of breast-feeding has been complemented by scare stories about using formula. During the past year, numerous stories have been written about the danger of using hot water to heat feeding bottles. *Practical Parenting* and *Mother & Baby* have warned mothers about the risks of scalding. These stories typically exaggerate the risks, suggesting that this is a common occurrence even though the figure they cite is 23 burn cases over a three-year period—that is, 7.6 cases per year.[19]

There are a lot of good arguments for breast-feeding a baby. But when a practical matter like breast-feeding is transformed into a crusade, advice turns into a form of moral blackmail. In 1996, zealous advocates of this cause in Dundee, Scotland, used their influence to ban health visitors from teaching mothers how to make up bottle-feedings in prenatal classes, unless specifically requested to do so. An editorial in *Nursing Standard* argued that the clinical judgment of frontline professionals was being compromised by top-down edicts and that women who had chosen to bottle-feed were being ostracized or made to feel ashamed of their choice. The editorial singled out the activities of the Baby-Friendly Initiative for its insensitive campaigning. Many health professionals justify their stance on the ground that teaching parents how to make up formula feeds in prenatal classes "sends out the wrong message." It seems that professional campaigners have taken it upon themselves to prevent mothers from making an informed choice about feeding their babies.

The heavy-handed campaigning of breast-feeding fanatics is not only intrusive and intimidating but also a source of unnecessary worry and apprehension for many women. Numerous mothers have complained that they find it difficult to gain access to quality information about bottle-feeding. Their attempts are often met with a look of incomprehension, as if to suggest, "Surely a responsible mother like you would not be so selfish as to put her baby at risk by using formula." Many new mothers are placed in an impossible situation. Matters are made even worse for those who for one reason or another simply cannot breast-feed. The frenzied climate of hostility against the bottle can only make them feel guilty about not doing what's right for their new baby.

Breast-feeding fanaticism does not only undermine the confidence of those mothers who opt for bottle-feeding. The transformation of a practical feeding matter into a huge public issue has the effect of fostering an atmosphere of anxiety over nurturing babies. Since advice is, by its very nature, predicated on the latest bit of research, it is by definition provisional and highly unstable. In a world where every experience seems to give rise to a risk, every health benefit is potentially linked to some unexpected side effect. Breast-feeding is no exception to this rule. How is a mother to react when she hears claims that she may be inadvertently giving her baby doses of toxic pollutants through her milk? A Dutch study, published in 2000, reported that the breast milk of many European women contains levels of polychlorinated biphenyl high enough to damage a child's immune system. The authors of this study stated that such babies were several times more likely to contact chicken pox, ear infections, and other illnesses. Supporters of breast-feeding immediately contested their findings, but in a climate where insignificant feeding risks are elevated into a major public health issue, a new focus for parental anxiety had been constructed.[20]

The instability of child-rearing advice encourages public conflicts of professional opinion. Take the issue of co-sleeping. Supporters of breast-feeding have traditionally supported the practice of parents sharing their bed with their baby since this form of feeding encourages co-sleeping. However, in recent years a group of experts have claimed that there might be a link between bed sharing and sudden infant death syndrome (SIDS). Matters are not helped by the tendency to confuse practical child-care problems with the moral concerns of different groups of parenting experts. It is difficult to avoid the conclusion that such advice is often driven more by the agenda of the advice provider than the desire to tackle practical issues. The alleged link between crib death and bed sharing brings to the surface a potential tension among the objectives of three distinct groups of campaigners: supporters of bed sharing, supporters of breast-feeding, and campaigners against crib death.

Whether a parent sleeps with the baby should be treated as a minor issue best left to the inclinations of those concerned. Sharing a bed or breast-feeding works for some but not for others. But instead of leaving it at that, bed sharing threatens to turn into a highly charged discussion with the moral overtones that characterize the spanking controversy. Advocates of co-sleeping tend to preach rather than inform. Deborah Jackson's *Three in a Bed: The Benefits of Sleeping with Your Baby* makes many useful points and even tries to be nonjudgmental, saying that it is preferable "to put your baby in a cot [crib] happily, than to sleep with him begrudgingly." But instead of just sticking to the benefits, she appears to portray parents who do not sleep with their children as opting for second best. The implicit message of the book is that parents who do not sleep with their children are missing out on a wonderful and important experience. Leaving a baby in his cradle in a separate room is represented as an "obvious explanation for infant misery." Jackson warns working parents that "there could be a crisis looming" if they don't sleep with their children, since such separated infants could grow up "more closely bonded to their minders than to their parents."[21]

Child professionals who believe that allowing infants to sleep in a room separate from their parents is unnatural have argued that bed sharing is essential for parent-child bonding. In the early 1990s, American anthropologist James McKenna carried out research suggesting that bed sharing helps babies' breathing and has other health benefits that reduce the risk of crib death. This argument convinced many child experts to advocate bed sharing. Mary Newburn, head of policy research at the National Childbirth Trust, states that the closer a baby is to adults, the safer he is, because hearing the heartbeat and breathing of his parents will stimulate his own system. According to Newburn, this helps to avoid crib death in those cases where the child has simply forgotten to breathe. In 1999, this case for bed sharing was called into question by research carried out in Britain and the United States alleging that this practice actually increased the risk of crib death. As a result, the Federal Consumer Product Safety Commission issued the warning that sleeping together posed a significant risk of accidental smothering or strangling to the infant. In Britain, the Foundation for the Study of Infant Deaths advises that a baby should always be returned to her crib if the parents have been drinking, taking drugs, or are particularly tired or obese. Advice is now divided on this subject, and parents have been left on their own to pick up the pieces.[22]

Since the debate on co-sleeping has been subjected to conflicting moral agendas, it is easy to overlook the fact that we simply do not know what, if any, risks are associated with either bed sharing or sleeping separately. The alleged risks based on the authority of research are statistically insignificant, and in any case, no one has been able to show any causal link between how a family sleeps and the incidence of crib death. As in the case of breast-feeding, the controversy is fueled by ideology rather than practical considerations. Many opponents of bed sharing, such as Spock and Brazelton, are concerned about the effect of parental nudity and of the possibility of the child witnessing her parents having sex. Others worry about the exacerbation of Oedipal conflicts. It has been claimed that co-sleeping puts a child's development of independence at risk. Supporters of bed sharing take the view that this practice is natural and essential for the emotional development of children.

Virtually every child-care issue—feeding, quality time, watching television, early education, discipline, and so on—is subject to conflicting advice. New fashions and fads come and go with ever-increasing frequency. Parents who are not aware of this whole process are left to interpret the latest claim about some newly discovered risk to their child's health. Advice is always presented to them as a matter of choice. Parenting manuals continually insist that it is up to parents to decide what is best for them. The first words of Dr. Spock's book were "Trust yourself." This nonprescriptive rhetoric runs through almost all the current literature, but underneath the rhetoric, the advice is highly prescriptive and, with rare exceptions, contains the implication that you better do what has been suggested—or else.

With so much conflicting advice and such a large volume of research transmitted into the public domain, parents are continually made to feel vulnerable and ignorant. Most of us are not aware that the moral uncertainties of our society, and the agendas of competing groups of professionals and experts, fuel much of this supposedly unbiased information.

So what are we to make of all this information? It is worth asking the question "What do experts really know?" What do we actually know about the impact of parenting on children? For parents who are interested in the answer to this question, there is both bad news and good news. The bad news, which will be outlined in the next section, is that most advice is based on speculation and common sense, not science. In a nutshell: we actually know very little about the impact of parenting on children. The good news, the *really* good news, is that parents are no more ignorant than the experts. And since the experts know so little about so many of their claims, we might as well ignore them and act on our instincts. Parents usually know better than anyone else what is the best way of bringing up their children.

Prejudice Masquerading as Research

Parenting advice is usually presented as a result of the latest scientific studies. The appeal to the authority of science endows it with immense prestige. Individual experts such as Dr. Spock or Dr. Penelope Leach exercise a formidable influence over the way parents behave with their children. Their views are treated as incontrovertible facts based on rigorous science. Many such experts try to formulate their advice conscientiously, and they do their best to communicate sound information after sifting carefully through the available knowledge. However, it is difficult to reinterpret scientific knowledge and turn it into effective parenting advice. This is not simply due to the fact that scientific knowledge is incomplete. Parenting is not reducible to a scientific endeavour. It involves a unique relationship that does not always readily fit into a general formula.

Child-rearing research and advice is also affected by prevailing moral and cultural attitudes. The expert is influenced by these attitudes and invariably selects and presents information in a manner that reflects them. Individual authorities are products of their own experience as children, adolescents, family members, and fathers and mothers. These personal details invariably shape their outlook and often influence the quality and orientation of their advice. Most of the time, parenting information is based on a combination of common sense, prejudice, and insights provided by research and interpreted through the prism of current moral values. Although many experts are unaware of it, their advice is frequently little more than prejudice masquerading in the guise of research.

Whereas experts can be highly critical of the prejudiced parenting advice of the past, they flatter themselves into believing that their advice is sound, objective, and beyond reproach. They do so even though such advice is continually contradicted by so-called new discoveries. The field of psychology is littered with parent pathologies announced as a major discovery only to be discarded as nonsense a few years later. In the fifties, the schizophrenic and the refrigerator mother were blamed for producing autistic children. The sixties was the decade of maternal deprivation, when working moms were held responsible for causing irreparable emotional damage to their children. Today, these pathologies stand discredited—instead psychologists have invented new ones, such as attachment disorder.

A close inspection of child-rearing literature shows that the experts themselves are continually shifting their arguments from science to what they consider common sense. Take the discussion of the lessons gained from brain research for child development. A leading feature in *Newsweek* enthused that this research confirmed what parents already knew. "Cutting-edge science is confirming what wise parents have always known instinctively: young children need lots of time and attention from the significant adults in their lives."[23] For the author of this report, the line between intuition and science is arbitrary. Cutting-edge science is presented as the validator of well-known home truths. If science simply tells us what we already intuit through common sense, what's the point of appealing to its authority other than to boost an argument? The experience of the past tells us that when science is used to provide legitimacy to preexisting speculation, there is always the possibility that researchers will find what they set out to confirm. Looking for research-based evidence to justify a cause is sometimes openly acknowledged by some of the researchers themselves. And returning to the issue of co-sleeping, according to newspaper reports, a team at Durham University led by anthropologist Dr. Helen Ball is embarking on a study to back up some of the positive claims made about this practice. The team is hoping to discover the benefits of co-sleeping. It is highly likely that they will stumble across the evidence they seek. When researchers set out to prove a case, they usually succeed. But in such instances, the role of science is to provide a fig leaf to cover opinion.

Advocates of particular child-rearing techniques often display a disturbingly instrumental approach toward research and science. Many supporters of infant determinism welcomed the claim that research proved listening to classical music had a powerful effect on the intellectual development of young children. It proved the wisdom of what they had long suspected. "We've always known that music is great for kids but now research shows that music should be an essential part of childhood," enthused Elizabeth Stilwell, the director of the Early Childhood Center at Cornell University. Music teachers were even more delighted by the news. An article in *Teaching Music* recognized the impact that the authority of scientific research was likely to have on parents. It noted that the "long-term effect on public opinion about music and education has been favorably altered to benefit all of us" (meaning music teachers). When the scientific claims made about the Mozart effect were questioned by further research, its advocates changed their tune: the benefits of listening to music were so obvious that it did not matter that their claim was not supported by science. One supporter wrote in *Time* magazine that maybe the case was not "based on rigorous neuroscientific research," but it was "pretty good advice nonetheless." When it serves the cause, science is upheld as the last word on the subject—when it doesn't, then science is an irrelevant distraction.[24]

The debate on spanking directly parallels that on the Mozart effect. Opponents of spanking are continually searching for research-based evidence to substantiate their objectives. The more scrupulous campaigners acknowledge that such evidence does not exist and argue "So what?" American psychologist Leonard Eron has argued that the job of social scientists is to step out of their role as pure scientists and become advocates for social change. Others agree, choosing to oppose spanking on ethical grounds rather than to rely on evidence-based research. Nevertheless, they too advocate more research since they rightly believe that the success of their enterprise requires the support of science.[25]

Since science confers legitimacy on the views of professionals, advice continually appeals to its authority. It has become commonplace to use the formula "research shows that . . ." Supporters of infant determinism continually adopt this approach. The proposition that love boosts brainpower or that babies develop more quickly if they are systematically stimulated during their early years is often backed up by claims of evidence drawn from brain research. In actual fact, there is no evidence for these claims. Invariably the advice offered on the basis of brain research is the same as that offered by proponents of infant determinism twenty or thirty years ago. The celebration of attachment and bonding is simply framed in scientific jargon about brain development.

Charlatans who know that they can cash in on it sometimes manipulate the hunger of parents for scientific facts. But most often it is not dishonesty that drives professionals to misuse the authority of science. Rather, it is a case of people failing to distinguish their opinions from what research actually states. Surveys of parenting literature confirm that the information presented has little to with serious research findings. Such studies have noted that there is often a lack of correspondence between scientific knowledge and the information that is conveyed to parents.[26] Cultural change and moral values influence the selection and communication of parenting advice. Research itself is subject to similar influences. That is why it is important for parents to understand that media reports of research findings should not be interpreted as synonymous with scientific knowledge. Often parenting research is driven by an explicit agenda. And even when it is not, research has a habit of validating prevailing cultural practices.

There are good reasons why parenting and family research is so unreliable. Thirty years ago, Michael Anderson, editor of the widely cited textbook *Sociology of the Family*, said every sociologist "knows at the outset too much about what he is supposed to be studying."[27] In this respect researchers are no different from ordinary mortals. Since most of us have had some experience of family life, we all have opinions on the subject. It is often difficult to separate the profound intimate experiences that shape our imaginations from the objects of our study. The difficulty of maintaining objective distance has plagued family research. Prevailing cultural values influence what researchers define as the problem and the kinds of questions they ask. Research is invariably driven by social, ideological, and moral concerns. Take the effect of maternal employment on children. Research on this topic was initiated at a time when there was widespread disapproval of this practice. The clear expectation was that children would receive inferior parenting if they grew up in a family where the mother went out to work. Is it any surprise that many researchers who went out to explore this topic looked for nothing but problems? Their questions were framed in such a way so as to solicit information about symptoms of anxiety, dysfunctional behavior, and disruption to family life. The possibility that maternal employment might bring some benefits to family life was simply not entertained.

These days, when maternal employment has become a reality, research questions about its impact are no longer posed so one-sidedly. There are many researchers who believe that this practice may have some positive outcomes for family life and frame their questions accordingly. However, they often fall into the same trap as their opponents and allow value judgments to shape their research. In an important study on the subject, two New Zealand academics, John Horwood and David Fergusson, conclude that questions like "Is maternal labor force participation harmful or beneficial?" may be misleading. They believe that what is required is research into "patterns of family life, child supervision, and support that may lead maternal labor force participation to have harmful or beneficial effects."[28]

All research is subject to value judgments. But parenting research is almost entirely prisoner to such judgments. Often this research rests on the unproven assumption that what parents do explains the development of the child. It is only recently that psychologists have begun to popularize the notion that children are quite capable of exerting an important influence on their own development. During the past twenty years, sociologists have also begun to question the idea that parents are the most powerful influence on their children. The lack of evidence of any significant connection between parenting and children's behavior has led sociologists to look at other influences, in particular those of other children.[29] Sadly, parenting research has not seriously engaged with this insight and continues to be driven by the ideology of parental determinism.

How children develop is only in part determined by the behavior of their parents. Children's lives are rooted in a complex network of social, cultural, environmental, economic, and family relationships. Research findings are specific to particular communities, cultures, and social arrangements. Conclusions drawn from work carried out in Slovenia are not necessarily valid or relevant to the experience of children in Los Angeles. Even work carried out within one society may provide little insight. It is difficult to ascertain the virtues of breast-feeding over the bottle since the children studied may not be directly comparable. Breast-feeding is more widely practiced by middle-class than working-class mothers, and claims made about the benefits of this practice may be due to differences in socioeconomic status and other variables. With so many influences to consider, it is impossible to isolate the effect of parenting on child development. As children grow older, the variety of influences on them increases and becomes more complex: friendship circles, quality of education, amenities provided by the community, and most important of all, a child's own role in shaping her life.

Serious researchers are characteristically tentative about drawing hard conclusions. Objective research requires that others replicate its findings.[30] The history of research into parenting is characterized by nonreplicated results. Contradictory findings are sometimes due to different methods of data gathering. But most often they are due to the fact that parenting involves so many unpredictable and unexplainable influences that it can never be an exact science. That is why reputable researchers rarely draw a causal relation between parenting and child behavior. Parenting experts and professionals are rarely able to exercise such restraint, giving the impression that they know far more about the influence of mothering and fathering than the research warrants.

Most of what goes by the name of parenting research is best described as advocacy research, which is devoted to raising awareness of particular problems. Such research aims to influence public policy, and this objective overrides all other considerations. Advocacy research does not set out to discover what's not known; it seeks to influence public opinion. Its starting point is a belief that something is a good thing, and its aim is to marshal arguments to persuade a doubting public. Campaigners against corporal punishment promote advocacy research to convince parents and politicians to outlaw spanking. Child-protection advocacy groups continually publish surveys and reports in order to raise awareness about the subject of their concern. In September 2001, it was widely reported in newspapers that up to four hundred thousand children a year are involved in the United States sex trade. These reports were based on advocacy research produced by University of Pennsylvania's School of Social Research. A closer inspection of the study indicated that it was based on guesstimates and speculation.[31] There is nothing inherently objectionable about advocacy. It has a long and honorable tradition of highlighting important social issues. However, such a cause-driven enterprise is in the business of propaganda and not of communicating scientific truths. Parents in particular need to know that most of the surveys they read about children's problems are the products of people's opinions and not of science.

Moral Confusion

Parenting advice and research bear the stamp of moral and cultural values and concerns. In contemporary times, matters are further complicated by the lack of consensus about moral norms and values. Changes in relations between men and women and the structure of family life have created a situation where important questions about everyday life have become the subject of debate. We live in an era of moral confusion—where the absence of consensus encourages competition between moral values. Debates about "family values," lone parenting, the roles of women and men, homosexuality, and parental responsibility are often embedded in competing moralities.

Moral confusion fuels a situation where parenting advice becomes subject to the competition of values. The instability of this advice reflects the tension between different attitudes to personal life and codes of conduct. In a time of moral uncertainty, it is difficult to resist opting for oversimple solutions. Improved parenting seems such a simple answer to our lack of clarity about how to conduct our everyday affairs. Confusions about how to rear children are superficially resolved by the demand for more and better parenting. So although we find it difficult to agree about the values and rules that should guide our lives and those of our infants, we can find common ground when it comes to children. Expanding parental responsibility is one way of retaining a measure of control over a difficult situation. We may not be clear about how to rear our children and what rules and values we want to impart to them, but we can give them more attention. We may feel unsure about giving children an inspiring vision of a good world, but we can spend a lot of time supervising their activities so that they don't get into any trouble. Parents who live this life of confusion but want to do what's best for their children are therefore prey to the pressure to parent more. Children do need a lot from their parents, but in most British and American homes, the one thing they can do without is more supervision.

Paranoid parents are ordinary people who are forced to pay the price for society's failure to provide them with a relevant moral outlook to guide their lives. In the absence of such guidance, mothers and fathers seek to find some measure of control over their predicament by over-parenting. As the next chapter suggests, this approach empowers not mothers and fathers but the parenting professional.

10 Professional Power and the Erosion of Parental Authority

From the government downward, everyone involved in the parenting debate reiterates the need to support parents and families. Parents do need support, but not the kind that is generally offered. Parents need access to quality child care, and we need child-friendly communities. Most important of all, they need to know that the decisions they make about the future of their children will be supported and not undermined by the rest of society. However, the term *support* is often a euphemism for prescriptive advice about how parents should behave. Parenting education is primarily oriented toward altering adult behavior and providing mothers and fathers with skills they allegedly lack. Unfortunately, projects that aim to transform incompetent adults into skilled parents tend to disempower mothers and fathers and empower professionals.

The intervention of professionals in family life has done a lot to consolidate paranoid parenting. Although child professionals mean well, they continually put to question the authority of the parent. The caring professions profess to uphold the interests of children and families, but no matter how well-meaning, most professional groups promote their own interests, and the parenting and child-protection industry is no exception. It has a vested interest in discovering new crises to solve and in inflating problems associated with parenting. Professional intervention often involves putting parents in their place as inept amateurs. Occasionally it involves blaming parents for the problems they face. At the very least, professionals demand a privileged status for themselves as experts and make parents dependent on them.

Creating Demand for Support

The past decade has seen a concerted campaign to convince the American public that mothers and fathers desperately need the support of parenting professionals. Parents reading alarming surveys of family life in the press are often not aware that what they take to be disinterested studies are actually public relations campaigns designed to create a demand for the parenting professional. Take a report published by the Commonwealth Fund in 1998, *Survey of Parents with Young Children*. This report placed great stress on the difficulties faced by parents and asserted that it found widespread demand for more information and services to help parents with child rearing. It is not surprising that this report came to such conclusions, since the survey was framed in such a way as to invite maximum agreement with the need for greater professional support. Parents who are asked if they need more support and information are unlikely to answer in the negative. Such surveys do not simply aim to find out what parents want—they are also designed to widen the demand for professional services.

It should not come as a shock that so many resources are devoted to creating a demand for the services of parenting professionals. Professionals frequently complain about the relatively small number of busy parents who are interested in their services. A survey of parenting programs by Celia Smith states that there is a mismatch between what professionals and parents think about the need for support services. She remarks that advertised courses have had to be cancelled because of lack of interest. Although some of the professionals she interviewed believed that there was potential for expanding attendance, this was "not always demonstrated by parents queuing up to attend."[1] Parenting education and associated projects are evidently not driven by demand. That is why so much time and energy are devoted to promoting the idea that parents need these services. If mothers and fathers had indeed been queuing up to join parenting classes, there would be little need for public relations campaigns.

Promoting the case for the parenting professional is not confined to official and specialist agencies. One of the defining features of contemporary child-rearing literature is the advice to seek more advice. Parenting literature continually reassures us that there is help available and that asking for help and support is a positive step, often directing the reader to other sources of support, including long lists of help lines and support networks. Sometimes it seems that providers of child-rearing advice are more interested in convincing parents that they should seek professional support than in offering practical solutions.

In the past, child-rearing manuals sought to provide advice that could help parents cope with everyday challenges and also with difficult problems. Although experts believed that there were limits to what parents could do, they assumed that with sound advice most problems could be solved. Today's experts take a radically different approach. They assume not only that parents haven't a clue but also that they are unlikely to be able to cope on their own. Informing parents that they can't cope alone and that therefore they should seek support is a central theme of contemporary child-rearing literature.

To create a demand for their services, professionals often argue that parents lack the skill and knowledge necessary for raising children. A major survey carried out by the Canadian Invest in Kids Foundation in April 1999 claimed that parents were woefully ignorant about the "basic facts necessary for fostering healthy development." According to Carol Crill-Russell, the vice president of this organization, parental knowledge is "a mile wide and an inch deep."[2] The premise that parents are too ignorant to do what their child requires informs the Commonwealth Fund's survey of parents with young children. "Despite medical evidence about the importance of breast-feeding, many mothers do not breast-feed their infants," it reports.

In a tone of disbelief, it observes that "only 39 percent of parents read or looked at a picture book with the child at least once a day within the week before the interview. . . . Many mothers do not plan the birth, seek prenatal care, or take childbirth or parenting classes." The conclusion—How dare they!—is seldom made explicit in this exposure of parental misdemeanors, but the message is clear.[3]

A survey commissioned by Prevent Child Abuse America, published in 1998, is even less subtle. It indicated that 37 percent of American parents had reported insulting or swearing at their children within the previous twelve months. The survey also claimed that 50 percent of parents had neglected their child's emotional needs and that the majority of these parents indicated that this neglect took place "almost every day."[4] Vastly exaggerated claims of parental neglect constitute a powerful argument for professional intervention.

Campaigns designed to expand the demand for parenting services are driven by the conviction that enlightened professionals know what's best. Professionals often compare their crusade to campaigns against drunk driving or smoking. The fervor with which they pursue their objectives could give the impression that parenting programs make a positive difference. Parents are never told that there is no evidence that these programs actually work.

Robust claims about the effectiveness of parent education programs have little foundation. Such programs are rarely evaluated, and when they are, they provide little indication that they are effective. A study of such programs in Texas found they made little impact on the children of middle-class parents.[5] Celia Smith's review of British programs also failed to find evidence that they are effective. Nevertheless, instead of conceding the point, she minimizes the absence of evidence by blaming the difficulty of mounting research in this area. So although Smith acknowledges that "we still do not know enough about the effectiveness of parenting programs," she concludes that the absence of evidence does not mean parenting programs are ineffective but "rather that their effectiveness has been exceedingly difficult to demonstrate." In other words, she assumes that such programs are effective—and that it is only a matter of time before the evidence will be found. In the meantime, she draws attention to the "wealth of anecdotal evidence and the practically universal praise from the parents who participate in this project."[6]

The failure to demonstrate the efficacy of parenting programs is a source of worry to some child professionals. Some researchers have concluded that parenting programs do not work because parents are too stupid to be able to transmit the ideas to their children. Recently it was reported that "speeding the cognitive development of small children by training their parents is likely to be no more successful than teaching algebra to eighth-graders by enrolling their mothers and fathers in the class." Dale C. Farran, an education professor at Vanderbilt University, claims that his research shows that focusing on parents has "been a resounding failure." Some professionals who are disillusioned with the experience want to cut out parents altogether and orient their programs directly at children. Matthew Melmed, executive director of the Washington-based advocacy group Zero to Three, believes that "for programs to be effective, what seems to matter is the child's direct involvement in the services."[7]

Given the inconclusive state of research about the impact of parenting on children and the absence of evidence that shows that parenting programs work, it is worth asking from what the experts involved in these projects derive their expertise. It is certainly not an expertise based on science and research. Nor is it rooted in practical experience. Most professional child experts do not advertise themselves as model parents who know every trick in the book. Parenting expertise is one of those mysterious arts seldom asked to account for itself. Sadly, many mothers and fathers who lack confidence in their own resources are prepared to defer to the claim of authority. They don't ask the obvious question—"Why should this expert presume to know more about the needs of my child than I do?" How long before someone cries out that the emperor has no clothes?

Disempowering Parents

Professional intervention into child rearing is portrayed as disinterested support that aims to help parents gain confidence. Modern-day experts insist that they are not in the business of judging parents and prescribing formulas. Their advice is often conveyed in a nondirective, nonprescriptive form. "There is no right way to bring up a child," parents are told, before being reminded that unless they act according to the expert's guidelines, their child will suffer long-term consequences. It is very difficult to trust your instincts when you are continually reminded of the grave consequences that your mistakes can have on the development of your child. The ideas associated with infant determinism have a particularly detrimental effect on the confidence of mothers and fathers. Since so much of a child's future is determined in the early years, parents cannot afford to make mistakes. Parents have no second chance to repair the damage if mistakes made during the first three years of a child's life have incalculable consequences for her long-term development.

The proliferation of advice on every detail of a child's life has the double effect of undermining the confidence of parents and of promoting the authority of the expert. It is hard to trust yourself if feeding your child the wrong food might affect his intellectual development. It is difficult to feel empowered by new claims based on neuroscience when you are advised to stimulate, but not to overstimulate, your infant. The main effect of this advice culture is to reinforce the dependence of parents on experts.

, Parenting programs are deliberately packaged to come across as nonauthoritarian. The buzzword is *partnership*—experts and parents working together. Program designers contend that they are in the business of involving parents and insist that their role is to facilitate rather than instruct. These claims overlook the fact that parenting programs assume a relation of inequality and that they are based on an agenda formulated by professionals and professionals alone. Parent input has a perfunctory and entirely decorative function. The parenting profession's lack of sensitivity to the way in which its expertise can undermine parental authority is particularly disturbing.

Back in the fifties, the renowned British child psychiatrist D. W. Winnicott warned about the danger of allowing experts to come between a mother and her child. In 1976, a report by the Committee on Child Health Services echoed his concern. It reported that the "growth in the number and variety of professions connected with child rearing, however necessary in our kind of society, has in some measure undermined the self-confidence of parents." Even two committed advocates of parenting education, writing in 1984, could acknowledge that "a recurring theme in talking to groups of parents and reading research reports and accounts of group discussions is that the attitudes of many professionals are tending to undermine parent's self-confidence and their belief in their own parenting abilities."[8]

In recent years, professionals have become far less concerned with the negative impact they may have on parental confidence. They apparently believe that their crusade is too important to worry about the upset they might cause to the life of the odd mother or father. Having vastly inflated the complexity of child rearing, they also view their own role as indispensable and decisive. In the past, professional intervention in family life was focused on problem families. Such intervention was targeted toward specific people who were deemed to be unfit or exceptionally ignorant parents. This relatively modest role has given way to a far more ambitious project designed to support all parents. Time and again, experts remind us that every mother and father needs the services of a parenting professional. This shift from focusing on the small minority of problem parents to targeting all parents suggests that the professionalization of parenting has its own inner dynamic. At meetings and conferences, professionals frequently argue for universal parent education. From their perspective, there are no normal, average parents capable of responsible child rearing. A responsible parent today is someone who is prepared to actively solicit the indispensable advice and support offered by the professional.

The very concept of parent education militates against a genuine partnership. It is founded on the premise that mothers and fathers are too ignorant to understand their own needs and those of their children and therefore need to learn these skills from an expert. Professionals define parent education and support as "a range of . . . measures which help parents and prospective parents to understand their own social, emotional, psychological and physical needs and those of their children and enhance the relationship between them."[9] Parenting education is not designed to provide useful tips and sound practical advice. It assumes a far more ambitious goal—changing the way that mothers and fathers think about themselves and their children. "Parent ed is coming to be thought of as education in family life, marriage, and parenthood, a type of educational activity separate and different from child development research on the one hand and nursery education on the other," was how the director of the National Council of Parent Education put it back in the 1930s.[10] Helping parents realize their needs was the explicit objective of this movement. In no other area of life would adults routinely be told that they are not in the best position to decide what their real needs are. And in no other area of life would adults be prepared to put up with lectures from strangers who presume to instruct them about intimate aspects of their lives.

What Professionals Really Think of Parents

Mothers and fathers must realize that experts tend to regard them as either inept amateurs or as a potential source of risk to their children. Sometimes they see parents as the problem and assume that they are the solution. Earlier, such professionals expressed these views openly.[11] One British expert, Jean Ayling, wrote: "Most of the children of my acquaintance are already badly damaged at an early age." Her solution was to limit the role of parents, since they have a "strictly bounded domain of usefulness," and to assign the wider task of child socialization to the helping professions.[12] Ayling's patronizing assumptions about parental incompetence dominated professional thinking in the post–World War II period. Winnicott alluded to this trend when he warned that normal parents faced "petty regulations, legal restrictions, and all manner of stupidities" from intrusive professionals. He believed that many professionals were "by no means uniformly confident in the mother's ability to understand her child better than anyone else can." And he cautioned that "doctors and nurses are often so impressed with the ignorance and stupidity of some of the parents that they fail to allow for the wisdom of others."[13]

Today, the caring professions are even more suspicious of parental authority. Doctors and nurses are invited to spy on parents. A policy statement on prenatal visits endorsed by the American Academy of Pediatrics instructs professionals to gather information on "cultural beliefs, values, and practices related to parenting, including attitudes regarding tobacco, alcohol, and other drug use" and to identify high-risk situations, including single mothers or a gun in the home.[14] Checking out the character and competence of parents-to-be appears to be a key function of a profession that is convinced it has the moral authority to judge the ability of adults to rear children.

Judging and finding parents wanting is a regular feature of advice columns. Take the "Dear Abby" column. "Whatever happened to parenting?" asks a reader who manifestly believes that parents are to blame for the failures of the American education system. Abigail "Abby" Van Buren replies sympathetically: "It's unfair to demand that schools teach children that which should be taught at home by parents." This remark is followed by a mini-lecture, where Abby explains that parenting "takes patience, setting a good example," and so on. And with a note of unconcealed contempt she concludes that "for parents who feel the knack is beyond them, many books have been written on the subject."[15] Is this useful advice to parents "who feel the knack is beyond them," or just another patronizing rant against the incompetent parent?

Child-care advisers believe that if you do not practice the parenting skills they prescribe, you may not be a fit parent. An emotional health check is one way of imposing quality control over future parents. Another far more insidious proposal is to weed out the unfit by licensing parents. Jack Westman, a professor of psychiatry at the University of Wisconsin, has been a vociferous advocate of licensing parents. His proposals have been widely debated by academics, parenting professionals, and politicians.[16] Westman, like many professionals in his field, supports the regulation of parenting because he believes that children are often damaged by their mothers and fathers. From the perspective of the caring professional, there is no such thing as a normal parent. This inability to distinguish between the vast majority of responsible and intelligent adults and a tiny minority of out-of-control abusive parents can benefit no one. The very idea that parents need to be vetted sends the message that mothers and fathers cannot be trusted. Such a message inevitably undermines their authority. There is considerable anecdotal evidence that many mothers and fathers have internalized the expert's version of contemporary parenthood. This makes it difficult for them to trust other parents. Such parenting pathology sows mistrust and plays a critical role in parental paranoia.

Cannot Be Taught

Parenting advice has become a growth industry. Lamentably, we rarely pause and ask the question, "Is this doing any good?" The reluctance to evaluate the role of this industry is all the more surprising since there is little evidence that it has helped men and women to become better fathers or mothers. On the contrary, its growth has coincided with the intensification of paranoid parenting. Although the professionalization of parenting is not the cause of this phenomenon, there can be little doubt that it continually exacerbates problems and undermines the confidence of mothers and fathers.

There are several ways in which the professionalization of parenting makes parental paranoia worse. Professionals have helped to construct the idea that parents are likely to be incompetent. A lack of belief in parental competence has been absorbed by contemporary culture and is regularly communicated to the public through sensational accounts about the failures of fathers and mothers. The very idea that parenting is a complicated skill has weakened child caretakers' sense of self-sufficiency.

The majority of caring professionals genuinely do their best to support parents. They would claim that they are not in the business of blaming parents but reassuring them that we all need help and support. What they fail to realize is that this reassurance is anything but reassuring. Just because all parents are deemed potentially incompetent does not make any individual caretaker's job easier. On the contrary, the message that parents cannot cope on their own is readily interpreted as an indication that society has little confidence in their ability to parent. Extremist proposals such as the call to license parents vividly confirm the lack of professional confidence in the potential of grown-ups to care for their children. But even more moderate proposals transmit the same message.

Even with the best will in the world, professionals cannot help but undermine the status and therefore the confidence and authority of parents. Professional authority competes directly with the authority of the parent. Rhetoric about partnership can rarely obscure this reality. The terms of any unequal partnership will be set by the party that possesses the skills and expertise. Of course, grown-ups continually have to deal with experts. Mothers and fathers engage with teachers, doctors, and car mechanics. In these encounters, most sensible adults do not presume a relation of equality. They seek out experts precisely because they trust their knowledge and authority. Such experiences with authoritative experts need not create problems for adults who lack knowledge about the subject of their inquiry. When a parent takes a child to the doctor because he knows that the doctor will be able to treat the child's allergy, it has no effect on the parent's confidence. He expects the doctor to know about allergic reactions. That is the function of a doctor. Matters are different when it comes to the relationship between a parent and a parenting professional. This relationship involves a direct conflict of authority about who knows what's in the best interest of a particular child. Let's look at this relationship more closely.

Effective child rearing relies on authoritative parenting. The relationship between the child and the parent evolves from a physical one to an emotional and social one through a succession of stages. A child's sense of security depends on the unconditional trust she develops in her parent. In her early years, the omniscient parent becomes the point of reference through which she makes sense of her experience. What a parent says and does really matters to the child. In turn, parents rely on their unquestioned authority to nurture and to subsequently encourage the habit of independence in a child. That is why the prerequisite of effective parenting is self-confidence and belief in their role. Without this confidence, the exercise of parental authority is fraught with problems.

The role of the parent changes if authority shifts to the professional. The parent now has to listen and defer to outside opinion. To ignore such expertise is to court public mistrust and the accusation of irresponsibility. The literature on child rearing is surprisingly silent on the potential problems caused by the sharing of parental authority. However, once authority for parenting is accorded to a group of professionals, the legitimacy accorded to the status of mothers and fathers is likely to diminish. Parents who are expected to defer to the expert are likely to have a weaker sense of authority than those who do not. It is not possible to share some of the authority hitherto accorded to the parent without weakening this authority overall.

The pressure to share authority with the child-rearing professional has profound implications for modern parenting. The very existence of an outside authority places parents under permanent trial. Those who are uncertain about their authority are likely to find child rearing an intensely unsettling and trying task. Even the most confident mother or father is negatively influenced, since the weakening status that society accords to parental authority influences the way that child caretakers approach their everyday tasks.

The caring professions regularly advocate the virtues of responsible parenting. Yet their encroachment on parental authority is most likely to have the opposite effect. The link between weakened authority and a reluctance to exercise parental responsibility is strikingly evident in relation to the troublesome problem of discipline. Although they don't say so in so many words, many parents often feel defeated even before they try to impose a measure of discipline over a truculent child. The cry "What can I do?" reflects the consciousness of uncertain authority. Unfortunately, too often the expectation of defeat leads parents to look for other sources of authority—teachers and schools—to discipline the young. Normalizing parental failure can only lower parents' expectations of themselves. Shared authority is a disincentive to responsible parenting.

The professionalization of parenting impairs the confidence of mothers and fathers. It also promotes an expertise that is of dubious value to our community. It has already been noted that much of what constitutes this expertise is prejudice masquerading as science. The lack of substance in this research is not surprising, since the very idea of parenting as a science is flawed.

The core assumption of the parenting profession is that child rearing consists of a set of practices that mothers and fathers need to learn. Of course, no one could dispute this assertion. Every human relationship involves learning and gaining an understanding of the other person. A parent needs to learn how to engage the imagination of a child, how to stimulate him, and when and how to restrain him from doing something harmful. Effective parents are always learning on the job. However, the most crucial lessons that they are learning have to do not with abstract skills but with the relationship they have with their children. Learning how to manage this relationship in order to guide a child's development represents the crux of effective parenting.

The issue is not whether parenting needs to be learned but whether it can be taught. Everyday experience suggests that not everything that has to be learned can be taught. Parenting can't be taught because it is about the forging and managing of an intimate relationship. And when it comes to a relationship, people tend to learn from their own experience. Children and grown-ups are often subjected to very good advice about whom they should mix with and whom or how they should love. However, in the end, people learn through their interactions with the other party in the relationship. Each relationship contains unique elements that are only grasped by the parties involved. People learn through experiencing the joy and the pain, the exhilaration and the disappointments of their interaction with someone who is significant to their lives.

When it comes to a relationship, learning what is right is inseparable from the act of individual discovery. Parents learn what is right for their children through interacting with them. Men and women are not born with an innate understanding of parenting. They certainly don't gain such understanding through books and parenting classes. Until they have a child, even basic parenting questions remain unfocused and unspecific. As many parents confirm, what they learned from books and from professionals actually bears little relationship to their subsequent experience. The birth of their baby throws up the first real problems that they will have to solve practically. It is at that point that learning begins, and it is the experience of the parent-child relationship that teaches men and women how to go about fulfilling their responsibilities.

When it comes to science, it is possible to teach facts without the student, having to personally experience and discover them for themselves. It is possible to teach skills that can be applied in all scientific experiments. This is not the case with parenting. The very instability of parenting advice and the regularity with which yesterday's authoritative recipe is dismissed as hopelessly inaccurate indicate that what is going to be taught today will be rejected as irrelevant tomorrow.

People are bombarded with advice about how they should conduct their relationships. The popularity of self-help schemes and advice literature indicates that there is a genuine demand for learning about relationships. Just how much these books and schemes teach us is a matter of debate. There have never been so many publications devoted toward instructing people how to have a more fulfilling sex life. There have also never been so many people who have eagerly sought to learn the skills and knowledge provided by these publications. Does that mean that more and more people have learned to have a more fulfilling sex life? Just posing the question indicates how ludicrous is the claim that fulfillment in a sexual relationship can be taught. People can no more be taught how to have good loving relationships than how to be good parents.

The very concept of parenting "skills" obscures the essence of a child-parent relationship. This technical approach toward parenting has little to do with the needs of children. Children do not benefit from the erosion of their parent's authority. Recasting human relationships as sets of skills that can be learned—or taught—makes a statement about our culture and how adults are viewed in it. We seem almost to expect people to be too immature to handle their relationships with each other. Caring professionals and educators advocate relationship education, with special classes teaching relationship skills for married or soon-to-be-married adults.

Apprehensions about the ability of people to manage their affairs have also led to calls for teaching parenting skills to schoolchildren. Trying to teach schoolchildren how to become good parents in the future indicates that the caring professions have lost the plot. Schools can play an important role in providing children with the high-quality education they need for becoming successful adults. Educated adults with good jobs stand a good chance of learning to become effective parents. Instead of providing lessons about parenting, schools could achieve a lot more by concentrating on the task of making sure that their students become educated adults.

It is very difficult to conduct intimate relationships under public scrutiny. A relationship between a parent and child is not only complicated by but also changes when conducted under shared authority. A mother or father who is forced to keep one eye on the expert and the other on the child is forced to play to two different scripts. This distraction can create an unnecessary barrier between parent and child and weaken the ability of the caregiver to learn from a unique experience. Undermining the confidence of the parent is the inexorable consequence.

There is a case for professional support for families. But that support should be unobtrusive and targeted toward the small minority of parents who have genuinely failed to establish their authority over their children. Not distinguishing between the problems faced by this small minority and those confronted by most mothers and fathers is the outcome of the assumption that all normal parents need support. This approach fails both groups of parents. When all parents are treated as potential failures, it is the children who pay the price.

There is a lot that parents can learn from experts. They can learn about practical skills having to do with health and nutrition. If they choose, they can learn important insights about child development. But the one thing they cannot learn from experts is how to conduct their relationship with their children. There are no relationship experts. Mothers and fathers are likely to learn far more from other parents and family members who have shared their experience and whom they trust. But in the end, parents also need to understand that most of the time they and they alone know what is in the best interest of their children.

The Politicization of Parenting

The parenting professional has found an eager ally in the politician. All the main political parties regard the so-called problem of parenting as their issue. Politicians have absorbed the ideology of parental determinism: parenting determines the behavior of children. It is frequently proposed that all forms of antisocial behavior—crime, drugs, teenage pregnancy, illiteracy, and poverty—are linked to incompetent parenting.

During the Clinton years, early learning and childhood development research were used as a justification for formulating new government policy. White House conferences on children provided a platform for politicians and professionals to lecture mothers and fathers on their responsibilities. In May 2000, an entire White House Conference on teenagers was devoted to informing the public that teenagers need the guidance and support of their parents. At this event, Hillary Rodham Clinton announced that the National Partnership for Women and Families along with the Families and Work Institute would "lead a campaign to promote the importance of spending time with your teenagers."[1] At the summit, politicians were free with folksy advice about the need for "parents to take stock of their own lives and work habits and look for ways to make more time for their children." Evidently, it was now the job of politicians to instruct parents about the importance of spending time with their children.

From the perspective of the Clinton administration, the solution to a variety of social problems was to get parents to eat evening meals with their teenagers. "Sitting down to dinner can have enormously positive impact," declared President Clinton. Why? Because "teenagers that had dinner with their parents five nights a week are far more likely to avoid smoking, drinking, violence, suicide and drugs."[2] The corollary of this argument is, of course, that when problems do arise, it is the fault of those parents who skip the odd evening meal.

The politicization of parenting is driven by a profound sense of moral malaise. Society is deeply concerned by the prevalence of crime, antisocial behavior, the breakdown of trust, and the apparent decline of the family. Many long-established institutions—from the family to local communities—appear exhausted and disoriented. Bewilderment about moral values is widespread, and many people feel that society is losing its way. Such concerns are generated when life seems unpredictable and out of control. The absence of a sense of community is a constant source of insecurity. We all feel a sense of estrangement, at least some of the time, and often ask the question "Where do I belong?"

Moral confusion creates a demand for quick-fix solutions. Parents provide an ideal focus for those seeking a ready-made target. It is much easier to personalize a moral problem than to understand it as the erosion of an abstract system of values. Immoral people are simpler to recognize than the failure of institutions to transmit meaningful values about the difference between right and wrong. So we pounce on immoral people. And since most immoral people have been brought up by their parents, it is tempting to blame their behavior on their mothers or fathers. After all, if people's behavior is determined by the actions of their parents, whom else should we blame?

In the past, politicians were only interested in indicting the so-called problem parent. The main concern was with the problem posed by a small group of marginalized poor families. Later, the weakening of the institution of marriage and the apparent decline of the family led some politicians to represent single mothers as the symbol of moral decay. During the nineties, the deadbeat dad became the subject of moral concern. Gradually, with the intensification of moral uncertainties, other parents were brought into the frame. The yuppie parent who was more concerned about career than family life soon joined the working mother. Today, political scrutiny is no longer fixed on a specific group of mothers and fathers. All potential parents face the attention of policy makers.

Of course, society does face important moral issues. But to blame parents for the present state of moral malaise is to confuse the symptom with the cause. How parents behave is informed by the cultural, moral, and social influences that bear down upon them. The values they transmit to their children are not their personal property; they appropriate them from everyday life in their community. Parents can do a lot to prepare their children to become good citizens. But adopting a different child-raising strategy will do little to put right a society uncertain about its moral universe. It is a testimony to the moral illiteracy of the political class that instead of confronting the big questions, they prefer to give lectures on parenting skills.

There is a strong streak of opportunism behind the politicization of parenting. America faces a variety of social problems. It is far more expensive to improve the quality of education, health, and social services than to exhort parents to spend more time reading to their children, cuddling them, or breast-feeding them. No doubt sound parenting practices can have positive effects on children's lives. But these effects pale into insignificance compared with what can be achieved through an excellent public system of child care and education. Parenting as a tool of social policy is likely to be ineffective, but it has the merit of being very cheap. Increasingly, social policy oriented toward helping disadvantaged children has been transformed into a campaign to influence and alter parent behavior.

Initiatives like Head Start and Early Head Start target the parenting and home environment. Supporters of these programs claim that their participants show "more supporting parenting behaviors."[3] The assumption that underlies this evaluation is that the problem lies with the quality of parenting rather than the difficult social circumstances facing the child.

Politicians have been quick to embrace new ideas about early child development. Child experts are now regularly consulted, and infant determinism informs the new policy initiatives surrounding early intervention. The parent figures prominently in contemporary social policy making. The Bush presidency has continued where Clinton left off. In July 2001, a White House Summit on Early Childhood Cognitive Development assigned to the child caretaker the role of putting right the problem of social deprivation. According to one speaker, "many risk factors that presage academic failure can be trumped by providing parents, grandparents, child-care providers, and early childhood educators with solid information about how to best engage kids systematically in the use of language and the joy of reading."[4] Federally funded research oriented toward educating parents to stimulate their children transforms child rearing into a political issue.

The politicization of parenting is influenced by a genuine concern for the many problems associated with family life. Unfortunately, well-meaning and even constructive proposals can do very little to solve the problems faced by parents. State policy is too crude an instrument to deal with the management of the intimate emotional relationship between parent and child. Parental anxieties and the complex relations between adults and children are not problems that are susceptible to public policy solutions. Why? Because the problems of human relationships are too specific and too personal to be tackled by policies, which are by definition general in character.

Focusing public attention on private troubles has the potential for making matters worse. Even well-meaning but intrusive family members can exacerbate an already unsettled situation. In the past it was recognized that such interference could be harmful and that parents must be allowed to bring up children their own way. Today this insight has been lost. Public policy now assumes that intervention into family life can only improve the situation. Yet public intervention is likely to go much further than the intrusion of busybody relatives in complicating parenting. By legitimizing the professionalization of parenting, public policy can have the unintended consequence of disempowering parents further. It is evident that one of the main causes of parental paranoia is the way in which intimate family relations have become subject to public scrutiny. Such pressure, whether in the form of helpful advice, periodic health warnings, or the intervention of professionals or of politicians, continually erodes parental confidence. Those who are genuinely concerned about parents and their children need to realize that their problems are not susceptible to political solutions. Taking the issue of parenting out of the sphere of political life would make a valuable contribution toward restoring the confidence of many parents.

Not the Business of the State

Unfortunately, responsible public figures often overlook the fact that the professionalization of parenting is fraught with danger for the conduct of family life. Take the recent case of a Montgomery County, Maryland, family who lost its bid to keep a one-year-old autistic daughter at home after county social workers convinced a judge that the girl would be safer in a group home. This dispute did not involve any allegation of child abuse or neglect. Indeed, Judge Stanley Klavan pointed out that the parents, Caleb and Ann Chang, are "nice people" and that they "have done nothing wrong." Their only crime was that they disagreed with officialdom over the best treatment for their severely disabled child. The Changs wanted to keep their family together. The officials believed that the child's developmental needs would best be met in a residential program. Local officials could not comprehend the possibility that the Changs could know better than anyone else what was in the best interest of their child.[5]

One of the arguments constantly reiterated by government officials and the caring professions is that parenting is one of the most important jobs in the world, and yet so little is done to support it. Of course, parenting is an important matter. So are love affairs, marriages, and all intimate relations between people. But just because something is important does not mean that it requires the regulation of the state. Whenever public policy encroaches into the domain of personal relations, it is likely to undermine them. Human relations thrive on emotion and sentiment. They involve personal attachment, commitment, and responsibility. Sentiment plays an important role in binding people together. When it is subject to formal procedure, sentiment becomes less effective in binding together relations of trust.

The idea that politicians and officials know what's in the interest of children better than their parents is an affront to the dignity of every mother and father. Parents work very hard to fulfill their responsibilities and most of the time do a very good job. What they do is not the business of the state. Politicians have no authority to claim that they possess special insights into the conduct of private affairs. The role of public authorities should be confined to those exceptional circumstances in which a child faces real harm. Society has a legitimate interest in the protection and welfare of its children. But it has no interest in encouraging the politicization of parenting.

Whenever politics intrudes into the sphere of parenting, problems are exaggerated and parents are put on the defensive. The politicization of parenting is an outcome of the failure of political imagination. Unable to work out effective social policies that can tackle the real problems facing American society, some politicians have been persuaded that if they can reeducate parents, everything will turn out fine. Politicians who have failed to provide the nation with a decent system of education assume that nevertheless they are fit to educate parents. Since most of the time parents are intensely defensive about their role, they have remained silent about this affront to their self-respect.

Parents have nothing to learn from politicians about child rearing. The pronouncements of public figures are often driven by political expediency. Even when they try to be helpful, they have no more to contribute to the subject than any other parent. Often their reflections on family matters are naïve and even patronizing. Talking down to parents was the predominant tone of the July 2001 White House Summit. One contributor, Dorothy Strickland, took it upon herself to offer the following tips to parents and grandparents:

1. Talk with your child.
2. Listen to your child.
3. Sing and chant nursery rhymes and childhood songs you remember.
4. Turn ordinary, everyday trips into interesting excursions.
5. Play language games with your child.[6]

When participants at a White House Summit advise parents to talk and listen to their children, it is evident that the political imagination is in trouble. But even more worrying is the tendency for officialdom to hide its political failures behind parents. A culture of parent-blaming is the inexorable outcome of official intrusion into the domain of child rearing.

It is vital to take politics out of parenting. Official intervention into the sphere of parenting offers no solutions. It only fuels parental paranoia, distracts people from tackling genuine problems, and magnifies parenting difficulties. This danger was clearly anticipated by D. W. Winnicott when he warned that "whatever does not specifically back up the idea that parents are responsible people will in the long run be harmful to the very core of society."[7] The politicization of parenting serves as an everyday reminder that parents need officialdom to remind them of their responsibility. It has helped create a climate of suspicion and mistrust. The consequence for parents and their children is the subject of the conclusion.

Conclusion

Whoever invented the word *parenting* was not primarily interested in the lives of children. Until recently, the term *to parent* referred exclusively to the act of begetting a child. Today, it is deployed to describe the behavior of mothers and fathers. That is why so many of the issues surrounding paranoid parenting have surprisingly little to do with children's lives. Fears about adult identity are often transferred to children, who then bear the brunt of our anxieties. Public concerns about parenting are grounded in adult confusions about their lives. These confusions have a disproportionate impact upon those responsible for rearing children.

Many of the forces behind the growth of parental anxieties are unrelated to practical issues of child rearing. The tendency to increase our emotional investment in our children is in part a reflection of difficulties with relations between mature men and women. These difficulties, previously described as the emptying out of adult identity and the weakening of adult authority, exist independently of child-care issues and shape the lives of all grown-ups. Of course, the fact that adults find it difficult to conduct their affairs has a significant impact on the way we bring up our children. The decline of adult collaboration and responsibility for the welfare of youngsters has far-reaching implications. Insecurity inevitably permeates a parenting culture that relies so heavily on isolated mothers and fathers.

Deprived of the authority they require to carry out their responsibility effectively, parents possess only a weak sense of control over their children's lives. Unfortunately, the caring professions and policy makers have not grasped why parents face such a difficult predicament. Even with the best of intentions, child-care professionals add to parents' woes. Their interventions disempower parents by contesting their authority. The objective of supporting parents turns into its opposite. Deep inside, every sensible adult knows that the provision of support carries the implication of failure. We support failing schools, failing health care, and failing marriages. When it comes to child rearing, outside support risks inflicting an irreparable blow to the authority of the parent.

The politicians' failure to identify the right problems is not due to a lack of imagination. Policy makers look for problems that they can solve. However, the principal problems confronting parents are not susceptible to political solutions. Grown-ups' confusions are influenced by social, moral, and cultural processes. These cannot be tackled by a clever law. What we need is a change in adult attitudes toward the socialization of children. Instead of adding to the problems faced by mothers and fathers by transmitting the message of parental incompetence, politicians should address the big question: how to establish a society where adults are able to trust others with the welfare of their children.

What Can We Do?

Understanding the predicament faced by mothers and fathers in general helps place individual difficulties in perspective. We all need to know that most of the really big issues that plague parents have little to do with problems intrinsic to child rearing. Today's heightened sense of anxiety about children is not based on any practical discoveries about their lives. Almost all the forces that fuel paranoid parenting stem from unresolved tensions rooted in the world of adults. The emptying out of adult identity, the depreciation of adulthood, the loss of parental authority, uncertainties about moral values, the professionalization and politicization of parenting, and the weakening of adult solidarity are outcomes thrown up by developments in the wider society. These influences disorient and confuse parents, who in turn transmit their insecurities through the way they interact with their children. In that sense, the wider cultural influences on adulthood have a direct bearing on child rearing. But these are problems that adults have to sort out among themselves, not with their children. Parents can do little to counteract these cultural influences. But they can minimize their impact on their family by doing their best to avoid confusing the problems of adulthood with those of childhood. Just remember that when you are about to say, "I could not live with myself if something happened to my child," you are principally concerned with your own state of mind rather than the welfare of your child.

Paranoid parenting can be seen as a form of collective displacement. The failures of grown-up society are visited on children. Lamentably, it is our children who pay the price for the difficulty that adults have in sorting out their problems.

It is always useful to recall that our obsession with our children's safety is likely to be more damaging to them than the risks they encounter in their daily interactions with the world. Children can recover from accidents very quickly. In a loving environment, even a traumatic episode need not prevent a child from bouncing back and developing into a confident adult. However, if parents stifle their children with their obsessions and restrict their scope to explore, then the young generation will become socialized to believe that vulnerability is the natural state of affairs. Letting go is always difficult for parents. However, freeing children from the obsessions of parental paranoia is essential for their healthy development.

There is simply no sensible alternative to letting go. Paranoid parenting actually accomplishes the very opposite of what it sets out to do. When youngsters are protected from risks, they miss out on important opportunities to learn sound judgment and build up their confidence and resilience. Such psychological resources ensure their safety far better than the current regime of constant adult supervision.

Instead of teaching children to distrust strangers and to regard the outside world with suspicion, parents need to nourish their children's belief in themselves. The best way to help children to learn to look after themselves is to instill them with a strong sense of what is right and wrong. Instead of concentrating on negative themes like stranger danger, parents must transmit to their children a positive vision of humanity. We have a responsibility to raise and not lower their expectations about what they can expect of themselves and other people.

One way that parents can temper their fears is by tackling the breakdown of adult collaboration. Parents need to take active steps to overcome their isolation. They need to cultivate friends, colleagues, and family members to serve as collaborators in the task of child rearing. In the present climate of suspicion, this is hard work. Parents need to create their own little community of stakeholders in their children's welfare. Some parents have more opportunity than others to construct a network of adult collaborators. But all parents can establish some such links, since in every community parents intuitively grasp that they need the help of one another. Parental cooperation helps to minimize the effects of isolation. But it is also the most effective alternative to the disempowerment brought about by professionalized parenting.

Parenting is not a complex science. It is not even a science at all. It is actually quite a natural undertaking. Sometimes boring, ordinary, and even banal, bringing up children is always demanding. Parents can afford to make mistakes, although they would do well to learn from them. As long as you do your best for your child you are unlikely to need any professional backup. No one is likely to understand the situation of your child better than you do—so you might as well do what you think is best.

In any case, most professional advice is at best good common sense or at worst someone's prejudice. Usually it is simply someone's opinion. Such advice is formulaic, very general, and nine times out of ten entirely useless. As noted previously, it is often based on prejudice masquerading as research. You need to be aware that the two principal ideas that dominate today's parenting culture—infant and parental determinism—are fundamentally flawed. They illuminate the job of child rearing as much as the idea that the world is flat helped overseas explorers. They are today's prejudice. Experience indicates that today's authoritative advice will probably be dismissed in five years as unenlightened opinion, so don't feel worried about not heeding it. The advice of friends and family members is likely to be far more relevant, since they are acquainted with your circumstances and actually know a bit about your child. However, in the end it is your call, so you might as well follow your instinct. Be prepared to call the child expert's bluff.

The aim of this book is not to offer superior advice to the anxious parent. It is motivated by the conviction that if parents can grasp why parenting has been turned into such a troublesome enterprise, then they can do something about regaining their self-confidence. Today's parenting culture systematically de-skills mothers and fathers. It places enormous pressures on parents to turn away from what only they can do. The good news is that if parents understand the pressures that bear down upon them, they can insulate themselves from it. They may still be anxious about their children's well-being, but at least it will be possible to put those fears into a more balanced perspective.

 **Notes**

Introduction

1 See "California Research Group Cites Toy Hazards," *Los Angeles Times*, November 22, 2000.

2 See "7 Steps to a Safer Summer," *Family Life*, June/July 2001.

3 See "Kids Spend More Time with Parents than 20 Years Ago," *Associated Press*, August 13, 2001.

4 See "When Is a Child Ready to Stay at Home Alone?," *Family Life*, March 1999.

5 "It's 4:00 P.M. Do You Know Where Your Children Are?," *Newsweek*, April 27, 1998.

6 J. Eichel and L. Goldman (2001) "Safety Makes Sense: A Program to Prevent Unintentional Injuries in New York City Public Schools," *Journal of School Health*, vol. 71, no. 5, p. 181.

7 "School/Playground New Survey Reveals Parents Lack Concern About Preventing Sports Injuries to Kids," National Safe Kids Campaign press release, May 4, 2000.

8 See *Time*, January 25, 1999.

9 See Dave Shiflett, "Summertime . . . ," *National Review*, May 28, 2001.

10 See Janny Scott, "When Child's Play Is Too Simple," *New York Times*, July 15, 2000.

11 See "More School, Structure Found in '90s Child's Life," *Washington Post*, November 9, 1998.

12 See "When Is a Child Ready to Stay at Home Alone?," *Family Life*, March 1999.

13 See David Alexander, "The Learning That Lies Between Play and Academics in After-School Programs," *21 Community News*, Spring 2000.

14 Cited in "Toy-Related Injuries Among Children and Teenagers—United States, 1996," *Morbidity & Mortality Weekly Report*, December 19, 1997, vol. 46, no. 59, p. 1190.

15 See "Popularity of Scooters Leads to Dramatic Rise in Injuries This Year," National Safe Kids Campaign press release, November 30, 2000.

16 Rachelle Vander Schaaf, "Safety Rules Even Good Parents Miss," *Family Life*, March 2001.

17 Cited in *U.S. News & World Report*, March 19, 2001.

Chapter 1: Making Sense of Parental Paranoia

1 See "The New Age of Anxiety," *Newsweek*, August 23, 1999.

2 For an illustration of this worrying trend, see R. Landau (1995) "The Impact of New Medical Technologies in Human Reproduction on Children's Personal Safety and Well-Being in the Family," *Marriage and Family Review*, vol. 21, no. 1–2.

3 NCH Action for Children (1999) *The Internet: A Parents' Guide*, London, p. 2.

4 See "Computers Rot Our Children's Brains: Expert," *Observer*, April 16, 2000.

5 Strasburger and Donnerstein (1999) p. 129.

6 System Three (1998) *Poll on the Safety of Children in Society in Scotland*, Edinburgh. Stickler and Simons (1995) p. 47.

7 See for example the claim made by the company Safety Shield marketing security products on their Web site.

8 See "Recess Is Over," *Christian Science Monitor*, October 5, 1995.

9 See "Government Wants Children to Shape Up," *Sun-Sentinel*, December 10, 2000.

10 Orpinas and Murray (1999) pp. 774–777.

11 This view is argued by Jean Richardson, professor of preventative medicine at the University of Southern California. She is cited in "Figuring Out When Children Are Ready to Stay Home Alone," *Christian Science Monitor*, July 9, 1996.

12 See "Home Alone Census," *Virginian Pilot*, October 31, 2000.

13 See "Unsupervised Teens Do Poorly in School," *U.S. Newswire*, March 6, 2001.

14 Alderson (2000) pp. 100–101.

15 Lindon (1999) p. 9.

16 Hardyment (1995).

17 Cited in "Against Innocence," *New Republic*, March 15, 1999.

18 Cited in Root (1997) p. 128.

19 See Hillman, Adams, and Whiteleg (1990) p. 84.

20 D. Norris (1999) *Protecting Our Children: A Guide for Parents*, London, p. 3.

21 "The Cost of Caution Fueled by Fear," *Omaha World-Herald*, August 11, 2000.

22 See "Smoke Without Fire," *Guardian*, January 12, 2000.

23 Cited in London *Times*, August 10, 1999.

24 See "Yes, It's the Pedophiles I Blame," *Guardian*, July 27, 1999.

25 See "As Scandal Keeps Growing, Church and Its Faithful Reel," *New York Times*, March 17, 2002.

26 See the *Telegraph*, September 26, 1997.

27 See Salvation Army (1996) *Safe and Sound*, London, p. 2.

28 Interview with Colonel Joy Paxton, September 9, 1998.

29 Home Office (1993) *Safe from Harm: A Code of Practice for Safeguarding the Welfare of Children in Voluntary Organizations in England and Wales*, London, p. 2.

30 England and Wales Cricket Board (1999) *Child Protection: Awareness and Procedures for All Adults Involved in Cricket for Children and Young People*, London, p. 9.

31 See *Daily Telegraph*, May 16, 1998.

32 Cited in *Daily Telegraph*, July 25, 1999.

33 Cited in *Guardian*, August 29, 1998.

34 See "Lord Puttnam: the Arts Chose Moral Ambiguity," London *Times*, June 1, 2000.

35 Emily Wilson, "The Touchy-Feely Kids," *Guardian*, November 3, 1999.

36 See NSPCC media release, "Cruelty to Children Must Stop," August 2, 1999.

37 See *Guardian*, April 21, 2000.

38 See interview in Furedi (2002), p. 22.

Chapter 2: The Myth of the Vulnerable Child

1 Furedi (2002) pp. 19–21.

2 Clinton (1996) p. 11.

3 Elliot (1996) p. 42.

4 "You Can't Play Here," *Daily Mail*, May 30, 2000.

5 See "Scourge of the Playground," *Time*, May 21, 2001.

6 See "Safety Makes Sense," *Journal of School Health*, May 2001.

7 Alderson (2000) pp. 100–101.

8 See "Helping Children to Play Stunts Creativity," *Independent*, June 13, 2000.

9 See "Injury Facts, Trends in Unintentional Childhood Injury Prevention," National Safe Kids Campaign, October 15, 2001.

10 See "Drug Found to Curb Kids' Debilitating Social Anxiety," *Washington Post*, April 25, 2001.

11 See I. Tofler, B. Stryer, L. Micheli, and L. Herman (1996) "Physical and Emotional Problems of Elite Female Gymnasts," *New England Journal of Medicine*, vol. 335, no. 4.

12 See "Blueprint for Change: Research on Child and Adolescent Mental Health," *National Advisory Mental Health Council's Workgroup on Child and Adolescent Mental Health Intervention, Development, and Deployment*, NIH publication, August 2001.

13 Interview, 1999.

14 See for example Ann Buchanan's claim that child disorders are caused by poor parenting in "The Background" in Buchanan and Hudson (1998) p. 3.

15 See Kagan (1998).

16 These ideas are explored in Scarr and Dunn (1987).

17 K. C. Parker, and D. Forrest (1993) "Attachment Disorder: An Emerging Concern for School Counselors," *Elementary School Guidance & Counselling*, February 1993, vol. 27, no. 3.

18 Scarr and Dunn (1987) p. 73.

19 Tizard (1997).

20 John Bowlby, M. Ainsworth, M. Boston, and D. Rosenbluth (1956) "The Effects of Mother-Child Separation: A Follow-Up Study," *British Journal of Medical Psychology*, vol. 29, p. 233.

21 See A. Clarke, and A. Clarke in Bernstein and Brannen (1996).

22 Ventegodt (1999) pp. 213, 220.

23 Cited in Schaffer (1998) p. 366.

24 Werner and Smith (1982) p. 159.

25 Schaffer (1998) pp. 376–379.

26 Cited in Schaffer (1998) p. 368.

27 Interview, May 2000.

28 Cited in "The Science of Cuddles," *Daily Telegraph*, November 15, 1997.

Chapter 3: Parents as Gods

1 See "Oregon State University Study Finds Parents' View of Their Children Key Factor in Child Abuse Risk," *Ascribe Newswire*, May 2, 2001.

2 "Parents Get Blame for Terrible Twos," *Daily Telegraph*, July 30, 1996.

3 See *Daily Telegraph*, March 17, 1995.

4 In 1997 and 1999, two Panorama documentaries were devoted to this subject.

5 "Postnatal Blues Can Lower IQ of Baby Boys," *Guardian*, January 22, 2000.

6 See *Observer*, November 21, 1999.

7 See "Screaming Parents 'Damage' Teenagers," *Independent on Sunday*, April 9, 2000.

8 See "Children Are Damaged by Quality Time," London *Times*, April 13, 2000.

9 "Over-Protective Parents May Be Causing Anorexia," *Independent*, February 1, 2000.

10 Kagan (1998) p. 146.

11 For a discussion of this event and its wider impact, see Bruer (1999) pp. 1–27.

12 See special edition of *Newsweek*, Spring/Summer 1997, on this subject.

13 *Time*, February 3, 1997.

14 See "Is It a Sign?," *Washington Post*, March 13, 2001.

15 See for example J. Briscoe, "Breaking the Cycle of Violence: A Rational Approach to At-Risk Youth," *Federal Probation*, vol. 61, no. 3.

16 Cited in "What Should Children Be Eating?," *Co-Ordinate*, January 1997, p. 10.

17 "Not in Front of the Children?," *Mother & Baby*, May 2000.

18 Cited in "Dummies: The Pros and Cons," *Parents*, September 1997, p. 33. See also "The Truth About Dummies," *Prima Baby*, Summer 1998.

19 See "Breast Way Forward" *Mother & Baby*, January 2000, and "Music to Your Ears," *Mother & Baby*, April 2000.

20 "Overture for Babies," *Guardian*, vol. 23, no. 6, 2000.

21 See "The Quest for Superkid," London *Times*, September 24, 2001.

22 "Mental Strength," *Parents*, August 1999.

23 "When They Are Old Enough to . . .," *Prima Baby*, April/May 2000.

24 "Speak," *Practical Parenting*, April 2000.

25 "Kill Your Television," *Baby*, March 2000.

26 "Enjoy Books," *Prima Baby*, April/May 2000.

27 Bruer (1999) p. 103.

28 Scarr and Dunn (1987) p. 187.

29 See *Lancet*, August 28, 1999, p. 749.

30 Gopnik, Meltzoff, and Kuhl (1999) pp. 201–202.

31 Bruer (1999) p. 185.

32 Ibid., p. 188.

33 Scarr (1992) p. 16.

34 Harris (1998).

35 "Attachment Parenting: A Style That Works," excerpted from William Sears, *Nighttime Parenting: How to Get Your Child to Sleep*, La Leche League International, 2000.

36 Duin and Sutcliffe (1992) pp. 114–115.

37 See HMSO (1991).

38 "How to Have a Brainy Baby," *Prima Baby*, June/July 1999.

39 Naish and Roberts (2000) pp. 9, 11, 111.

40 Anne Fleissig (1991) "Unintended Pregnancy and the Use of Contraception: Changes from 1984 to 1989," *British Medical Journal*, vol. 302, p. 147.

Chapter 4: Parenting on Demand

1 See Granju and Kennedy (1999).

2 See Young (1990).

3 Leach (1997) p. 144.

4 Dorothy Rowe, Foreword to Parker and Stimpson (1999) p. 1; Leach (1997) p. 144; and Jackson (1999) p. 41.

5 Jerome Kagan, "Our Babies, Ourselves," *New Republic*, September 5, 1994.

6 Goleman (1996) p. 199.

7 See John Gottman, "Are You a Good Parent?," *Daily Telegraph*, January 18, 1997.

8 See NSPCC (1998) *Positive Ways of Managing Children's Behavior: Notes for Group Leaders*, London, p. 6, and Parker and Stimpson (1999) p. 77.

9 "Her Growing Confidence," *Mother & Baby*, April 2000.

10 See *Practical Parenting*, May 2000, and *Baby Power*, April 2000.

11 See *Practical Parenting*, May 2000, and Jackson (1999) pp. 77–105.

12 "Touch Early and Often," *Time*, July 27, 1998.

13 Cited in Cassidy (1998) p. 87.

14 Lasch (1977).

15 "Parents Step Up Roles in Schools," *Charleston Daily Mail*, October 10, 2001.

16 See "Strong Children a Result of Hands-On Parenting," *Washington Times*, July 2, 2001.

17 See "Parents Take on 7 Hours Homework," *Daily Telegraph*, March 27, 2000.

18 See "Teachers Threatened by 'Parents from Hell,'" *Daily Telegraph*, April 27, 2000.

Chapter 5: Parenting Turned into an Ordeal

1 Cited in "Fact Sheet," produced by Rocky Mountain Family Council, Denver, CO, 2001.

2 London Sunday *Times*, May 25, 1997.

3 Cited in "The Myth of Quality Time," *Newsweek*, May 12, 1997.

4 "Pushyparent Going Public," *Guardian*, April 19, 2000.

5 Nestle Family Monitor No. 3 (1998), "The School Summer Holiday: At Home," p. 2.

6 See "More Time Together," *Los Angeles Times*, March 27, 2000.

7 J. Gershuny (1997) "Time for the Family," *Prospect*, January, p. 56, and "Men Wear the Aprons as Wives Work More," *Daily Telegraph*, April 16, 1998.

8 S. Hofferth (1999) "Changes in American Children's Time, 1981–1997," *Brown University Child and Adolescent Behavior Letter*, vol. 15, no. 3, pp. 1 and 5.

9 Ibid, p. 5.

10 See "Kids Seeing More of Mom and Dad," *Washington Post*, May 9, 2001.

11 See "New National Survey on Parents of Kids 2–5," *PR Newswire*, August 21, 2001.

12 See *Complicated Lives: A Report by the Future Foundation for Abbey National*, London, 2000.

13 Ibid.

14 Arlie Russell Hochschild, "There's No Place Like Work," *New York Times* magazine, April 20, 1997.

15 Maushart (1999) p. 10, and Jeffers (1999).

16 "An Overview, Analysis and Response by Psychologist Dr. Maureen Marks," Johnson & Johnson Limited press release, December 13, 1999.

17 ICM Research, "Mothercare 2000," press release, November 10, 1999.

Chapter 6: Why Parents Confuse Their Problems with Those of Their Children

1 See Galinsky (1999).

2 Chernofsky and Gage (1996).

3 Hardyment (1995) p. 299.

4 See advice leaflet issued by the Staff of Counseling and Mental Health Center, University of Texas, June 30, 1999.

5 Leach (1997) p. 145.

6 Cassidy (1998).

7 Hamand (1994) p. 18.

8 See Pittman (1995) "How to Manage Your Kids," *Psychology Today*, vol. 28, no. 3, p. 42.

9 Cassidy (1998) p. 43.

10 Zelizer (1994) p. 3.

11 Cited in Zelizer (1994) p. 9.

12 "The Over-Scheduled Child: Avoiding the Hyper-Trap," *Brown University Child & Adolescent Behavior Letter*, April 2001.

13 Rosenfeld, Wise, and Coles (2000).

14 See "Kids Need Time to 'veg out' with Family," *Herald-Mail ONLINE*, April 16, 2002.

15 See Elkind (1998).

16 Sennett (1998) p. 146.

17 Bushnell (1996) p. 2.

18 Firestone and Catlett (1999).

19 Swidler (1987) p. 117.

20 Ibid.

21 Jenks (1996) p. 107.

22 Zoë Ball's interview in *Marie Claire* is discussed in "Doomed from the Start," London *Times*, March 24, 2000.

23 Beck and Beck-Gernsheim (1995) p. 37.

24 Kagan (1998) p. 129.

25 Zelizer (1994) p. 265.

26 *Complicated Lives: A Report by the Future Foundation for Abbey National*, London, 2000, p. 6.

Chapter 7: Confusions About Facing Up to Adulthood

1 Jacobson (1996) pp. 582–588, and Martha Wolfenstein, "Fun Morality: An Analysis of Recent American Child-Training Literature," Mead and Wolfenstein (1955).

2 Hewlett and West (1998) p. 126.

3 Calcutt (1998) p. 236.

Chapter 8: The Problem of Holding the Line

1 Bob Franklin, "The Case for Children's Rights: A Progress Report," Franklin (1995) pp. 14–15, and Alderson (2000) pp. 24–25.

2 See Gordon (1975) p. 123; Leach (1997) p. 528; and Ringen (1998).

3 Franklin (1995) p. 14, and Ringen (1998).

4 McCord (1996) p. 832.

5 Baumrind (1996) p. 828.

6 Hymowitz (2000) p. 63.

7 Cited in D. Barasch, "Defiance," *Family Life*, June/July 1999, p. 45.

8 See "Giving Guidance on Child Discipline," editorial, *British Medical Journal*, January 29, 2000.

9 "Why Smack?," *Nursery World*, July 29, 1993.

10 Leach (1997) pp. 528–534.

11 For a discussion of this controversy, see "This Book Says You Should Beat Your Children, Not Cuddle Them," *Daily Telegraph*, February 22, 1998.

12 Leach (1999) p. 19, and M. Strauss, (1996), "Spanking and the Making of a Violent Society," *Pediatrics*, vol. 98, no. 4, p. 842.

13 See Hyman (1996), and Eron (1996), p. 822.

14 See "When to Spank," *U.S. News & World Report*, April 13, 1998.

15 See Robert Larzelere (1996) "A Review of the Outcomes of Parental Use of Nonabusive or Customary Physical Punishment," *Pediatrics*, vol. 98, no. 4, and Baumrind (1996).

Chapter 9: Unclear Rules

1 Isaacs (1960) p. 2.

2 Mead and Wolfenstein (1955) p. 145.

3 Ibid.

4 J. Davey, "When You Feel Like Smacking," *Parents*, March 1995.

5 See NSPCC (1999).

6 Parker and Stimpson (1999) p. 81.

7 Cited in "Advise and Consent," *Newsweek*, Spring/Summer 1997, special edition.

8 See *Guardian*, June 17, 2000.

9 For these conflicting views see "Lights on at Night May Harm Children's Sight," *Daily Telegraph*, May 20, 1999, and "Nursery Lights Do Not Damage Young Eyes, Say Scientists," *Daily Telegraph*, March 9, 2000.

10 See "Dishing Out Dirt," *Guardian*, October 12, 1999.

11 Cited in "New Advice for Parents," *New York Times*, October 18, 2000.

12 "Parenting with an Edge," *Arkansas Democrat-Gazette*, February 28, 2001.

13 See "Parenting Author Offers a Different Take on Self-Esteem," *Charleston Gazette*, April 24, 2001.

14 See Kathryn Carpenter, "Childcare Selections to Grow On," *Library Journal*, January 8, 1992.

15 On Spock's views see Etaugh (1980) p. 314. Changing attitudes toward maternal employment are documented by Young (1990) p. 21.

16 Allan Carlson, "Trojan Horse of Child Care," *Executive Speeches*, June/July 1998.

17 See Young (1999) p. 23.

18 See *Baby* magazine, March 2000, and *Mother & Baby*, May 2000.

19 See "What's Stopping You Breastfeeding?," *Prima Baby*, Summer 1997; *Prima Baby*, Summer 1998; "How to Have a Brainy Baby," *Prima Baby*, June/July 1999; *Parents*, May 1999; *Practical Parenting*, May 2000; and *Mother & Baby*, May 2000.

20 See "Breast-Feeding Mothers May Pass Toxins to Babies," Sunday London *Times*, April, 30, 2000.

21 Jackson (1999) p. 175.

22 For an outline of McKenna's research see M. Small and M. Hellweg, "A Reasonable Sleep," *Health & Hygiene*, April 1992. Newburn is cited in "Should the Baby Sleep in Your Bed?" *Express*, December 9, 1999. The Federal Consumer Product Safety Commission's report is discussed in "Baby in Parents' Bed in Danger? U.S. Says Yes, but Others Demur," *New York Times*, September 30, 1999.

23 See "Off to a Good Start," *Newsweek*, Spring/Summer 1997, special edition.

24 Stilwell is cited in S. Lang, "Music—Good for Not Only the Soul, but the Brain," *Human Ecology Forum*, Spring 1999, p. 24. See "Music Beats

Computers at Enhancing Childhood Development," *Teaching Music*, June 1997.

25 See Eron (1996).

26 See Smith, Van Loon, DeFrates-Densch, and Schrader (1998).

27 Anderson (1973) p. 8.

28 Horwood and Fergusson (1999) p. 1023.

29 These points are developed by Dr. Alan Prout (1999) "Living Arrows: Children's Lives and the Limits of Parenting," *Parenting Forum*, no. 15; *Practical Parenting*, May 2000; and *Mother & Baby*, May 2000.

30 See Schaffer (1998) *Social Development* pp. 4–5.

31 For a critique of the methodology used in this report see "Exploited the Exploited," *Vital Statistics*, October 2001.

Chapter 10: *Professional Power and the Erosion of Parental Authority*

1 Celia Smith (1999) *Developing Parenting Programs*, London, p. 33.

2 Cited in *Alberta Report*, April 19, 1999.

3 See "Survey of Parents with Young Children," available on the Web site of Healthy Steps, 1997.

4 "Survey of Parents on Abuse," Prevent Child Abuse America, www.childabuse.org.

5 See Owen and Mulvihill (1994).

6 Smith op. cit., pp. 93, 97.

7 See "An Early Start on Education," *Washington Post*, August 14, 2001.

8 Pugh and De'Ath (1984) pp. 13–14.

9 See *Parenting Forum Newsletter*, no. 2, 1996.

10 Cited in Grant, Julia. *Raising Baby by the Book: The Education of American Mothers*. New Haven: Yale University Press, 1998, p. 165.

11 See ibid, p. 33.

12 Ayling (1930) pp. 204, 213.

13 Winnicott (1991) pp. 173–174.

14 See "The Prenatal Visit," *Pediatrics*, June 2001, vol. 107, no. 6.

15 See "Lessons Best Taught at Home Are Crowding School Classes," *Chattanooga Free Press*, January 11, 2000.

16 For an overview of this debate, see *Society*, November 1996.

Chapter 11: The Politicization of Parenting

1 See "Remarks by the President and the First Lady at the White House Conference on Teenagers: Raising Responsible and Resourceful Youth," White House Office of the Press Secretary, May 2, 2000.

2 Ibid.

3 See "Specific Effects of EHS on Development," *Early Childhood Report*, February 14, 2001.

4 "White House Summit on Early Childhood Cognitive Development," G. Reid Lyon, summary comments, July 27, 2001.

5 See "Autistic Girl Unsafe at Home," *Washington Post*, April 27, 2001.

6 "The Role of Parents and Grandparents in Children's Cognitive Development: Focus on Language and Literacy," Dorothy S. Strickland, White House Summit on Early Childhood Cognitive Development, July 27, 2001.

7 Winnicott and Klaus (1991) p. 175.

Bibliography

Books

Alderson, Priscilla. *Young Children's Rights: Exploring Beliefs, Principles, and Practice.* London: Jessica Kingsley Publishers, 2000.

Anderson, Michael, ed. *Sociology of the Family: Selected Readings.* Harmondsworth, London: Penguin, 1973.

Archard, David. *Children: Rights and Childhood.* London: Routledge, 1993.

Ayling, Jean. *The Retreat from Parenthood.* London: Kegan Paul, Trench, Trubner & Co., 1930.

Beck, Ulrich and E. Beck-Gernsheim. *The Normal Chaos of Love.* Cambridge, MA: Polity Press, 1995.

Bellah, Robert Neely, editor. *Habits of the Heart: Individualism and Commitment in American Life*. Berkeley, CA: University of California Press, 1996.

Bernstein, Basil and J. Brannen, eds. *Children, Research, and Policy*. London: Taylor & Francis, 1996.

Brazelton, T. Berry. *On Becoming a Family: The Growth of Attachment Before and After Birth*. Boston: Delacorte/Seymour Lawrence, 1981.

Bruer, John. *The Myth of the First Three Years: A New Understanding of How Learning Occurs Throughout Life*. New York: Free Press, 1999.

Buchanan, Ann and Barbara L. Hudson, eds. *Parenting, Schooling, and Children's Behavior: Interdisciplinary Approaches*. Aldershot, Hampshire: Ashgate Publishing, 1998.

Bushnell, Candace. *Sex and the City*. London: Abacus, 1996.

Calcutt, Andrew. *Arrested Development: Pop Culture and the Erosion of Adulthood*. London: Cassell, 1998.

Campion, Mukti Jain. *Who's Fit to Be a Parent?* London: Routledge, 1995.

Cassidy, Anne. *Parents Who Think Too Much: Why We Do It, How to Stop*. New York: Dell, 1998.

Chernofsky, Barbara and D. Gage. *Change Your Child's Behavior by Changing Yours: Effective Solutions for Common Parenting Problems*. Chicago: Crown, 1996.

Clinton, Hillary Rodham. *It Takes a Village and Other Lessons Children Teach Us*. New York: Simon & Schuster, 1996.

Damon, William. *Greater Expectations: Overcoming the Culture of Indulgence in Our Homes and Schools*. New York: Free Press, 1995.

Davis, Anne. *Confident Parenting: A Hands-On Approach to Children*. Brighton: Souvenir, 1997.

Duin, Nancy and J. Sutcliffe. *A History of Medicine*. London: Simon & Schuster, 1992.

Elkind, David. *The Hurried Child: Growing Up Too Fast Too Soon*. New York: Addison Wesley, 1998.

Elliot, Michele. *501 Ways to Be a Good Parent: From the Frantic Fours to the Terrible Twelves*. London: Hodder & Stoughton, 1996.

Eyer, Diane. *Motherguilt: How Our Culture Blames Mothers for What's Wrong with Society*. New York: Random House, 1996.

Firestone, Robert. *The Fear of Intimacy*. Boston: American Psychology Association, 1999.

Franklin, Bob. *A Handbook of Children's Rights*. London: Routledge, 1995.

Fukuyama, Francis. *The End of Order*. London: The Social Market Foundation, 1997.

Furedi, Frank. *Culture of Fear: Risk Taking and the Morality of Low Expectation*. New York: Continuum, 2002.

Future Foundation. *Complicated Lives: A Report by the Future Foundation for Abby National*. London: Future Foundation, 2000.

Galinksy, Ellen. *Ask the Children: What American Children Really Think About Working Parents*. New York: William Morrow, 1999.

Goleman, Daniel. *Emotional Intelligence: Why It Can Matter More than IQ*. London: Bloomsbury, 1996.

Gopnik, Alison, Andrew Meltzoff, and Patricia Kuhl. *The Scientist in the Crib: Minds, Brains, and How Children Learn*. New York: William Morrow, 1999.

Gordon, Thomas. *P.E.T.: Parent Effectiveness Training*. New York: Plume, 1975.

Gottman, John. *The Heart of Parenting*. London: Bloomsbury, 1997.

Granju, Katie Allison and Betsy Kennedy. *Attachment Parenting: Instinctive Care for Your Baby and Young Child.* New York: Pocket Books, 1999.

Hamand, Jeremy. *Father Over Forty: Becoming an Older Father.* London: Optima, 1994.

Hardyment, Christina. *Perfect Parents: Baby-Care Advice Past and Present.* Oxford: Oxford University Press, 1995.

Harris, Judith Rich. *The Nurture Assumption: Why Children Turn Out the Way They Do.* New York: Free Press, 1998.

Health Education Authority. *Birth to Five: A Guide to the First Five Years of Being a Parent.* London: Health Education Authority, 1992.

Hewlett, Sylvia Ann and Cornell West. *The War Against Parents: What We Can Do for America's Beleaguered Moms and Dads.* Boston, MA: Houghton Mifflin Co., 1998.

Hillman, Meyer, John Adams, and James Whiteleg. *One False Move: A Study of Children's Mobility.* London: PSI Publishing, 1990.

HMSO. *Fourth Report of the Health Committee: Maternity Services: Preconception,* Vol. 1. London: HMSO, 1991.

Hymowitz, Kay S. *Ready or Not: What Happens When We Treat Children as Small Adults.* San Francisco, CA: Encounter Books, 2000.

Isaacs, Susan. *The Nursery Years: The Mind of the Child from Birth to Six Years.* London: Times, 1960.

Jackson, Deborah. *Three in a Bed: The Benefits of Sleeping with Your Baby.* London: Bloomsbury, 1999.

Jeffers, Susan. *I'm Okay, You're a Brat! Free Yourself from the Guilt-Making Myths of Parenthood.* London: Hodder & Stoughton, 1999.

Jenks, Christopher. *Childhood.* London: Routledge, 1996.

Kagan, Jerome. *Three Seductive Ideas.* Cambridge, MA: Harvard University Press, 1998.

La Fontaine, Jean. *Child Sexual Abuse.* Cambridge, MA: Polity Press, 1990.

Langford, Wendy. *Revolution of the Heart: Gender, Power, & the Delusions of Love.* London: Routledge, 1999.

Lasch, Christopher. *Haven in a Heartless World: The Family Besieged.* New York: Basic, 1977.

Leach, Penelope and Jenny Matthews. *Your Baby and Child.* London: Penguin, 1997.

Leach, Penelope. *The Physical Punishment of Children: Some Input from Recent Research.* London: NSPCC, 1999.

Lewis, Jane. *Individualism and Commitment in Marriage and Cohabitation.* London: Lord Chancellor's Department, 1999.

Lewis, Jane, David Clark, and David Morgan. *Whom God Hath Joined Together: The Work of Marriage Guidance.* London: Routledge, 1992.

Linden, Jennie. *Too Safe for Their Own Good? Helping Children Learn About Risk and Lifeskills.* London: The National Early Years Network, 1999.

Maccoby, Eleanor and J. Martin. "Socialization in the Context of the Family: Parent-Child Interaction," in *Handbook of Child Psychology,* fourth ed., edited by E. Heatherington. New York: John Wiley, 1983.

Maushart, Susan. *The Mask of Motherhood: How Becoming a Parent Changes Everything and Why We Pretend It Doesn't.* London: Pandora, 1999.

Mead, Margaret and Martha Wolfenstein, eds. *Childhood in Contemporary Cultures.* Chicago: University of Chicago Press, 1955.

Mental Health Foundation. *Bright Futures: Promoting Children and Young People's Mental Health.* London: MHF, 1999.

Naish, Francesca and Janette Roberts. *Healthy Parents, Better Babies: A Couple's Guide to Natural Preconception Care.* Dublin, Ireland: Newleaf, 2000.

Norris, Dan. *Protecting Our Children: A Guide for Parents.* London: House of Commons, 1999.

NSPCC. *Baby's First Year.* London: NSPCC, 2000.

NSPCC. *Get Ready! Preparing Yourself for Your Baby.* London: NSPCC, 1999.

Parker, Jan and Jan Stimpson. *Raising Happy Children: What Every Child Needs Their Parents to Know—From 0 to 7 Years.* London: Hodder & Stoughton, 1999.

Pittman, Frank. *Man Enough: Fathers, Sons and the Search for Masculinity.* Los Angeles: Perigreen, 1994.

Priya, Jacqueline Vincent and Michel Odent. *Birth Traditions and Modern Pregnancy Care.* Dorset, England: Element Books, 1995.

Pugh, Gillian and E. De'Ath. *The Needs of Parents, Practice, and Policy in Parent Education.* London: Macmillan, 1984.

Ringen, Stein. *The Family Question.* London: Demos, 1998.

Rodger, John. *Family Life and Social Control: A Sociological Perspective.* Basingstoke, Hampshire: Macmillan, 1996.

Rosenfeld, Alvin, M.D. and Nicole Wise. *Hyper-Parenting: Are You Hurting Your Child by Trying Too Hard?* New York: St. Martin's Press, 2000.

Scarr, Sandra and Judith Dunn. *Mothercare/Other Care: The Child-Care Dilemma for Women and Children.* London: Penguin, 1987.

Schaffer, Rudolph. *Making Decisions About Children.* Oxford: Blackwell, 1998.

Schaffer, Rudolph. *Social Development.* Oxford: Blackwell, 1998.

Sennett, Richard. *The Corrosion of Character: The Personal Consequences of Work in the New Capitalism.* New York: W. W. Norton, 1998.

Spock, Benjamin. *Baby and Child Care.* New York: Pocket, 1961.

Straw, Ed. *Relative Values: Support for Relationships and Parenting.* London: Demos, 1998.

Tizard, Barbara. *Adoption: A Second Chance.* London: Open Books, 1997.

Werner, Emmy and R. Smith. *Vulnerable but Invincible: A Longitudinal Study of Resilient Children and Youth.* New York: McGraw-Hill, 1982.

Westman, Jack C. *Licensing Parents: Can We Prevent Child Abuse and Neglect?* New York: Perseus Press, 1994.

Winnicott, Donald and Marshall H. Klaus. *The Child, the Family, and the Outside World.* London: Penguin, 1991.

Woodhead, Martin, Dorothy Faulkner, and Karen Littleton, eds. *Cultural Worlds of Early Childhood.* London: Routledge, 1996.

Zelizer, Viviana. *Pricing the Priceless Child: The Changing Social Value of Children.* Princeton, NJ: Princeton University Press, 1994.

Zucker, Paul. *Loving Our Children, Loving Ourselves.* New York: GLE Publications, 1998.

Articles

Baumrind, Diana. "A Blanket Injunction Against Disciplinary Use of Spanking Is Not Warranted by the Data," *Pediatrics,* Vol. 98, No. 4, 1996.

Baumrind, Diana. "The Influence of Parenting Style on Adolescent Competence and Substance Use," *Journal of Early Adolescence,* Vol. 11, No. 1, 1991.

Bigner, Jerry and R. Yang. "Parent Education in Popular Literature: 1970–1990," *Family & Consumer Sciences Research Journal*, Vol. 25, No. 1, 1996.

Burgess, Edward. "The Family in a Changing Society," *The American Journal of Sociology*, Vol. 53, No. 6, 1948.

Clarke-Stewart, Alison K. "Historical Shifts and Underlying Themes in Ideas About Rearing Young Children in the United States: Where Have We Been? Where Are We Going?" *Early Development and Parenting*, Vol. 7, No. 2, 1998.

Eron, Leonard. "Research and Public Policy," *Pediatrics*, Vol. 98, No. 4, 1996.

Etaugh, Claire. "Effects of Nonmaternal Care on Children: Research Evidence and Popular Views," *American Psychologist*, Vol. 35, No. 4, 1980.

Gardels, Nancy. "The Crime of Quality Time," *New Perspectives Quarterly*, Vol. 15, No. 3, 1998.

Holloway, Susan and B. Fuller. "Families and Child Care: Divergent Viewpoints," *Annals of the American Academy of Political Science*, Vol. 563, May 1999.

Horwood, John L. and David Fergusson. "A Longitudinal Study of Maternal Labor Force Participation and Child Academic Achievement," *Journal of Child Psychology and Psychiatry*, Vol. 40, No. 7, 1999.

Hyman, Irwin. "Using Research to Change Public Policy: Reflections on 20 Years of Effort to Eliminate Corporal Punishment in Schools," *Pediatrics*, Vol. 98, No. 4, 1996.

Jacobson, Lisa. "Revitalizing the American Home: Children's Leisure and the Revaluation of Play, 1920–1940," *Journal of Social History*, Winter 1996.

Mahoney, Gerald and A. Kaiser. "Parent Education in Early Intervention: A Call for a Renewed Focus," *Topics in Early Childhood Education*, Vol. 19, No. 3, 1999.

McCaslin, Mary, and H. Infanti. "The Generativity Crisis and the 'Scold War': What About Those Parents," *Teachers College Record*, Vol. 100, No. 2, 1998.

McCord, Joan. "Unintended Consequences of Punishment," *Pediatrics*, Vol. 98, No. 4, 1996.

Ojemann, Ralph. "A Functional Analysis of Child Development Material in Current Newspapers and Magazines," *Child Development*, Vol. 19, 1948.

Orpinas, Pamela and N. Murray. "Parental Influences of Students' Aggressive Behaviors and Weapon Carrying," *Health Education and Behavior*, Vol. 26, No. 6, 1999.

Owen, Margaret and B. Mulvihill. "Benefits of a Parent Education and Support Program in the First Three Years," *Family Relations*, Vol. 43, No. 2, April 1994.

Powell, Douglas and K. Diamond. "Approaches to Parent Teacher Relationships in U.S. Early Childhood Programs During the Twentieth Century," *Journal of Education*, Vol. 177, No. 3, 1995.

Root, Amanda. "Walk, Don't Drive: Why Are Children's Journeys to School Increasingly Made by Car?," *New Economy*, Vol. 4, No. 2, 1997.

Rutter, Michael. "Psychosocial Adversity and Child Psychopathology," *British Journal of Psychiatry*, No. 174, 1999.

Scarr, Sandra. "Developmental Theories for the 1990s: Development and Individual Differences," *Child Development*, Vol. 63, 1992.

Smith, Cecil, Preston Van Loon, Nancy DeFrates-Densch, and Thomas Schrader. "Content Changes on Parent Education Books for Parents of Adolescents," *Family & Consumer Sciences Journal*, Vol. 27, No. 2, 1998.

Stickler, Gunnar B. "Worries of Parents and Their Children," *Clinical Pediatrics*, Vol. 35, No. 4, 1996.

Stickler, Gunnar B. and Patricia Simons. "Pediatricians' Preferences for Anticipatory Guidance Topics Compared with Parental Anxieties," *Clinical Pediatrics*, Vol. 34, No. 7, July 1995.

Strasburger, Victor and E. Donnerstein. "Children, Adolescents, and the Media: Issues and Solutions," *Pediatrics*, Vol. 103, No. 1, 1999.

Strauss, Murray. "Is It Time to Ban Corporal Punishment of Children?," *Canadian Medical Association Journal*, Vol. 161, No. 7, 1999.

Ventegodt, Soren. "A Prospective Study on Quality of Life and Traumatic Events in Early Life—A 30-Year Follow-Up," *Child: Care, Health, and Development*, Vol. 25, No. 3, 1999.

Young, Kathryn T. "American Conceptions of Infant Development from 1955 to 1984: What the Experts Are Telling Parents," *Child Development*, Vol. 61, 1990.

Index